Respectable Rebels:

Middle Class Campaigns in Britain in the 1970s

Respectable Rebels:

Middle Class Campaigns in Britain in the 1970s

Edited by
Roger King and Neill Nugent

**DISTRIBUTED BY
HOLMES & MEIER
PUBLISHERS, INC.
New York   London**

HM

British Library Cataloguing in Publication Data

Respectable rebels.
  1. Middle classes – Great Britain – History
  – 20th century
  I. King, Roger   II. Nugent, Neill
  301.44′1   HT690.G7

ISBN 0 340 23164 5 Boards
ISBN 0 340 23165 3 Paper

Phototypeset in V.I.P. Times by
Western Printing Services Ltd, Bristol.

Printed in Great Britain for Hodder and Stoughton
Educational, a division of Hodder and Stoughton Ltd,
Mill Road, Dunton Green, Sevenoaks, Kent, by Richard
Clay (The Chaucer Press) Ltd, Bungay, Suffolk.

Contents

The Editors

Roger King
Principal Lecturer in Sociology, Huddersfield Polytechnic

Neill Nugent
Senior Lecturer in Politics, Manchester Polytechnic

The Contributors

Dallas Cliff
Senior Lecturer in Sociology, Huddersfield Polytechnic

John McHugh
Senior Lecturer in Politics, Manchester Polytechnic

Timothy May
Principal Lecturer in Politics, Manchester Polytechnic

Acknowledgments

This book could not have been written without the assistance of many people. Since much of our interest was with very recent events, relatively little material was documented and hence we were heavily dependent on the cooperation of officials and members of the various organisations we studied.

Unfortunately it is not possible to publicly thank everyone who provided us with information. We would, however, like to place on record our particular gratitude to those who, often at no small inconvenience to themselves, gave up much of their time to be interviewed and, in some cases, re-interviewed. In 'chapter order' they are:

Chapter 2: G. H. Alexander, Mrs J. Baty, R. G. Booth, Mrs L. Harrison, Mrs M. Hobbs, A. Napper, T. Peart, I. M. Scott, W. Spoor

Chapter 3: J. Blundell, Mrs T. Gorman, P. G. Ruffley

Chapter 4: G. Berg, G. Hartup, N. McWhirter, C. Tame

Chapter 5: Dr M. Gillibrand

Chapter 6: Miss M. Addleshaw, Mrs H. Bates, A. Bush, Dr S. E. Ellison, O. R. Johnston, Mrs V. Riches, Miss F. Tulloch, Miss A. Whitaker

Chapter 7: G. Block, N. Budgin MP, R. Cryer MP, G. Finsberg MP, J. Gorst MP, A. Hopkinson, K. Hovers, G. Howells MP, P. Knowlson, D. Mitchell MP, A. Rowe, N. Seligar, R. Wainwright MP, J. Varley

Amongst others who went out of their way to assist us, we should like to mention: D. Galleymore, J. Gouriet, D. Kelly, J. McGeorge, E. Martell, J. Monks, D. Morrison and G. Sparks.

For their valuable comments on sections of the manuscript we are grateful to Alan Bruce, Ruth Levitas and Michael Moran. Special thanks are offered to Tony Barker, who, though faced with his own publisher's deadline, kindly set aside time to carefully read and criticise the entire typescript.

Finally, thanks are also due to those who had perhaps the most burdensome task of all, our typists: Christine Harrison, Mary Knowles, Maureen Nugent, Margaret Riley.

Naturally none of the above bear any responsibility – or very little, at least – for such faults or omissions as the book may contain.

Roger King
Neill Nugent
May 1979

Roger King

1.   The middle class in revolt?

Introduction

It has become fashionable to suggest that the 1970s have witnessed a 'middle class revolt' in Britain. Political columnists warn governments not to 'underestimate the potential strength and seriousness of the middle class revolt'[1] and television programmes investigate the 'mangling of the middle classes'.[2] *The Times* sombrely explains the phenomenon of a mutinous middle class as based on groups whose 'normal ambitions are opposed by powerful forces.'[3] A suspicion that these 'powerful forces' include a Labour government is reinforced when Sir Keith Joseph, echoing other Conservatives, describes a Healey budget as marking 'the twilight of the middle classes'.[4] Sympathetic observers, such as Patrick Hutber in *The Decline and Fall of the Middle Class: and how it can fight back*, darkly refer to 'this time of crisis for the middle classes, who are subject to unprecedented pressures and, at the same time, to unprecedented denigration'.[5] All are agreed that the middle classes are no longer prepared to accept with their traditional forbearance the alleged erosion of hard-won living standards, the declining influence of traditional morality and the depredations of socialist governments.

At first this 'threat' to the middle classes is puzzling. If the middle classes are revolting, what could they be revolting against? Their lot appears a happy one. They dominate our social and political institutions and provide the leadership of most pressure groups. Politicians from all the major parties defer to their interests. Middle class political and cultural dominance is reflected 'in the relative ease with which the Conservative Party has been able to capture the mantle of the national interest while at the same time continuing to serve the specific interests of the middle class as a whole very effectively'.[6] The ascendancy of capitalist economic criteria which protects middle class control over property and the inequality of the labour contract is matched by unequal access to the use of state power and middle class entrenchment in local politics.

But the term 'middle class' hides a variety of occupational groups. It could be objected that the ascendancy ascribed to them is limited to a distinct middle class elite, a 'haute bourgeoisie', whilst the rest are in the same unrepresented and powerless boat as everyone else. It is well attested that the traditional middle class – the petite bourgeoisie and independent professional – has long been alienated by the organisational developments of modern industrial society and is squeezed between the millstones of big business and powerful trade unions. The plethora of small business organisations in the 1970s, which are outlined by McHugh in Chapter 3, testifies to the continuing feeling that their interests are not properly safeguarded in the counsels of state.

They are not alone. Various sections of the middle class have begun to defend more militantly interests they believe to be ignored by economic and political leaders. For some occupational groups, such as airline pilots, banking staff, teachers and doctors, this involves eschewing 'middle class' or 'professional' norms and threatening strike action. Middle class militancy is matched by the increase in unionisation. The density of white collar unionism rose from 29 per cent in 1964 to 40 per cent in 1974, as May points out in his chapter on middle class unionism.

In this introductory chapter a brief survey of this variety of recent middle class activism is offered, followed by the text of a thesis that certain aspects of this activism comprise a 'middle class revolt'. This is then examined against empirical evidence.

In their role as citizens the middle class display an increased willingness to organise outside conventional party alignments. The ratepayers' associations which mushroomed after the massive rate increases in 1974 are more vigorously critical of the major parties than their staider predecessors. Some of the cultural/religious defenders of Christian morality, in the National Viewers and Listeners Association (NVALA) or the National Festival of Light (NFOL), for example, suspect an unholy alliance by national leaders to advance the permissive society. Cliff in Chapter 6 suggests that the Conservative Party in particular is now viewed more sceptically than before. It is feared that the commercial soul of the Party too easily overcomes its sympathy for traditional ethics. Disaffected Tories in the National Association for Freedom (NAFF) – explored at length by Nugent in his chapter on the 'freedom groups' – feel the need for a collective defence of middle class Toryism outside the Conservative Party.

These organised signs of increasing middle class disenchantment with the Conservative Party, examined in greater detail in the chapter on the 'middle class revolt' and the established parties, are a relatively recent feature of the British political scene. Unlike a number of European countries, there have been few attempts to form middle class associations outside the major parties. Bechhofer *et al.* remark that 'for the most part the political interests of non-manual groups have found expression through the Tory Party and almost always within the framework of conventional parliamentary politics'.[7] But the loss of two general elections by the Conservatives in 1974, the enormous increase in the Liberal vote in the same year, and the bustle of proudly 'non-partisan' organisations is evidence of middle class political turbulence.

This new belligerence is not confined to Britain. A strike by the self-employed in June 1975 deprived Belgians of the services of doctors, dentists, lawyers, barbers, garage owners, taxi drivers, publicans, electricians, tobacconists, restaurateurs and hoteliers – all complaining about increases in tax and social security contributions. In France, where middle class militancy has a long tradition, a businessmen's protest movement – the Union of Business Proprietors and Managers – was launched in December 1975. It warned the government that entrepreneurs and managers had suffered enough harassment by 'minority' trade unions and magistrates with working class sympathies. Shades of the British 'ratepayers' revolt' could be seen in the United States in 1978 with the support for Proposition 13 which reduced property taxes by an average of 57 per cent in a state-wide referendum held in California. Mogens Glistrup, leader of the anti-tax Progress Party in Denmark, has won much public support for protesting against levels of taxation, and the party is the second largest in the Danish parliament. Even Japan has had a strike of small businessmen.

John Gorst's Middle Class Association (MCA), founded in November 1974, typified, in this country, the feeling that politicians are failing to represent middle class interests adequately. The MCA sought to unite 'professional, managerial, self-employed and small business occupations' against 'spiteful' tax increases at a time when the middle classes were 'suffering disproportionately from inflation and massive erosions of savings and investment'. Its members resented the militancy of trade unionism which tilted at the 'measure of comfort' worked for in socially and economically valuable lifetimes. The doctors, accountants and architects who dominated the membership resented being made to play 'the role of scapegoat' for Britain's economic ills. On the contrary, the gadarene rush to equality of reward threatened the source of vitality, independence and creativity provided by middle class man.[8]

The MCA also opposed the growth of collectivism – 'the collectivised society in which the individual counts for nothing and the state for everything'.[9] In this they were responding as much to Heath's abandonment of market principles in favour of corporatism as to the new Labour government. Heath's phrase, 'the unacceptable face of capitalism', was particularly deplored. Not surprisingly, the MCA welcomed his replacement, Margaret Thatcher, with great enthusiasm.

The Association reached almost 5,000 members; yet it was short-lived. Supporters quarrelled over the term 'class' – many disliked its 'socialist' connotations – and after a coup by a militant anti-communist the organisation became the Voice of the Independent Centre before finally merging in 1976 with NAFF. Its early demise highlights the difficulty of organising the variegated middle class into one general association. Certainly it is much more problematic than organising single-issue or specific interest groups such as the self-employed or ratepayers' associations, and these, as is shown in Chapters 2 and 3, experience enough internecine difficulties of their own. The specific policies of the MCA were little more than those of the Conservative front bench: opposition to the 'crushing' burden of taxation, calls for cuts in public expenditure, and advocacy of income tax indexation. This reflected the Conservative hue of the organisation. At the same time, many Conservatives disliked the idea of a separate extra-parliamentary body representing the middle class, whilst 'Heathites' regarded it as a stalking horse for Thatcher's brand of Toryism.[10]

If the term 'middle class revolt' does have meaning it is that in recent years sections of the middle class, hitherto reluctant to organise, are beginning to do so. Their organisations are more militant and less prepared to work through and accept the wisdom of conventional party politics, particularly the leadership offered by the Conservative Party. This may involve cooperation 'across' class boundaries. The 'ratepayers' revolt' of 1974 and 1975 included more than a sprinkling of manual workers in the urban industrial areas, whilst members of the National Federation of the Self-Employed include a number of skilled artisans. Similarly, as May indicates in Chapter 5, in terms of tactics there is increasingly less reluctance to act collectively and use methods long employed by manual workers.

Although much of the evidence remains impressionistic, middle class participation appears to have increased in recent years. Motorway protesters disrupt official inquiries and innumerable environmentalist organisations have developed rapidly in the last decade. This is not completely novel. Middle class radicalism of the 'left' in the 1950s and early 1960s took its most visible form in the Campaign for Nuclear Disarmament, whilst ratepayers' associations, small business organisations, religious-moral defenders of traditional culture, and 'economic freedom' groups all have their antecedents too.

Nevertheless there has been a clear change in the extent and nature of participation since the late 1960s. As Crouch notes, 'there has been a movement away from established institutions of participation (primarily the political parties but also trade unions and other bodies) to various others: ad hoc community-level or unofficial groupings, special interest lobbies, new radical movements of urban protest and direct action'.[11] Much participation, especially of the direct action variety, has tended to be associated more with the 'left' than the 'right' of the political spectrum, and to have had greater impact on the Labour and Liberal parties – e.g. the increasingly radical demands of students and of a vigorous youth movement.

Yet the upsurge in political activism in the 1970s reflects a wider disenchantment with conventional politics, particularly the major parties, and is not confined to the young or the well-educated. The centralisation and remoteness of centres of decision-taking, the development of 'administrative' politics in Whitehall and town halls of an almost invisible kind, affect more than the deprived and underprivileged. Shopkeepers, ratepayers and white collar workers are amongst those who have become involved in a cluster of new and militant organisations. In part this is a response to the willingness of the well-educated and the unionised sections of the working class to advance their claims and the fear that this may result in an assault on established privileges and comfortable ideologies. This awakening is both a general reaction to the egalitarian and 'permissive' tendencies of the late 1960s and also a consequence of specific and genuine grievances. Ratepayers experienced huge rates increases in the mid-1970s; since 1975 the self-employed and small businessmen have been outraged by a national insurance surcharge that appears to them manifestly unfair; managers and other non-manual workers feel that manual unions have been eroding their hard-earned differentials. More generally, there is despair at the failure of political allies and spokesmen, particularly in the Conservative Party, to help. The National Association for Freedom and the Middle Class Association were formed directly out of Heath's embrace of collectivism and abandonment, in 1972, of individualistic, free enterprise policies. Moral watchdogs like NVALA, although well-established by the early 1970s, also expressed increasing disenchantment with the 'commercialism' of a Conservative government.

Consequently the Conservatives suffered most from a widespread disen-

chantment with the major parties in the 1974 general elections. Crewe *et al.*
point out that 'in their election victories of the 1950s the Conservatives won
almost half of the vote; by October 1974 the Conservative figure was down to
only a little more than a third (36·7 per cent), the lowest level in its history as a
mass party'.[12] And although the Labour Party suffered substantial losses too
(there was 'a clear dealignment of major-party support' which Crewe *et al.*
suggest marks the February 1974 election as a 'watershed' election[13]), the
striking disenchantment with the specific policies of the Heath administration
led to substantial middle class disaffection with Toryism. 'Not for 20 years –
perhaps more – had the middle classes displayed less partisan solidarity than
the working class.'[14] As Chapter 7 shows, the Tories have made strenuous
attempts to regain lost support, but some of their efforts, particularly the
wooing of small businessmen, have failed to alleviate suspicions of Conservative intentions when in power.

Clearly not all middle class activism is a product of a 'populist' backlash, but
most of the organisations discussed in the following chapters are those seized
upon by middle class polemicists as evidence of a 'middle class revolt'. Mostly
they have in mind the vociferousness of ratepayers and self-employed groups
which reached their height in 1974 and 1975. Yet there is an overriding
impression that, despite the ebbing of much of their support since then, they,
and the other groups we examine, are a more permanent feature of British
society than could have been envisaged in the 1960s. Most share a persisting
dislike of higher taxation, bureaucratisation, the growth of government power
and the decline in individualism. By no means do they form a coherent or even
clearly identifiable political grouping. The middle class unionists seem uncomfortable bedfellows with the petits-bourgeois that comprise the bulk of the
support of many of our groups. Nevertheless they are an important element of
middle class political activism in the 1970s, and provide an interesting comparison with the more widely researched radicalism of the left and the well-
educated.

Many of these groups are 'outsiders'. Grant distinguishes between 'insider'
and 'outsider' groups on the basis of a group's relationship to government: is it
accepted as a legitimate spokesman that has to be listened to or not?[15] Insider
groups often receive assistance of various kinds from government, such as
provision of office accommodation. They have a permanent staff who have a
vested interest in maintaining and developing the existing network of contracts
with government, and they approach any proposals for change of tactics
cautiously and incrementally in order to maintain their favoured relationship
with government. They prefer 'a strategy of responsibility'.

Environmentalist organisations provide examples of 'insider groups'. As
Grant points out, they tend to attract relatively large proportions of well-
educated members who have a fairly sophisticated appreciation of the way in
which the political system works. 'They realise that it is important that they
establish a credibility; that is, that they secure attention as a group which has
something to say and knows what it is talking about.'[16] Local amenity societies
also fall into the 'insider' category. They are part of the voluntary associations
movement that has come into existence to influence land-use planning by local
authorities and which specialise in conservation and amenity matters. A study

of 635 registered amenity societies by Barker and Keating testifies to their
recent proliferation. Eighty-five per cent had begun since 1957, including 37
per cent started between 1970 and 1974.[17]

In common with many 'middle class' organisations, amenity societies claim
to be socially representative and disavow class interests. Yet closer inspection
reveals the predominance of non-manual workers in their membership. Over
70 per cent of the societies in Barker and Keating's sample reported that they
did not have among their members 'even one third who do manual jobs' and
they had 'very few' council housing tenants. Sixty per cent of societies stated
that their members 'tend to live in the neighbourhoods with the best standards
of layout and amenity'.[18]

The amenity societies display two particularly interesting characteristics.
Firstly, they look with favour on local government officials, especially planning
officials, who are regarded as generally sympathetic to the views and values of
the societies. Secondly, they are generally 'pro-planning' in their outlook.
Many indeed regard the promotion of improvements and new developments as
their central concern. The nub of arguments concerns not the desirability of
planning as such, but rather 'good planning' and 'bad planning'.

This 'interventionist' position is explained principally by the fact that
environmentalist and amenity groups often contain professional workers such
as planners and architects. Many are public employees and less antipathetic to
the idea of planning than the 'older' sections of the middle class, particularly
the petits-bourgeois. In this they provide a contrast with many of the groups
who make up the 'middle class revolt' – such as the National Federation of the
Self-Employed (NFSE), NAFF, MCA, and the National Association of
Ratepayers' Action Groups (NARAG) – for these find the axis of their support
amongst the small businessmen or the self-employed and are hostile to anything which smacks of bureaucracy, planning or socialism. They tend to be
'outsider' groups in Grant's terminology.

'Outsider groups' are so called because they are unlikely to have developed
close relationships with government and are not committed to a 'strategy of
responsibility'. Many are politically unsophisticated. One such example is
NARAG which was founded in June 1974 following the massive rate rises
which spawned the 'ratepayers' revolt'. It tended to attract sections of the
middle class who had little political experience and this was reflected in its early
campaigns. It submitted naive evidence to government departments and committees, it exaggerated its influence, and it preferred noisy mass demonstrations to quieter, perhaps more effective lobbying. In Chapter 2 Nugent quotes
an interview with NARAG's chairman where he says that they sought publicity
because it was obvious that 'respectable' ratepayer groups had not got anywhere.

McHugh indicates how the NFSE has pursued a similar 'razzmatazz' campaign. It was sparked into existence in 1974 by the Bill (later the Social Security
(Amendment) Act 1975) which levied an extra 8 per cent National Insurance
contribution on the self-employed, and was boosted further by grievances over
VAT, rate increases, and the increasing administrative burdens imposed by
government legislation. Membership approached 50,000 by the end of 1975.
Like NARAG, it has generally preferred to seek media coverage for its claims

rather than cosy chats in Whitehall. Like NARAG, however, it experienced difficulty in maintaining its initial momentum, and personality disputes and policy differences rendered it virtually powerless for a considerable time. By 1978 it had sufficiently put its house in order to be once again a significant pressure group.

Other signs of middle class resentment could also be detected in the mid-1970s. A rumbustious agricultural dimension to the tide of militancy that swelled across the country in 1974 was provided by rioting farmers at Holyhead protesting against Irish cattle and pig imports. A military flavour was added by the activities of two retired officers who formed civil militia to defend the nation in the event of such dire emergencies as a general strike. General Sir Walter Walker's Civil Assistance was the largest of these 'patriotic' organisations, although its claim to have more than 100,000 members was very dubious. Disassociating itself from the political parties, Civil Assistance described itself as 'non-party, non-political and non-class'.[19] GB75, an organisation of 'apprehensive patriots' founded by Colonel David Stirling, also claimed to be 'apolitical' although it was particularly bothered by 'extremism' in the trade union movement and the parliamentary Labour Party. Nothing came of its plans to train 800–900 men to run the power stations, nor of its cry for a Bill of Rights 'to preserve individual freedoms' and for a 'drastic re-ordering of the curriculum' in the schools.[20] Both of these 'private armies' aroused severe criticism from the major parties and the police, who were alarmed at the conflict that could ensue from the para-military activities of individuals not under government direction. This alarm and ridicule effectively squashed the 'private armies' and by April 1976 they had collapsed.

There is thus clearly a sense in which parts of the middle class feel ignored by the major parties, particularly the Conservative Party. For NAFF this translates itself more specifically into opposition to 'Heathite' Conservatism, with its accommodation to the trade unions and apparent helplessness in the face of collectivism. Although a non-party organisation, it seeks to 'ginger-up' the Conservatives by forcing them to return to more individualistic economic policies, to firmer commitments on defence against the communist threat, and to reducing trade union influence, especially through the legal prohibition of the closed shop.

That so many groups have felt compelled to advance 'middle class' interests is in part indicative of the economic distress experienced by certain sections of the middle class in the inflationary 1970s. Whilst retail prices rose by 25 per cent between 1965 and 1970, they jumped by 16 per cent in 1976 alone. Such inflation threatens the economic rewards of saving and thrift – the classic middle class virtues. As Gamble points out, inflation makes capital values rather than earnings the source of real wealth, and this encourages a boom in speculation and breaks the relationship between effort and reward.[21] It is noticeable that many of the 'middle class' organisations articulate populist grievances against speculators, big business and finance capitalism. And although some small businessmen and farmers have been helped by the boom in property prices – the classic middle class capital asset – and have had their mortgage indebtedness reduced by rising inflation, those on a fixed income have seen its value eroded whilst groups with bargaining power, such as powerful trade unions, have kept their incomes abreast of inflation. Larger rate bills and higher mortgage charges have added to middle class difficulties.

Political factors have reinforced middle class grievances. Public expenditure soared in 1974 and 1975 under a Labour government believed to be in thrall to the trade union movement, and taxes were raised to pay for it. Denis Healey, Chancellor of the Exchequer, promised to squeeze the better off 'until the pips squeaked' and new taxes were introduced or threatened. Capital Transfer Tax replaced the much-avoided estate duty and taxed gifts made during the lifetime as well as at death. Capital Gains Tax was imposed and a Wealth Tax proposed. The self-employed had the new eight per cent National Insurance levy to pay.

It is not, however, simply fiscal policy that has aroused middle class apprehension. Resentment at trade union power has helped to link the traditionally anti-union small businessman with parts of the 'new' middle class, such as the middle manager who has seen trade union authority considerably advanced by the 1974 Trade Union and Labour Relations Act and the 1975 Employment Protection Act. The middle class as consumer has also been irritated at trade union power that is seen as pushing up its bills by wage and public expenditure demands and creating inconvenience by causing strikes. Doctors, too, bitterly resent attempts by unions such as the National Union of Public Employees (NUPE) to accelerate private ward closures in national health hospitals, one of the few remaining opportunities for the state-employed 'medic' to practise as an old-time professional. The closure of private wards is regarded as part of a general attempt by the unions to erode professional authority, aided and abetted by a Labour government.

Yet, as Chapter 7 makes clear, the 'middle class revolt' is not simply a response to Labour governments, nor just the invention of politicians and newspaper editors anxious for a Conservative administration. Many of the 'middle class' associations either possess a genuine belief in non-party politics or despair of all politicians. Some were disenchanted with the last two years of Heath's government. Peter Walker's local government reorganisation upset ratepayers by creating what appeared to be large, inefficient authorities which enhanced the career prospects of local government officials and pushed up rate bills. The NFSE are bitterly critical of the Conservatives for introducing the Class 4 National Insurance levy on the self-employed in the Social Security Act 1973. NAFF reflects a continuing suspicion of collectivist tendencies in Conservatism and their collaborative efforts with the big-business-dominated Confederation of British Industry (CBI) and also the Trades Union Congress (TUC).

A middle class rebellion?

How correct is the assertion that the middle class are in revolt? Do organisations such as NARAG, NVALA or even the Association of Scientific, Technical and Managerial Staffs (ASTMS) form part of a sufficiently coherent protest movement justifying this description? The experience of the ill-fated MCA, the only serious attempt to mobilise on an openly middle class basis, is hardly encouraging. Other organisations, such as the NFSE, have been racked by internal feuding as well as having poor relations with similar groups such as the Association of Self-Employed People (ASP).

An ideal typical representation of a 'middle class revolt' against which the activities of these groups may be compared should perhaps exhibit the following characteristics:

(*a*) organisations draw individuals from a clear location in the class structure, viz. the middle class, and seek to defend or advance specific or general interests associated with that class position;

(*b*) individuals in these organisations display a common class consciousness;

(*c*) these organisations recognise other classes, particularly the working class, as possessing interests in conflict with their own.

These specifications form a 'pure' representation of a 'middle class revolt' and consequently one would not expect it to be fully reflected in the empirical evidence. However, it provides a yardstick against which to measure the thesis that certain aspects of middle class political activism in Britain constitute a 'middle class revolt'.

The middle class in the class structure

It is commonplace for observers of the middle class to apologise for not providing a watertight definition of the term 'middle class'. The sympathetic Lewis and Maude quickly concluded in 1949 that 'there is no single middle class', although this did not prevent them from listing a variety of occupations 'that most people would agree were middle class'. These included the professions, business men, managers above the grade of foreman, most farmers, the majority of the public service, the majority of shopkeepers, a substantial number of clerks, other non-manual workers, and some independent craftsmen.[22] After thirty years many would agree that this list still contains most of the middle class occupations, although they would probably be hard put to it to explain why.

Hutber, another middle class sympathiser, is sceptical of the 'sociological' preference with occupation as the basis of class and prefers that of 'motivation'. 'Middle class' motivation involves the readiness to postpone satisfactions, and a desire for independence – 'an obstinate belief that it is natural to stand on one's own two feet'. In contrast, Hutber suggests, the working class attitude 'starts from a different frame of mind'. Satisfaction is taken today and is extracted from consumption. Consequently there is less commitment to independence and self-reliance and a preparedness to accept state largesse and control.[23]

Both Hutber and Gorst, founder of the MCA, are attracted to Reisman's phrase 'inner directed' in their conception of middle classness as a 'state of mind'. For Gorst this involves a 'me not we mindedness' which transcends occupational position. The self-employed gardener is more middle class in his self-directedness in this characterisation than the corporate lawyer or the pension-protected civil servant who at best are 'weakly motivated members of the middle class'. But even middle class sympathisers produce very different definitions. Some stress ideological as opposed to social criteria. Margaret Thatcher argues that the working class have 'middle class values' for they also deplore violence, truancy and the decline of discipline and are strong in their support of family life, individual freedom and property accumulation.[24] Occasionally these class characterisations slip into romantic hyperbole. At least one Conservative member sees in the 'instinctive nationalism' of working men's clubs and football supporters working class values entirely consonant with a middle class ethos.[25]

Yet these alleged virtues provide a source of anxiety for middle class polemicists. They argue that middle class values are intolerably strained by the decline in the work ethic and the spread of the hippie, hedonistic culture which marked the 'swinging sixties'. This view is developed by sociologists as diverse in their political positions as Bell, Habermas and Carroll.[26] They point to a legitimation crisis in capitalism, a decline in the appropriate motivation required for expanding industrial production. A decline in traditional morality and the spirit of Protestantism poses serious threats to the ideas of work discipline, deferred gratification and career advancement through personal effort.

However, for those who believe there is such a thing as a 'middle class revolt' a characterisation of class in terms of attitudes helps to overcome sticky problems of definition. Although lacking in sociological rigour, this formulation has the political benefit of spreading the range of possible supporters and helps its user to avoid the possibility of being labelled a narrow, self-interested class, who sell their labour power to these capitalists. The middle classes are is used enables political entrepreneurs 'to direct their appeal to a very wide audience, to encourage mutual identification and unity among diverse non-manual groups'.[27]

Marx provides the starting point for most sociological accounts of class structure with his description of classes as social groups placed in a similar relationship to the means of production. They are distinguished by access or non-access to productive property rights. Class structure is essentially dichotomous and in capitalist society there are two fundamental classes: the bourgeoisie – owners and controllers of productive property – and the working class, who sell their labour power to these capitalists. The middle classes are viewed as transitional, destined to merge with the two major classes, although in his historical studies Marx recognises both the persistence of the 'old' middle class of farmers, artisans and professionals, and the development of a new middle class of white collar employees, managers and administrators with the growth of the state and large corporations. But these are destined to be proletarianised with the extension of capitalism.

Weber adds two elements to the notion of stratification: status, involving specific 'styles of life', which may cut across class relationships, and party, which is oriented towards the acquisition and maintenance of political leadership. The amount and kind of property owned also gives rise to differences, as small businessmen demonstrate in their frequent hostility to bigger concerns. Differing skill levels may also create social differences, and Weber suggests that the middle classes are not transitory but reflect this persisting multidimensionality of social stratification.

Later sociologists have naturally taken into account the growth of professional, managerial and white collar employment. Although the 'old' middle class of small businessmen has not declined at the rate that earlier theorists suggested – its diminution has been steady though at a reduced pace in recent years – the advance of the white collar sector in industrial societies has excited sociological interest. In Britain the non-manual proportion of the labour force rose from 30 per cent to 45 per cent between 1931 and 1971, and the proportion of lower white collar employees from 18 per cent to 30 per cent. Whereas the initial enlargement of the white collar sector mainly concerned the expansion of clerical and sales occupations, in recent years professional and technical workers have shown the highest rates of development. There have been other changes, too, within the occupational composition of the middle classes in the post-war period, particularly the shift from independent to employee status, from small-scale to large-scale work settings, from private sector to public sector, and from profit-making to non-profit-making occupations.

Bechhofer *et al.* describe changes in the occupational structure as 'the result of two interacting processes, changes in the overall economic and industrial structure and changes in the employment patterns within particular sectors of the economy'. In the last twenty years employment in manufacturing, especially in primary industries such as construction and processing, has steadily declined whilst the growth of public sector employment reflects large increases in education, insurance, banking, finance, and professional and scientific services. Levels of private and personal service employment, however, have remained virtually unchanged.[28]

· Clearly, therefore, it is difficult to view the middle class as a coherent occupational category. It is large and complex, containing a variety of groups with identifiable interests. Furthermore, white collar workers are now drawn heavily from manual backgrounds, including older men who move into these jobs after spending most of their working lives in manual employment. Younger clerks often view their jobs as short-term prospects to be endured on the way to management careers, whilst an increasingly larger proportion of white collar occupations are taken now by married women, often on a part-time basis.

However, although the middle classes are not drawn from a similar location in society, there is one experience that members of the middle classes have come to share in common – state control. State regulation increasingly affects all sections of the middle class. Large and small business activity is subject to a variety of legislative and taxation requirements. Many professionals, such as doctors, accountants and lawyers, have forfeited their customary independence and are state employees subject to the control of administrators in large, bureaucratised work settings. It is hardly surprising that many should turn to collective action involving direct confrontations with government. Middle managers, aware of the challenges to managerial authority by trade unions, and the routinisation of their working lives, adopt more querulous attitudes to employers.

Interpretations of these changes vary. Bechhofer *et al.*, and Roberts *et al.*,[29] are among those who argue that the middle class is increasingly fragmented. Bechhofer *et al.* write: 'The middle class in Britain today is a less established, less unified middle class . . . the speed of change has been such that there has not yet emerged clear stable patterns of relationships between these new positions or between them and longer established occupations.'[30] Testimony to these differences within the middle class is offered by the experience of John Gorst's Middle Class Association, which managed to attract members from 214 occupations. That it failed to persist as a champion of a unified middle class is hardly surprising.

Yet other theorists, notably certain French marxists, insist that the middle class retains congruity because its various parts are unified through ideological and political relations. Poulantzas, for example, argues that the 'new' white collar workers share the same class position as the traditional petits-bourgeois. Both are neither fully bourgeois nor proletarian and feed off the surplus value produced by the working class. Together they form the 'swing group' of modern capitalism, not possessing a class ideology of their own but borrowing, adapting and twisting elements from the major classes of capitalism.[31]

This view is unnecessarily inclusive. The shopkeeper and small employer differ from white collar workers in their possession of capital. It is capital marked by low material and social technology, involving small workplaces and a restricted span of authority, but it is nevertheless sufficient to distinguish them from the propertyless employee. Indeed, some writers envisage a much more radical political role for the salaried white collar worker compared with the repressive, fascist-inclined small businessman. Mallet claims that the salariat are a form of the working class that emerges in advanced industrial societies.[32] He argues that technically and professionally qualified workers in the most modern societies are particularly opposed to the capitalist organisation of industry and have taken up most vigorously the traditional working class struggle to transform the ownership and management of economic enterprises. There is, however, little evidence to support these claims.[33]

A further interpretation suggests that the middle classes and manual workers are becoming fused into one amorphous mass. 'Mass society' theorists argue that the disintegration of communal identification has resulted in undifferentiated, consumer-fixated societies. Individuals are happy to be manipulated by a military-industrial-political complex utilising modern media and propaganda techniques.[34] Galbraith rejects this 'powerlessness' of the middle class thesis and suggests that they form a new ruling class differing from the 'old' middle class elites in their ethic of social responsibility. The bureaucrats and managers who comprise the new rulers – through their possession of authority rather than ownership of property – lack the dictatorial capacity of Mills's 'power elite'. They act more as 'veto groups' or arbiters in the bargaining between competing interests which characterises modern pluralistic society where the conditions of class cohesiveness are being eroded. The manual worker, if not fully embourgeoisified, comes to share the privatisation and instrumentality of the middle class.[35]

Galbraith's characterisation of the class structure in advanced industrial societies shares with the mass society approach a sense of the fragility of class ties. But whereas for Mills the term 'middle class' refers to the great mass of the increasingly white-collar-dominated non-elite, Galbraith is inclined to use it to refer to a more exclusive 'haute bourgeoisie' of top executives, owners and financiers whom Mills places in his 'power elite'. This illustrates both the diversity of the middle class and the confusion that the term engenders.

Another study, by Rallings, from an analysis of the Nuffield data, also concludes that white collar employees do not form a sufficiently distinct ideological grouping to comprise the basis for middle class political action.[36] Nor do they sufficiently share the ideological universe of the traditional petits-bourgeois to establish firm political alliances with them. They possess an 'essential intermediateness' whose attitudes and opinions do not accord strictly with those of either the traditional middle or working classes.

Consequently we are unable to state that the middle class are clearly located in the class structure. They are characterised by a variety of occupational interests, some of which may conflict. The civil servant, although worried by the size of his rates bill, may be disinclined to share the call of the small independent entrepreneur for a 'rolling back of the state' and a reduction in the number of public employees because of the threat to his occupational interests. Nor is it likely that the routine white collar worker reacts with the same antipathy to the advance of trade unionism as the middle manager or businessman. It is impossible to indicate clear interests associated with an identifiable 'middle class' position. Hardly surprisingly, then, attempts to form a comprehensive middle class organisation have been singularly unsuccessful. The chapters that follow examine these occupational differences 'in action', and throw light on their implications for one of the major propositions that we are investigating. Does the militancy of small businessmen, ratepayers and white collar trade unionists, for example, have sufficient in common to overcome these variegated interests and gell into a cohesive 'middle class revolt'?

A common class consciousness?

A distinguishing characteristic of many of the groups we examine is their internal divisiveness, fragmentation and, in some cases, brief existence. There is little sign of a common class consciousness, an awareness of belonging to a class with specific interests. Even the very idea of class appears grossly offensive, and the MCA was seriously undermined by the controversy over its use in its name. Although some, such as Gorst, wished for a bolder advocacy of 'middle class values', others regarded the very use of the term 'class' as divisive and as offensive to those who, whilst from a manual background, yet possessed an independence of outlook.

The short-lived existence of the MCA would not surprise historians. Such associations have been formed before, usually when the middle class have feared that a 'socialist' government has been about to appropriate them. For example, a Middle Class Defence League was formed in 1906, emerging out of the remains of the Liberty and Property Defence League of 1882, to safeguard the middle class from the industrial and political organisations of the working class and the threat posed to small entrepreneurs by larger concentrations of manufacturing and retailing units. The League developed more than forty branches and was particularly active in the 1907 London City Council elections. Its members often talked of forming a new 'Centre' party, and were put into a state of fevered excitement by Lloyd George's 'People's Budget' of 1909 which the *Daily Mail* described as 'plundering the middle classes'. Yet the organisation soon faltered and was virtually extinct by the outbreak of the First World War.

A similar body, the United Kingdom Property Owners' Federation, claimed in the short period of its existence before the First World War that 'the middle classes were the backbone of the country and were singled out for ever-increasing burdens' which, unless resisted, 'would wipe them out altogether'.[37] In 1948 Lewis and Maude set out to write a book on the 'Decline and Fall of the Middle Classes' in post-war socialist Britain, but decided that the middle classes were protesting so much that they could hardly have declined very far![38] More sourly, a series of articles in *The Economist* in the same year came to the conclusion that there was 'no hope for the middle classes to be expected from the Conservative and Labour parties, one of which was wedded to the FBI and the other to the TUC'. The author saw little hope in the Liberal Party either – 'the party of lost deposits' – and argued for a separate middle class 'Centre' party.[39]

Yet independent political action by the middle class outside the Conservative Party on the scale of the 'Poujadistes' in France or the Mittelstand associations in Germany has never materialised. This failure may lie in the highly amorphous, regionally varied and relatively open British class structure, with its gradations of power and the early incorporation of the small employer into municipal politics and the major parties.[40] However, as Bechhofer and Elliott point out, the traditional small business stratum is still an important constituency for middle class pressure groups, 'for in the similarity of their market and work situations there is some foundation for shared beliefs and common experiences'. It also has a long tradition of organisations and associations, such as those representing landlords and shopkeepers, from which to build these groups.[41]

But the petit-bourgeois politically 'has proved an uneasy stratum: its politics have been the politics of survival'.[42] Changing its political loyalties from radical to Liberal to Tory, it has sought to minimise the threats of an increasingly hostile world in defence of its own interests. This volatility reflects the ambiguous work situation of the small shopkeeper, normally part-owner and part-worker and drawn from a variety of social backgrounds. Furthermore, his anti-collectivism and belief in individual effort militates against a common basis for action. Small business organisations find difficulty in moving from particular grievances in times of economic hardship – over specific tax burdens, for example – to a congruous political philosophy.

A further feature of small business organisations, one shared with most 'middle class' political groups, is a 'non-political' and 'non-class' posture. They disagree 'radically with the whole conceptual basis of the "working class"/"middle class" dichotomy, whether manifest in common usage or in more formal sociological theory',[43] and are at pains to claim that their memberships represent a cross-section of the community and are not simply drawn from the middle class. They delight in pointing out that most socialist parties – despite claims to be working class organisations – are led primarily by middle class intellectuals and have memberships which are often more completely middle class than their own.

Sociologists are inclined to overplay the class category and too cynically disregard the middle class belief in 'non-class' politics. Webb, however, convincingly demonstrates the situational aspects of class in his survey of an occupationally heterogeneous suburb of Liverpool.[44] He discovered that when respondents were asked to describe their positions in the social structure, without the 'class' category being volunteered by the investigator, they were much less likely to place themselves into either the working or middle class. This was particularly noticeable for non-manual respondents. But when specifically asked which class they thought they belonged to, most non-manual workers considered themselves to be middle class. The weakness of self-rated middle classness is similarly revealed when we note that of those who rated themselves as belonging to the middle class, 59 per cent failed to think in this way when asked to freely describe themselves. Specific occupational and status categories ('professional', 'architect') predominated, thus indicating the high degree of formal 'middle class' job differentiation.

This reluctance to admit 'middle classness' is traced by some to a longgestating sense of guilt at class advantage which feeds the pejorativeness of terms such as 'middle class' or 'suburbanite'. Hutber suggests that this sense of sin is a simple defensiveness, 'a feeling that perhaps it is, after all, quite simply wrong to have anything which not everybody has. This imparts a kind of furtiveness to middle class life.'[45] Understandable shyness at proclaiming class advantage is reinforced by fear at arousing expectations in other groups that cannot be fulfilled. Lewis and Maude trace middle class 'angst' back to the 'Age of Guilt' associated with the spread of equality in late Victorian England. This coincided with a 'great mass of people being imbued with a craving to compete' but at a time when the older middle class was losing its asceticism in favour of possessions, enjoyment and status competitiveness. And this at a time when better social services were demanded from a British capitalism no longer as supreme as it had been.[46]

Clearly the middle classes contain groups which differ markedly in their preparedness to support their class ideologically. Some, notably students and intellectuals, recognising that they are middle class and not liking it, may even advance ideas which, far from serving middle class interests, are opposed to them. Many others refuse to accept class labels despite the growing tendency by some middle class polemicists to argue more openly for middle class virtues. Gorst, as the name of his association indicates, attempted to openly proclaim middle class interests, although with little success, whilst Hutber, despite recognising that the label 'middle class' may be inadequate, feels that 'it cannot be discarded if the values are to be preserved'.[47]

Often it is the basis of class that middle class groups find objectionable. Although claiming to dislike class labels, there is little denial of social and personal differences. But these differences do not simply centre around the unequal access to life chances of manual and non-manual employees respectively. Most of the organisations would echo the sentiments expressed by the Association of Self-Employed People (ASP) which admits that we are a 'class ridden society' but goes on to suggest that 'there are only two classes, the producers and the parasites'. The producers of wealth are those productive individuals trading in the free market and include businessmen, farmers, doctors and artisans, whilst the 'parasites' are those 'living off the taxes extracted from the producers'. The latter, in the words of ASP's journal, contain 'government bureaucrats, politicians, the Chrysler car company, and the unemployed'. Furthermore, some of the 'middle class' organisations object to the designation 'working class' being assigned solely to manual employees. They are regarded as simply one section of the 'real' working class which includes such contributors to national wealth as the self-employed and the small businessman.[48]

This adherence to the original class anlysis of the early Liberals and radicals is reinforced by the changes occurring within the middle class. Roberts *et al*. remark that 'in the process of growing the middle class has become a different type of social formation than the middle class with which Lewis and Maude sympathised'.[49] Lewis and Maude's original model of middle class representatives were self-employed businessmen and independent professional people such as solicitors and accountants. They carried a distinctive set of middle class values and culture, the sense of independence that allowed the middle class to become the moral and political backbone of English society. Their spokesmen in organisations such as ASP and the NFSE frequently view the new salariat with little short of contempt. The latter's values are not those of the self-reliant, freedom loving petit-bourgeoisie, but those of the dependent, soulless, rule-following roundhead unsmilingly engaged in destroying a diminishing band of cavaliers. In consequence the 'middle class revolt' almost resembles a war between the middle classes. 'Middle class mandarins' in the corporations and the civil service are held responsible for the administrative blight that besets small entrepreneurial life, and for conniving with bigger employers and the trade unions in an extension of the corporatist welfare state. The 'nanny state' so caustically described by Boyson[50] helps not so much to destroy the middle class as to bureaucratise it. The 'newer' middle class are frequently regarded by middle class apologists as traitors to the middle class cause. Instead of revolting against socialism they adapt themselves to it by entering state employment and extracting as much as they can from employers with devices such as inflation-proof pensions. But the self-employed are different. They resent the Socialists taxing them into the ground. And as the new middle class expands and the old middle class declines they feel that 'the less attractive middle class characteristics – snobbery, obsequiousness, pettiness, complacency, social conformity, insensitivity and authoritarianism –' predominate.[51]

Thus it is clearly difficult to refer to a 'middle class consciousness'. The evidence from Webb and elsewhere casts doubt on whether the middle class generally have any sense of common cause. Whether those 'in revolt' have one is a question we set ourselves in the following chapters. Although we lack survey evidence of participants' reasons for joining organisations, the internal struggles that characterised Gorst's MCA suggest that this is unlikely.

If a 'middle class identity' ever existed, the differentiation of the middle class occupational world has ensured its passing. Sociologists mostly refer to the middle class*es*, to types of middle class images of the class structure. Roberts *et al*. distinguish four such types:[52]

(*a*) compressed middle class
(*b*) middle mass

(*c*) proletarian

(*d*) ladder

The compressed middle class imagery is generally associated with the traditional middle class, such as the small businessman, or the white collar worker with few formal qualifications. They tend to regard themselves as belonging to a small group which is squeezed between a large working class and a powerful upper class. The most common variety of class imagery displayed by Roberts's white collar respondents, however, involved individuals placing themselves in a large category located around the centre of a social hierarchy, which was distinguished only from the very poor and the very rich. Somewhat surprisingly, these 'Mr Averages' were rarely bothered by working class encroachment, nor were they especially ambitious. A further minority of respondents positively identified themselves with the working class and were typically employed in routine white collar jobs. These 'proletarians' perceived the class structure in similar fashion to 'proleterian' manual workers, with a clear divide between themselves and the more privileged middle class. Finally a small number of highly educated respondents employed a 'ladder' imagery of the social order which was characterised as a series of fine gradations with no dominant class. They tended to be radical in outlook.

These images highlight the absence of a single 'middle class consciousness'. The petit-bourgeoisie is most clearly aware of trade union and working class challenges to its market and status positions, but is also resentful of the 'trendy' radical middle class and the 'haute bourgeoisie'. Small business and some ratepayers' associations may provide the best basis for 'middle class' political action – they persist for longer than most general middle class associations – but their diversity, competitiveness and gauche distaste for diplomatic politicking tend to produce an agglomeration of individual interests rather than a common class cause.

It is thus doubtful whether the common 'attitude of mind' identified by middle class sympathisers really does exist to unite the middle class. The love of independence, desire for self-improvement and postponement of immediate satisfactions, which allegedly distinguish the middle class from the pleasure-seeking working class, are less accurate descriptions of this or that group than characteristics found in all social classes. Roberts's middle class and working class respondents reveal less divergence in orientations to social mobility and attitudes to educational attainment by their children than the traditional stereotypes predict. Whilst manual parental aspirations for their children were modest in absolute terms, compared with white collar respondents, in relative terms, when levels of parental aspiration were measured against the respondents' own starting points, the relationship between occupational status and ambition disappeared.

Unsurprisingly, therefore, would-be mergers between 'middle class' organisations frequently fail. Gorst's efforts to set up a working party that would link the MCA with a host of other organisations such as NURA, NARAG, NFSE, and the Society for Individual Freedom (SIF), soon floundered on their reluctance to engage in cooperative action.

Class enemies?

The 'middle class revolters' robustly recognise their arch-enemies and are rarely reluctant to condemn them publicly. But these enemies are difficult to classify in class terms. Groups clearly associated with the detested state machinery, such as civil servants, politicians, planners, and their cultural allies in education and the mass media, are persistent objects of anger. But they are part of a wider aglomeration of 'non-producers' which includes the unemployed, financiers and aristocrats. This collection cuts across the manual/non-manual dichotomy generally employed by sociologists. It captures populist resentment against powerful forces by groups who feel that their position is under attack from the major parties, big business and Whitehall.

Despite patronising accounts of working class life, 'middle class' groups are not obsessed with a working class *bête noir*. Many dislike class labels, which makes it difficult for them openly to portray the working class as a class enemy. For example, NARAG persistently denies that it is a middle class organisation and NAFF claims to be a 'broad alliance that appeals to people from all social backgrounds'.[53] Those who are frequently behind much 'middle class' protest – the small employers and the self-employed – are characterised by their marginality, hovering precariously between the classes. Property and the ability to control his work schedule give the shopkeeper the 'hallmarks' of 'middle classness', yet he often shares the level of income and conditions of work of his working class customers. He may resent his need to defer to status inferiors with increasing purchasing power, yet full identification with the 'establishment' is prevented by the precariousness of his own position.[54]

This is not to suggest that the implied target of much 'middle class' political activity is not the working class and particularly the organisations that represent them. Attempts by NAFF to outlaw the closed shop strike directly at the institutional interests of the trade unions. The Employment Protection Act is strenuously opposed by the small business organisations as a trade-union-inspired measure that unfairly tilts conditions in the labour market in the direction of the worker. Ratepayers complain, too, when council house rents are frozen or Clay Cross councillors appear to escape the consequences of their defiance over the Rent Act.

The philosophers of the new right who seek to articulate a coherent ideology for 'middle class' groups based on the doctrine of a more competitive and individualistic society can hardly complain if the working class take them at their word and compete for a greater share of goods and resources. It is part of the claim by Sir Keith Joseph, for example, that all benefit from a less fettered capitalism, as the corresponding increase in productivity enables even the poorest to enjoy a higher standard of living than would be available from an egalitarian redistribution of existing wealth.[55] The logic of the argument is that there is no moral justification for any particular distribution of rewards provided they have been produced in a 'free economy' which in turn is believed to ensure the maximisation of individual liberty.

Finally, we must guard against the impression that a diffuse middle class is to be contrasted with a single working class identity or self-consciousness. The class structure as a whole is fragmented and middle class diffusiveness is paralleled elsewhere. There is no one collectivist, welfare-oriented, trade-union-based working class. Some manual workers share the fears and aspirations of our middle class activists, and 'anti-permissiveness' in particular is by no means solely a middle class preoccupation. A companion volume on the working class would indicate that the inchoate nature of the middle class accords closely with the wider national picture which it so greatly influences.[56]

The chapters that follow explore some of the themes raised in this introductory chapter and take selected features of the increasing activism of organisations which specifically promote 'middle class' interests. They have been chosen not because they constitute an exhaustive enquiry into the 'middle class revolt' but because they examine some of its central and more interesting characteristics. The chapters attempt to hold in focus the thesis that the 1970s have marked a quickening of resolve and an increased militancy by groups commonly identified as possessing 'middle class' aspirations and personnel. Taken together they indicate the diversity of the so-called 'revolt'.

In Chapter 2, on the Ratepayers' associations, Nugent indicates that, although mainly drawn from the ranks of the middle class, the aggressive ratepayers' action groups that mushroomed in the 'revolt' of 1974–5 proved attractive to a wider audience than their 'geriatric' predecessors and were often associated with a more general community or local pride against the depredations of planners.

McHugh's examination in Chapter 3, of the 'revolt' of the self-employed and small independent entrepreneurs reveals a common characteristic of middle class political activism – the inability of its participants to pool resources, in this case to achieve the declared aim of becoming a third force between the TUC and the CBI. The National Federation of the Self-Employed reveals the classic cross-pressures on organisations never sure whether their most effective approach is to appear respectable and acceptable to policy-makers or to be more militant and aggressive, thus swamping objections with a sheer accumulation of well-publicised protest. But the two are not totally unconnected. To be taken seriously by government an organisation must normally demonstrate weight of support; but to secure this support and avoid the alienative consequences of bureaucratisation that can beset orthodox and established pressure groups may require the public flamboyance that disturbs 'inside' relationships with decision-makers.

Chapter 4, on the freedom groups, is concerned with a number of organisations in Britain whose central aim is to lobby for a 'free market' economy. The National Association for Freedom represents the most recent and the most 'populistic' of these groups. The chapter, amongst other things, indicates how close links may be established between certain types of 'middle class' groups where the small entrepreneur provides the nub of their support. NAFF also provides the ideological umbrella that clothes the more specific interests of a number of our 'middle class' groups.

Chapter 5 outlines the steadier development of middle class unionism as compared with other, more mercurial, forms of middle class militancy. Both TUC-style unionism and other collectively orientated bodies have grown since the mid-1960s and there is no evidence to suggest that they have experienced any great spurt in the 1970s. Yet, despite the apparent embrace of collective industrial organisation which is anathema to most other groups examined in the book, this development also reflects middle class apprehension at working class and trade union advance rather than a desire for class unity with them.

Although the book concentrates on middle class responses to economic threats, Cliff, in Chapter 6, reminds us of the resurgence of concern by those groups that see themselves as reacting to threats to moral standards. They also became more active and attracted greater support in the mid-1970s as the moral pendulum swung back from the permissive climate of the 'swinging sixties'.

The last substantive chapter, on the established parties, explores a number of themes raised in this introduction, particularly the impact of the 'middle class revolt' on the major parties. That the 'revolt' was a response to a new predatory Labour government is shown to be too simple an explanation, and the strong disillusionment with the Conservative Party following the Heath administration is emphasised. The ambiguity and suspicion that characterise relations between the middle class protesters and their putative allies in the Tory Party remains one of the more fascinating features of the British political scene.

Finally, the Conclusion takes up the question posed throughout this Introduction. We draw together the threads of the preceding chapters and examine whether the organisations we explore are characterised by a sufficient commonality to justify the proposition that they comprise a 'middle class revolt'. The possibility of the existence of a *generalised* middle class revolt has already been shown to be doubtful. But this still leaves unresolved the question whether these recent manifestations of middle class dissent constitute a recognisable movement. The chapters that follow throw light on this.

NOTES

1 Watkins, A., London *Evening Standard*, 1 December 1974.
2 This phrase is taken from the ITV programme 'The Mangling of the Middle Classes' shown in 1975 and quoted in Roberts, K., *et al.*, *The Fragmentary Class Structure*, Heinemann, 1977, p. 107.
3 *The Times*, 11 January 1975, p. 13.
4 Ibid, 1 April 1974, p. 10.
5 Hutber, P., *The Decline and Fall of the Middle Class: and how it can fight back*, Penguin, 1977, p. 9.
6 Garrard, J., *et al.*, *The Middle Class in Politics*, Teakfield, 1978. See the Introduction.
7 Bechhofer, F., *et al.*, 'Structure, Consciousness and Action: A Sociological Profile of the British Middle Class', *British Journal of Sociology*, Vol. 29, No. 4 (December 1978). A good deal that follows draws on their work at the Department of Sociology, Edinburgh University.
8 These quotations are taken from the *Middle Class Association Bulletin*, May 1975.
9 Ibid.
10 Much of the information on the Middle Class Association was kindly given by John Gorst in an extended interview in March 1978.
11 Crouch, C. (ed.), *British Political Sociology Yearbook*, Vol. 3, *Participation in Politics*, Croom Helm, 1977, p. 2.
12 Crewe, I., *et al.*, 'Partisan Dealignment in Britain 1964–1974', *British Journal of Political Science*, 7 April 1977, p. 129.
13 Ibid, p. 182.
14 Ibid, p. 184.
15 Grant, W., 'Insider Groups and Outsider Groups', paper given at the European Consortium for Political Research Conference on 'Political Attitudes and Behaviour of the Middle Class in Europe', Berlin, March 1977. The paper was given to the workshop on Interest Group Strategies.
16 Ibid, p. 8.
17 Barker, A., and Keating, M., 'Public Spirits: Amenity Societies and Others', in Crouch, C. (ed.), *British Political Sociology Yearbook*, Vol. 3, *Participation in Politics*, Croom Helm, 1977, pp. 145–6. See also Barker, A., *The Local Amenity Movement*, Civic Trust, 1976.
18 Ibid, p. 151.
19 Letter by Walker to *The Times*, 10 September 1974.
20 *The Times*, 23 August 1974, p. 2.
21 Gamble, A., *The Conservative Nation*, Routledge, 1974, p. 127.
22 Lewis, R., and Maude, A., *The English Middle Classes*, Phoenix House, 1949, p. 17.
23 Hutber, op. cit., pp. 23–5.
24 See, for example, Mrs Thatcher's article 'My Kind of Tory Party', *Daily Telegraph*, 30 January 1975.
25 Clark, A., *Daily Telegraph*, 7 October 1975.
26 Bell, D., *The Cultural Contradictions of Capitalism*, Heinemann, 1975; Habermas, J., *Legitimation Crisis*, Heinemann, 1976; Carroll, J., *Puritan, Paranoid, Remissive*, Macmillan, 1977.
27 Bechhofer *et al.*, op. cit., p. 2.
28 Ibid, pp. 4–6.
29 Roberts *et al.*, op. cit.
30 Bechhofer *et al.*, op. cit., p. 12.
31 Poulantzas, N., *Classes in Contemporary Capitalism*, New Left Books, 1975.
32 Mallet, S., *La Nouvelle Classe Ouvrière*, Editions Sevil, Paris, 1963.
33 See, for example, Gallie, D., *In Search of the New Working Class*, Cambridge University Press, 1978.

34 Mills, C. W., *The Power Elite*, Oxford University Press, New York, 1965.
35 Galbraith, J., *The New Industrial State*, Penguin, 1969.
36 Rallings, C., 'White Collar Workers: Class and Politics – The Socio-Economic Characteristics and Political Behaviour of the Contemporary British Lower Middle Class', paper presented to the European Consortium for Political Research Workshop on 'Political Attitudes and Behaviour of the Middle Class in Western Europe', Berlin, March 1977, p. 7.
37 Lewis and Maude, op. cit., p. 75.
38 Ibid, Preface.
39 *The Economist*, January 1948. Series of articles on the middle classes.
40 See, for example, contributions by Nossiter, Fraser and Garrard, in Garrard *et al.*, op. cit.
41 Bechhofer, F., and Elliott, B., 'The Voice of Small Business and the Politics of Survival', *Sociological Review*, 26 February 1978, pp. 58–9.
42 Ibid, p. 62.
43 Letter from Chris Tame, Research Department, NAFF. Thanks to Mr Tame for permission to quote from our correspondence.
44 Webb, D., 'Some reservations on the use of self-rated class', *Sociological Review*, 21 (1973), pp. 321–30.
45 Hutber, op. cit., p. 87.
46 Lewis and Maude, op. cit., p. 70.
47 Hutber, op. cit., p. 169.
48 *Counterattack*, the publication of ASP, Vol. 1, No. 1 (March 1976), p. 2.
49 Roberts *et al.*, op. cit., pp. 105–6.
50 Boyson, R., *Daily Telegraph*, 7 December 1974.
51 Lewis, R., *The Times*, 17 February 1975.
52 Roberts *et al.*, op. cit., pp. 6–8.
53 Moss, R. (ex-Director of NAFF), in *Free Nation*, Vol. 2, No. 5 (17 March 1977).
54 Bechhofer, F., *et al.*, 'The Petits Bourgeois in the Class Structure: The Case of the Small Shopkeepers', in Parkin, F. (ed.), *The Social Analysis of Class Structure*, Tavistock, 1974, pp. 103–28.
55 Joseph, K., *The Business of Business*, Bow Group Publication, February 1977.
56 I am grateful to Anthony Barker for this point. Recent analyses of social mobility by Goldthorpe and his colleagues at Nuffield College, Oxford, suggests that one reason for the 'inchoate nature' of the middle class may lie in higher levels of inter- and intra-generational mobility into non-manual occupations by those with manual fathers since the last war. See particularly, Goldthorpe, J. H. and Llewellyn, C., 'Class Mobility in Modern Britain: Three Theses Examined', *Sociology*, Vol. 11, No. 2 (May 1977), pp. 257–87; Goldthorpe, J., 'Comment' on Bechhofer F., Elliott B., and McCrone D., *op. cit.*, pp. 436–8. R. Bourne's conversations with the Nuffield team in his article, 'The Snakes and Ladders of the British Class System', *New Society*, Vol. 47, No. 853 (8 February 1979), pp. 291–3, is also useful.

Neill Nugent

2. The Ratepayers

Introduction

The rating system is a controversial form of taxation, and criticisms have long ranged over virtually every aspect of its operation. Many have questioned the basic principles, arguing that a tax which raises revenue from levies on property takes little account either of the use made of services or of a household's ability to pay. Rates are thus claimed to be inequitable, regressive and unfair. Other critics have focused on more specific defects, arguing, for example, that small businesses are over-rated and that the system discourages improvement to property.

Despite these disadvantages, however, rating has only occasionally been a key political issue. At national level governments have been reluctant to tamper with a tax which is both administratively convenient and well established. Periodic bursts of ratepayers' activity have sometimes led to expressions of governmental concern – in the early 1960s, for example, controversy over property revaluations resulted in the establishment of the *Committee of Inquiry into the Impact of Rates on Households* (*the Allen Committee*) – but on the whole governments have preferred to leave well alone.[1] It is true that the general increase in local government expenditure in the post-war era, which has been accompanied by a decrease in the proportion of income received from rates, has resulted in greater attention being directed towards alternative forms of local authority finance. Until 1974, however, when there were massive rate rises in most parts of the country, this was not a divisive issue between the two main political parties. Nor was it regarded as being especially urgent, and the sudden establishment in July 1974 of the *Committee of Inquiry into Local Government Finance* (*the Layfield Committee*) owed more to the immediate pressure of that year's dramatic increases than to any long-term movement towards change.

At local level rates have naturally been of greater political importance. Ratepayers' associations have long been active in many parts of the country and in some areas have significantly affected local politics. More generally, even where associations have not existed, rates have been much more central to the political debate.

Even in local politics, however, the role of rates, certainly before 1974, should not be overstated. There are two reasons for this. Firstly, those Ratepayers' movements that did exist in the pre-1974 period tended to be ephemeral and poorly supported. Secondly, whilst it is true that much of the local political debate concerns levels of expenditure, and is thus rates-related, most survey evidence suggests that rate levels *as such* are of only limited electoral importance. Many politicians *believe* that rates influence elections, and thus move towards the 'saving' end of the 'save–spend' spectrum, but the uniformity of swing in local elections strongly suggests that national issues are in fact the major determinants.[2] Indeed, even where local variations in swing do occur, they are seldom explained by the impact of rates. This is illustrated, for example, by Gregory's study of Reading which shows that on the eight occasions between 1945 and 1967 when the national trend and the local trend in Reading departed from one another there was only one *possible* instance when rates *might* have been crucial.[3]

As Newton says, in summarising the findings of a number of local election studies,

> In short the sum total of research points to the same conclusion – that rates have had very little impact on local election results, that they have rarely been a contentious local issue, and that the majority of the electorate has not seen rates as a serious local problem.[4]

The reason for the limited political significance of rates is not difficult to find: they constitute a very small proportion of personal disposable incomes – around 2·5 per cent. That proportion has even fallen slightly in recent years despite a rapid growth in local government expenditure: from 8·6 per cent of gross domestic product in 1949 to 12·4 per cent in 1974. Rates have been held down by an increased central government responsibility for the financing of local services. In 1949–50 the total burden of local authority current expenditure came almost equally from three sources – government grants, 34 per cent; rates (domestic and commercial), 34 per cent; other income, 32 per cent. By 1973–4 these figures were, respectively, 45 per cent, 28 per cent and 27 per cent.[5]

At around 2·5 per cent rates compare very favourably with direct and indirect taxation which, in the mid-1970s for middle income earners of £50–£100 per week, *each* took an average of 14 per cent of gross household income. Indeed, for the middle and upper income earners, the most likely base of organised ratepayer activity, rates can even be seen as an acceptable arrangement, for, as the *Layfield Report* states,

> As it is, rating is progressive in its incidence . . . up to income levels of about £40 a week, is roughly proportional to income between £40 and £60 a week and is regressive at higher income levels.[6]

This relative marginality of rates helps to explain why they generated, before 1974, only limited political activity outside the normal channels of party politics. Certainly attitude surveys tend to suggest that whilst rates are widely viewed as being *unfair*, they are not significantly more *unpopular* than other taxes. This may be illustrated by reference to a study commissioned on behalf of the *Layfield Committee*. Conducted in May/June 1975, when it may be assumed that opposition to rates was at its height, the report stated:

> When asked to make a choice, 37 per cent of people said they would abolish VAT, 34 per cent rates and 28 per cent income tax. Of heads of household, 38 per cent would abolish VAT, 37 per cent rates and 23 per cent income tax. However, among those who knew most about the present rating system, a substantially higher proportion would abolish rates than would abolish VAT or income tax. . . .

Significantly fewer people agree that rating is a fair system than agree the same about VAT or income tax.[7]

But a satisfactory account of the limited impact of rates, and more importantly from our point of view the Ratepayers' movement, must go beyond the marginality of rates and the apparently less than fervent opposition to them. For there have been times and places, both before and after 1974, when a sudden sharp rise in rates or a property revaluation has caused an enormous outburst of indignation and a flurry of activity. The problem has been to maintain momentum. To explain this lack of 'staying power', organisational and ideological features of Ratepayers' associations must be considered.

Frequently, Ratepayers' associations are founded amidst great enthusiasm and excitement, with grossly exaggerated expectations of success. When this is not quickly achieved, disillusionment is apt to set in. For those who have not previously participated in political activity – and frequently they constitute a majority of newly formed Ratepayers' committees – the tedium and drudgery of many aspects of participation take their toll. The result is that many associations very quickly become highly dependent on a hard core of perhaps half a dozen members. In consequence they are highly fragile. Some completely disappear simply because they do not have the manpower to collect subscriptions or because the services of an efficient secretary are lost.

Local apathy is, of course, a problem not unknown to the major parties. Even with their broader range of interests and their greater ability to offer supporters political 'rewards', branches may still virtually cease to operate. But the problem can usually be covered, in part at least, by the services of the national organisation. With Ratepayers' associations this is not the case. Their intense localism, their general distrust of central direction, and their limited resources have limited the scope of national bodies and precluded the creation of a well-financed national framework. The National Union of Ratepayers' Associations (NURA), which was founded in 1921 and which, prior to 1974, was by far the largest national Ratepayers' organisation, has always been run on a shoestring and has never been in a position to offer physical help – of any kind – to an association experiencing difficulties. In fact, with affiliation being purely voluntary, it has usually had enough problems in extracting subscriptions from its member associations – which in the 1960s and 1970s have averaged around 500 – simply to maintain its already modest activities.

As a number of observers have argued, 'local' parties are much more likely to be subject to conflict and internal dispute than parties which have a national base and which are centred around producer interests.[8] Ratepayers' groups are particularly prone to such divisions and 'personality politics' and this in no small measure is due to their almost ideological commitment to 'non-party' local government. Whilst activists are usually pro-Conservative in their national sympathies they vigorously claim to be 'independent' or 'non-party' at local level. The party system is bitterly attacked for leading to a dogmatism and divisiveness that have no place in local affairs 'where the interests of all override political considerations'. In the council chamber party politics, it is alleged, simply produces 'automatons' and 'worthless political debate'. This non-party stance, however, whilst often useful in helping to create an early *esprit de corps* – of the 'us' against 'them' variety – frequently creates difficulties, leading to acrimony and division which can threaten the very existence of an association. Often this occurs when the initial burst of enthusiasm has passed and long-term strategy has to be agreed.

A particularly 'dangerous' situation can arise if it becomes apparent that the local political 'elite' – councillors and officials – are unsympathetic and unresponsive to the association's aims. Pressure may then build up for the adoption of alternative tactics so as to put the association 'on the inside'. Stacey has described the early stages of such a process at Banbury:

> The Ratepayers were from the start [i.e. 1966] a self-conscious pressure group. In 1968 they still seemed to feel outside the local power structure, and felt they should aim to get a representative of the Association on all possible committees 'so that they would be instrumental in decision making as opposed to being presented with a *fait accompli*'.[9]

A similar situation occurred in Newcastle in the late 1960s when a number of associations became increasingly despondent at their own ineffectiveness and also increasingly angry at the incompetence and lack of sensitivity of sitting councillors. As a result, one association, in Jesmond, which at the time of its formation in 1965 had had no desire to participate directly in council affairs, decided to contest local elections.[10]

It is possible, and this happened at Jesmond, that such a development can be the making of an association in that electoral success provides a more readily identifiable base for political activity and also offers to members and potential supporters a direct avenue to power and influence. More frequently, however, and it is in this sense that danger can arise, attempts to get on the 'inside' by contesting elections can create strains and even lead to splits. The 'non-political' stance inclines many ratepayer activists to the view that electoral politics are not appropriate. This may be because they genuinely believe that local government is in some way non-political; it may be because they are reluctant to damage relations with the established parties; or it may be because they have a prior commitment, if only at national level, to a political party – probably the Conservatives – and are thus divided in their loyalties. Whatever the explanation, electoral strategy is a very sensitive issue and those associations which decide to directly contest seats run a high risk of creating friction and alienating valuable support. They may help to sow the seeds of their own demise.

The 'old' associations

With rates themselves being something of a fringe issue prior to the massive increases of 1974–5, the more successful of the 'old' or established pre-1974 Ratepayers' associations were of two kinds. The first, a declining proportion from the 1950s, were 'concealed' Conservatives in that they were either not opposed by that Party in local elections or were part of an 'arrangement' whereby the two did not confront one another in particular wards. The second type attained success by tapping a variety of sources of discontent in their local community. As Grant observes, if 'genuine local parties', as opposed to 'concealed national parties', are to survive there must be a serious conflict which divides the citizens other than on national party lines; there must be 'underlying sustaining factors'.[11] Rates seldom provide such a source of division but other issues sometimes do. Thus environmental questions were frequently taken up by the 'old' associations to breathe new life into a flagging cause. In other cases a proposed road scheme, a new housing development, the extension of an industrial estate or something similar provided the initial *raison d'être* of an association. In this event the title 'Ratepayer' could just as easily have been 'Resident', 'Independent' or 'Citizen' (creating, incidentally, a problem of nomenclature which makes an exact monitoring of Ratepayers' activities well-nigh impossible).

Ratepayers' associations before the 1974–5 'revolt' were thus usually highly parochial and in consequence came in a variety of forms. A few examples, all drawn from associations which included 'Ratepayers' in their title, gives a flavour of the diversity of aims and strategies.

(1) Stanyer, in his account of Exeter politics in the early 1960s, when the Ratepayers won council seats, emphasises that they devoted almost all of their manifestos to a demand that the rating system should be reformed. They put themselves forward as 'Watchdogs of the Ratepayers' and in so doing emphasised that they were 'non-political and non-sectarian'. They were against parties in local government and in turn were opposed by all the parties.[12]

(2) In Newcastle, by contrast, the most influential association before 1974, the Jesmond and District Household and Ratepayers' Association, whilst also being opposed by all the political parties, only rarely concerned itself with rates as such. Its main interests were environmental and community issues. Thus its manifestos for the 1973 County and District elections (in which it won all the ward seats) made no call for a cut in rate levels despite the claim that Jesmond was the most highly rated residential area in the city. Rather was there a populist/parochial appeal to local identities and loyalties. Their candidate for the County Council concluded his personal manifesto with these words:

> *From Party 'yes-men', the voters of this Ward have hitherto been treated to a 'take-it-or-leave-it' and a 'there-is-nothing-we-can-do-about-it' attitude*
> IN MY OPINION, THERE IS NO ROOM FOR PARTY POLITICS IN LOCAL GOVERNMENT
> Previously, instead of proper representation, we have had continual exhibitions of 'toeing the Party line'. If elected, I shall make it my business to find out what the people of Jesmond want and, more particularly (in the present climate) what they do NOT want. For instance, I know they'd prefer the rates to be spent on education, health, *good* housing, more open spaces and better parks, clean and efficient public transport, smoke control and *improved* social services than on motorways that can only bring more and more traffic into the city and empty office blocks that are merely waiting for those mythical civil servants to move in from the South of England.
> If I become your new Councillor, THE MESSAGE WILL GO OUT LOUD AND CLEAR TO THOSE WHO ARE RESPONSIBLE FOR THE CREEPING ROT THAT IS RUINING JESMOND AND OUR CITY.[13]

(3) A classic concealed Conservative type is described by Richards in his study of Southampton politics. Between 1934 and 1954 power in the city switched between Labour and Ratepayers with the Conservatives not contesting. So complete was the identification between Conservatives and Ratepayers that in 1954 the two amalgamated and henceforth called themselves Conservative-Ratepayers; 'this amalgamation was carried through for reasons of administrative convenience, as the maintenance of separate Conservative and Ratepayer organisations was costly, cumbersome and inefficient'.[14]

(4) In Gateshead, in the years before reorganisation, 'Rent and Ratepayers' provided the main opposition in a strong Labour area. They too were concealed Conservatives in that the two parties did not openly compete against one another at local level, e.g. in 1971 there were fifteen contests in the borough; twelve were Labour v. Rent and Ratepayers, three were Labour v. Conservative. In 1972, the final year of elections before reorganisation, there were twelve contests, all Labour v. Rent and Ratepayers. In 1973, however, in the first elections to the new, enlarged, Gateshead council, the arrangement was substantially changed and though again there were no direct contests the Rent and Ratepayers were restricted to four wards in the Felling area – described in the local press as 'the home base' of the former opposition leader on the Gateshead council, 'a fiery Felling baker'. But though they were still, strictly speaking, of the concealed Conservative type, their manifesto differed in a number of respects from Conservative policy and was characterised more than anything by its parochialism.

> Being non-political and believing that no political party should control a council elected by the people, we think the new authority provides the opportunity to pull down the barrier of politics to work for the common good. However, we do not believe in miracles.
>
> We have some concern that Gateshead, with the ideology of 'bigger is best' will centralise everything in Gateshead to the detriment of Felling people. We will resist this.
>
> Our policy is to make available conventional houses for all families and make provision to enable council tenants to purchase.
>
> Regarding social services it is our continuing resolve to implement the 1970 Chronically Sick and Disabled Act without delay.
>
> We seek equal opportunity for all children to enjoy the highest standards of comprehensive education.[15]

(5) In Manchester in the late 1950s and early 1960s rates became, for a while, a key issue and various Ratepayers' groups emerged with the aim of securing representation on the council so as to cut expenditure and thereby lower rates. All claimed to be 'non-political and non-sectarian'. No candidates were in fact elected, but a noticeable feature of the campaign was the very close association the Ratepayers enjoyed with the Liberal Party in the city. The Liberal candidate elected to the council in May 1960, for example, was chairman of the Manchester Ratepayers' Council, and the chairman of the Ratepayers' Union was strongly supported by the Liberals.[16]

(6) Grant has described the activities of a typical retiree-based Ratepayers' movement in a resort town, Seaton, Devon.[17] In the early 1960s residents became increasingly concerned at the 'threat' posed by the provision of tourist amenities by the council. Accordingly an association was constituted, or rather an old one was reconstituted, which, though initially interesting itself in a range of matters, focused more and more on the danger of Seaton becoming a 'Blackpool of the South'. Necessarily this brought about a conflict with the local traders, as may be seen by quoting from a 1969 article in the Ratepayers' newsletters:

> The [official] 'policy' . . . is to fill the town in the season to overflowing, to allow holiday flats, chalets and camps to multiply, ostensibly to meet a need but calculated to create a demand. . . . The only section of our community which stands to gain from

this is a small, but articulate, part of the trading element. Residential property owners will lose heavily. The above would be undesirable even if the commercial section were paying for it; but they are not.[18]

These six examples, and many more could be given, illustrate the differing aims, contrasting strategies and varied distribution of the pre-1974 associations. They shared perhaps only four features:

(a) The'non-partisan' stance and the claim that party politics had no place in local government was almost universal.[19] Nowhere is this seen more clearly than in the evidence submitted by individual associations to the Redcliffe-Maud *Royal Commission on Local Government in England*. Whilst their many proposals for structural reform were enormously diverse, virtually all managed to voice their opposition to the dominant influence of party politics. The marginality of this to the terms of reference of the Commission, and the virtual impossibility of doing anything about party politics anyway, was frequently recognised but acted as no deterrent. The submission of the Bromley Ratepayers' Association, which may be regarded as typical, included the following:

> It would perhaps be impracticable to attempt to abolish party politics in local government, but as long as local government is subject to local party politics it will, often with good reason, be held more or less in disrespect by many citizens, who as a result will be even less inclined to take an active interest or part in local government.[20]

(b) There was general agreement that the rating system was in need of drastic reform. As we have seen, not all chose to give this top priority, for a variety of reasons, and there was no consensus on what should replace rating. Nevertheless few would have disagreed with the words of the Herne Bay and District Ratepayers and Residents' Association, in its submission to the Redcliffe-Maud Commission, that rating 'is intrinsically vicious'.[21]

(c) The great majority leant clearly towards the 'saving' end of the public expenditure spectrum. Such exceptions as there were, were usually not simply 'Ratepayers' but 'Rent and Ratepayers', 'Residents and Ratepayers', or even 'Tenants and Ratepayers'.

(d) Support was overwhelmingly drawn from middle class sections of the population. This is clear from both electoral analysis and leadership studies.[22] It is to be emphasised, however, that social composition in itself was not sufficient to produce a Ratepayers' association, for, as Grant observes, 'Ratepayers movements (particularly before reorganisation) were generally not successful outside middle class areas, but such movements did not develop in the majority of middle class areas.'[23] For an association to be successful there had to be a particular set of local circumstances which either had brought about an 'arrangement' with the Conservatives or had given rise to political conflict. These circumstances, in turn, had some bearing on the particular sections of the middle class who became active. For example, where environmental change in urban areas threatened property values, as in Jesmond, associations frequently had, amongst their leadership at least, a disproportionate number of professional people with appropriate skills, e.g. lawyers, planners, architects and accountants. On the other hand, in resort areas, such as Worthing, Hove and Weymouth, where the resident population included a high proportion of retirees from non-manual occupations, they frequently dominated an association.

The 'new' associations and the 'revolt'

The 'old' Ratepayers' associations thus came in many forms and displayed a range of interests and a variety of strategies. For many, rates had become almost a secondary issue. This was especially the case where representation on the council had been achieved, for then diversification was virtually unavoidable. Only a few associations thus fitted the stereotype of the 'enraged ratepayer' battling from the outside against 'town hall bureaucrats and party hacks'. Many had certainly started in this way but most had, over time, attempted to become, in one way or another, 'insiders' themselves.

By 1974 these Ratepayers' associations, at least as an electoral force, were on the decline. Many still flourished as local pressure groups – though 'Residents' was becoming an increasingly popular title – but fewer of their candidates were being elected onto councils. This reflected a broad pattern whereby 'non-partisans' of most persuasions – 'Ratepayers', 'Independents', 'Citizens', etc. – were squeezed as local party politics were increasingly 'nationalised'. Local government reorganisation, by creating larger electoral units, contributed to the process. So, whereas before 1973 two in five county councillors were 'Independents', in the new counties the proportion dropped to one in seven.[24]

The events of 1974, for a time at least, reversed these trends: rate levels, rather than environmental questions, took the centre of the Ratepayers' stage; many new associations were formed and virtually all adopted the classic postures of 'outsider' groups; and declining electoral fortunes were reversed as an increased number of Ratepayers, in 1975 and 1976, were elected to the new local authority bodies.

The 'revolt' was occasioned by the very large rate rises of 1974, which in turn were a result of inflation, local government reorganisation, and expansion of services. Against the background of a stringent Conservative statutory incomes policy the average increase in rates throughout England and Wales averaged a little under 30 per cent.[25] Within this figure there were enormous variations both within and between authorities. The 1974–5 rates bills varied from a reduction of 9 per cent to an increase of over 160 per cent. Increases were lowest in Wales, where 40 per cent of local authorities actually experienced decreases, and in London, and were highest in England, especially the North. Yorkshire and Humberside had the largest increases with 80 per cent of the districts in that region experiencing increases of over 50 per cent and nearly 17 per cent having increases of over 100 per cent. Of the 25 former county authorities with increases of over 100 per cent, the Yorkshire and Humberside region accounted for 20.[26]

Protests began early in 1974 as the size of the increases became clear. The reaction of one of the main architects of the newly formed Rates Action Group in Newcastle captures the mood of those who became active:

> My rates have gone up from £118 to £193 in a year. When I opened my rates demand my mouth just fell. I'm not paying until I get summoned. There are a lot of retired people around here and they are just flabbergasted. It seems to me that the only way we can fight is to unite.[27]

Countless public meetings were held throughout the country as established associations were resuscitated and new ones were formed. Significantly, many of the latter sought a more militant title than 'Ratepayers' Association'. 'Rates Action Group' was especially popular in the North; in London the 'Greater London Rate Revolt Committee' appeared. In many areas the developing activism was fuelled and encouraged by the local press. Thus in Wakefield the development of a militant Ratepayers' movement could be seen as a success for the *Wakefield Express* which had long campaigned against the 'metropolitan madness' of local government reorganisation and which, from the early months of 1974, had prepared its readers for 'big shocks in rate bills'. After associations were formed they were described as providing the 'virtual opposition to the Labour majority'.[28] In South Tyneside the activities of a highly vociferous Rates Action Group were constantly publicised in the *Shields Gazette*, even to the point of giving details of future meetings and telephone numbers of committee members in news reports. In Newcastle a leading article in the *Evening Chronicle*, under the headline 'The Great North Rate Revolt Starts', began:

> The great North East rates revolt is on.
> As shocked householders received their rate demands, feelings are running so high that many have already decided: 'We're not paying!'
> From all over the region come reports of protest meetings, petitions and rates strike threats, as the rebellion gathers momentum.
> Over the next few days action groups throughout the area are hoping to get together to launch an all out attack on the rates rise. . . .[29]

As to the geographical and social base of the 'revolt', generalisations, other than that it was overwhelmingly middle class, must be tentative. This is because of the limited availability of data and also because Ratepayers' support can be assessed in different ways.

If attention is restricted to the electoral level, most of the support for the 'new' associations in 1975 and 1976, the years of greatest success, appears to have been in middle class wards of predominantly Labour areas in the North, the Midlands, and South Wales. Thus studies of Wakefield and Walsall, where Ratepayers made a significant breakthrough, have shown that they were most successful in those parts of the district which contained a higher than average proportion of both owner occupiers and heads of households in non-manual occupations.[30] The weakness of the Conservative Party in such areas was also important in that it helped the Ratepayers to present themselves as the most vibrant alternative to Labour. This was particularly the case in South Wales where moderate successes in 1975 were followed by sweeping gains in 1976 following allegations of corruption amongst Labour councillors. In Swansea, where there was no Ratepayer tradition, but where the allegations were centred, 22 seats were gained in 1976 – 20 from Labour and 2 from the Conservatives – to give the Ratepayers 29 of the 50 seats and thus control of the council.

But there were, at the same time, many such areas where the Ratepayers made little headway. The importance of local, as well as general, explanations of success must not be overlooked. In Barnsley and Wakefield, for example, it was not simply that ratepayers experienced large increases but that their increases were amongst the largest in the country: 105 per cent and 98 per cent respectively; in Wakefield the Ratepayers' association harnessed not only resentment at these rate rises but linked it to community loyalties which had been severely bruised by reorganisation;[31] in South Wales, as we have seen, allegations of corruption in local government were a key factor.

A particularly important factor in all areas which witnessed Ratepayers' electoral activity was that individuals emerged who did not feel confined by existing party loyalties or 'non-partisan' commitments and who were quite prepared to launch election campaigns. Such circumstances of 'chance', though not very fashionable as explanations today, should not be underestimated, for there were many 'favourable' areas where elections were not contested precisely because key committee members opposed such a course of action. For example, in South Tyneside, where the 1974 increases averaged 82 per cent, and which in terms of socio-economic make-up and party balance is not dissimilar from Walsall, the Rates Action Group disaffiliated from the National Association of Ratepayers' Action Groups on the grounds that the latter encouraged its members to contest elections. Explaining the decision the chairman stated, 'All we are after is rate reform and anything outside this has nothing to do with us.'[32]

An assessment of support for the 'revolt' should not therefore be based on electoral success alone. For, if it were, the temptation would be to assume that whilst heat was generated in many middle class 'enclaves', more solid middle class areas, safely controlled by the Conservative Party, were quiescent. This, however, was by no means always the case. In Greater Manchester, for example, the Ratepayers' movement attracted most support, in terms of attendance at public meetings and paid up membership, in Trafford, the safest Conservative district in the county. But the Trafford Ratepayers' Association chose not to contest elections. Trafford, as with most other associations which took the same decision, claimed that such a move would jeopardise its 'non-political' position. Privately, many such associations were equally concerned to ensure that Conservative control of the authority was in no way jeopardised.

But though associations differed in their tactics, and though support varied according to local circumstances, a common thread can nevertheless be found in the Ratepayers' movement in the months following the 1974 rises: a general mood of anger and an increased disposition towards militancy. The chairman of the Wakefield City Ratepayers' Association, describing a meeting attended by more than 1,000 people, claimed: 'the feeling was to burn the Town Hall down. People were so incensed they had to be controlled, otherwise there would have been damage.'[33] A little dramatic, perhaps, but the sentiments his words evoke were echoed in many parts of the country as demands were made for immediate and direct action so as to resist the 1974 rises and to ensure that they would not be repeated in 1975. The 'new' associations in particular went on to the offensive and for a while petitions, marches and demonstrations were commonplace. Some, though by no means all, even advocated direct resistance: by, for example, only paying the 1973 demand plus a sum to cover inflation; by paying only at the very last minute, thus causing maximum administrative inconvenience; or even by holding a rate strike. (In the event these more drastic calls were rarely pursued right through and though there was, in 1974, a dramatic increase in the number of summons issued by local authorities for non-payment of rates this appears to have been as much a consequence of an increased inability to pay as of resistance on principle.)

Despite the excitement and the heat generated by the rate rises, the new associations offered remarkably little in the way of constructive suggestions as to how the increases might be kept down. Most contented themselves with general condemnations of 'town hall extravagance', 'bureaucratic empire-building' and 'wasteful overmanning'. In so far as specific items were identified they were frequently trivial: the cost of town hall furnishings, the provision and use of official cars, and, an issue which has attracted Ratepayers' ire since it was first introduced with reorganisation, the payment of allowances to councillors[34] (despite the fact that such payments average a mere 0·1 per cent of local government expenditure). The submission which the Durham Rates Action Group made to the Durham City Council in June 1974 may be regarded as typical of the remedies which were generally advocated. Five demands were made:

(*a*) Conference expenses should be reduced from £10,000 to £1,000.

(*b*) Councillors' allowances should be reduced from £55,000 to £10,000.

(*c*) Adequate space in the council magazine should be given to the group.

(*d*) All committees should have representatives from all parties.

(*e*) County and city councils should keep expenditure in 1975 within cost of living rises.[35]

Inexperienced and unsophisticated though the 'revolt' may have been, it did substantially affect both national and local politics. To consider therefore in a little more detail the exact nature of the 'revolt', its impact, and what happened after the initial outburst subsided, two case studies have been chosen. The first gives an account of the role of the main national body in the revolt: the National Association of Ratepayers' Action Groups. The second looks at what happened in an area where there were already sizeable Ratepayers' associations in existence before the revolt and where new, highly vocal, ones appeared: the metropolitan county of Tyne and Wear.

The National Association of Ratepayers' Action Groups (NARAG)

Although NURA had long been the only significant Ratepayers' group at national level it was unwilling to spearhead the revolt of 1974–5. Composed principally of long-established associations in the South of England and Wales, it held firmly to the view that the appropriate way to react to the sudden and dramatic rate rises was through traditional channels – writing letters to councillors and MPs, circulating policy statements, quietly discussing matters with officials, and encouraging those affiliated associations which wished to contest elections to do so. It was totally opposed to engaging in 'reckless, publicity-seeking adventures in the euphoria of the moment. They would merely serve to alienate the various decision makers who listen to us with great courtesy because we are responsible.'[36] (It might be suggested that they listened with courtesy precisely because the pressure was gentle. Certainly NURA could hardly point to a track record of blazing successes.)

Many of the 'new' associations which were formed as the 1974 rate demands made their impact did not subscribe to this view. Displaying all the hallmarks of the aggrieved outsider, they sought activities which would be much more immediate, direct and less easy for government, councillors and officials to ignore. On this groundswell the National Association of Ratepayers' Action

Groups (NARAG) was formed in June 1974. Its approach was quite different from that of NURA. As Ian Scott, a leading NARAG official from the early days and chairman since October 1975, has stated: 'The fact is, you've got to be a little bit sensational to attract attention. If you act sensibly and reasonably – having meetings and quietly lobbying – they don't want to know. If, however, you march on London with banners etc., then everyone listens.'[37]

On what Scott describes as 'a groundswell of feelings of injustice' the groups affiliated to NARAG proliferated and by the end of the year it was claiming to have, through its associations, a total membership of around 350,000 – only 100,000 or so less than that of NURA. Unlike NURA, however, which was firmly based south of Birmingham, NARAG drew most of its support from the North and the Midlands where many of the 'new' associations were formed.

Whereas most of the 'older' Ratepayers' associations were reluctant to change their settled patterns of behaviour – many regarded marching and demonstrating as bordering on the vulgar – most of the groups affiliated to NARAG had no such inhibitions. A venture of one group in Devon, affiliated to NARAG, encapsulates, or at least symbolises, the differing approaches. Unable to interest the media in a public meeting it was proposing to hold, it acquired a grey horse and sat on it a modern-day Lady Godiva. What exactly this had to do with rate increases was not completely clear, but it served its purpose by bringing both television and press to the meeting. For NURA, however, this merely illustrated the inexperience of such groups. 'They will not get the confidence of the government by making a noise and fuss.'[38]

It should be added that decisions of local associations to affiliate to one or other of the national bodies were not always based on calculated appraisals of their contrasting strategies. In many cases, especially in the newly formed associations, where officials frequently had little or no political experience, it was simply that 'we happened to hear of them'. This open situation, with new associations being formed and old ones being resuscitated, was naturally more favourable to NARAG because of its militant and aggressive posture. Its encouragement to affiliated associations to launch flamboyant campaigns based on mass meetings, demonstrations in council chambers, rates strikes etc., provided irresistible material for the provincial press, which increasingly referred to it as *the* national ratepayers' association. In this way NARAG quickly established itself, especially in the North where most of its officials lived, as the leading organ of the ratepayers' revolt.

The immediate aim of NARAG, and indeed of the revolt as a whole, was to reduce, or at least hold down, rate levels. In this it enjoyed early success. Appreciating the storm that had been created, and with an election on the horizon, the Government quickly took steps to defuse the issue. Special domestic relief, estimated at a cost of £150m, was introduced in July 1974 to mitigate the effects of the increases. Although there was some confusion in the operation of the scheme, relief was basically given to those domestic ratepayers whose total rate bills for 1974–5 had increased by more than 20 per cent as compared with 1973–4; the relief was 60 per cent of the excess over 20 per cent.[39] The Government followed this up, later in the year, by announcing the largest rate support grant ever accorded to local authorities: an increase from 60·5 per cent to 66·5 per cent. This was accompanied by a once and for all payment of £350m to cover underestimates of inflation. Anticipating that this would dampen the next round of rate increases, a national guideline of 25 per cent as the maximum rise for 1975 was announced by the Environment Secretary.

The Conservative Party, too, was quick to react to the newly invigorated Ratepayers' movement. From having previously been broadly content with the rating system it suddenly announced, in its October 1974 manifesto, a commitment to wholesale reform:

> First, we shall transfer to central government in the medium term, the cost of teachers' salaries up to a specified number of teachers for each local education authority. Expenditure on police and the fire services will qualify for increased grants from the Exchequer. We shall see that this saving is passed on to the ratepayer.
>
> Secondly, within the normal lifetime of a Parliament we shall abolish the domestic rating system and replace it by taxes more broadly based and related to people's ability to pay. Local authorities must continue to have some independent source of income.[40]

NARAG had clearly played its part in stimulating the quick responses of the Government and Opposition. But though that success was welcome it also created problems, for within months the organisation was racked by internal divisions. As has been noted, Ratepayers' associations at local level frequently break apart. A major source of dispute is definition of boundaries – how far does a concern with rates necessitate an interest in all local government activity? There are also difficulties over tactics, in particular whether the 'non-political' stance precludes contesting local elections. In NARAG's case such problems were exacerbated by the breadth and success of the organisation. In the very early days, when rates, which had brought it into existence, were the sole preoccupation, there were few problems: NARAG operated as a coordinating and advisory body. But as things settled down and as some members, perhaps encouraged by the euphoria of the initial momentum, began to press for the establishment of a broader base, then differences began to open up. Two developments, which were not unrelated to one another, created particular unrest.

Firstly, there was a movement to take up issues which were only marginally related to rates. The most notable example of this was the submission, in July 1975, of a resolution to 10 Downing Street. It urged, on behalf of the Association, a cut in public spending of 10 per cent and also suggested that the Government should stop tax repayments and social security to strikers and their families, with the proviso that children adversely affected must be given food, shelter and clothing. Not surprisingly, some saw this as part of a campaign to transform NARAG into a wide-ranging right-wing pressure group. Mrs Betty Armstrong for example, NARAG's press officer, resigned on the issue, claiming that the submission was wholly divisive. She thought it could prevent employers and employees from coming closer together, especially in the light of 'the hard work being done behind the scenes by intelligent trade union leaders to help the Government in tackling inflation'.[41]

Secondly, moves were set afoot, in July 1975, to broaden the organisational base. Delegates to a NARAG conference were invited to solicit support for an alliance which would embrace other interests such as the self-employed, small businessmen, and taxpayers. According to John Wilks, a prominent NARAG committee member, chairman of the National Union of Taxpayers, and prime mover of the 'opening up',

> The system of government today assures that the silent majority stay silent. We are inviting the co-operation of others who see the situation in the same way.
> If we get approval to set up an organisation, we shall ask other bodies to form a large federation. I am confident that members will approve and it could develop rapidly.
> Then, if the existing political parties will not listen and put the country before dogma, the people must find some other way of making their voices heard and their muscles felt.[42]

Discussions with other organisations duly took place but amidst a background of increasing dissension within NARAG as many became increasingly concerned at what they saw as an attempt to create a broadly based right-wing pressure group. Matters came to a head in October 1975 when, following a meeting of NARAG delegates, five of the six members of the executive, including the chairman, resigned. All had favoured the broadening out. According to Wilks, one of the five, they resigned for three reasons. Firstly, because moves to implement changes agreed by a majority of members were being thwarted. In this connection he claimed that a majority had supported, by postal ballot, a proposal to change the name to the National Association of Tax and Ratepayers' Action Groups. (In fact the ballot appears to have been very badly organised, with members being able to vote either as individuals or as members of a group.) Secondly, because they were unable to persuade groups to surrender some local sovereignty in the interests of national policies. Thirdly, because NARAG lacked financial support.

This was not quite how the new leadership saw matters. The chairman, Ian Scott, claimed: 'John Wilks is trying to use NARAG for his own extreme Right wing views.'[43] Though this was vigorously denied by Wilks, a hint of there perhaps being some substance to Scott's allegation is apparent in the resignation statement of the five committee members:

> NARAG has become a rabble of parochial glory seekers. We consider they are politically motivated in different directions and consequently incapable of forming or maintaining any coherent national policy on behalf of ratepayers.
> In our opinion NARAG is not at present a viable organisation, nor is it capable of offering leadership in the struggle to enforce drastic cuts in public spending and hence reduce rates and taxes.[44]

Under Scott's chairmanship things have settled down and the Association has restricted itself to rates-related matters. It has also become less sensational in its approach, though this has been due as much to circumstances as to conscious choice. After twelve months or so of public meetings, petitions, demonstrations etc., many of the affiliated groups, particularly those which did not gain council seats in the 1975 local elections, began to run out of steam and hence, in turn, so did NARAG. The decline in activity of local associations was partly because of the traditional organisational problems faced by Ratepayers' associations, discussed earlier. Partly, too, it was because the Government began to get rates under control. Generally speaking, the 1975 25 per cent guideline held, with the exception of the two areas where the 1974 increases had been lowest: London, where rates now rose by an average of 45 per cent, and Wales where the rise now averaged 56 per cent. In the following three years continued restrictions on local authority spending enabled the Government to recommend rate rises of no more than 10 per cent in 1976, 15 per cent in 1977, and 10 per cent in 1978. (In practice increases appear to have averaged around 7 per cent more than the recommendation.)

The case of the Trafford Ratepayers' Association, one of NARAG's original members, is typical. At the peak of the revolt it was claiming membership 'in the thousands', was packing town halls with highly successful public meetings, was attracting enormous publicity in the local press, and was boldly talking about the possibility of a 'rates strike'.[45] Yet within three years it had declined to the extent that only around thirty attended its 1977 annual general meeting. Its difficulties were such that it could not even raise the necessary manpower to collect subscription fees or deliver leaflets.

This situation, writ large, has inevitably restricted NARAG's activities since 1975. Whereas a full-time secretary was employed in the first year, 'when funds and offers of vast sums of financial help were flooding in',[46] that has subsequently been impossible. Meetings, both of the committee and of representatives, have been held less regularly as interest has declined and resources fallen. Since the end of 1976 NARAG has in fact been putting up 'a front' in that whilst it has claimed, like NURA, to be speaking for 'hundreds of thousands of ratepayers', it has in reality seen many of its affiliated associations fold and many more experience a dramatic loss of membership. It has increasingly faced a problem of credibility and has been forced to attempt to appear more powerful than it really is.

A further consequence of the decline in rate increases is that NARAG has inevitably moved away from its original, or at least immediate purpose – rate levels – towards the rating system itself. In so doing it has come to play an increasingly similar role to that of NURA: a fringe pressure group for the abolition of rates.

Both take as their starting point the fact that there are approximately 16 million ratepayers in Britain but 25 million taxpayers. The 9 million who escape rates are thus seen as being heavily subsidised. If they did contribute, it is claimed, the average amount required from existing ratepayers would be reduced by more than 40 per cent.

But though agreed on the inequities of the rating system, NURA and NARAG differ on the solution to the problem. NURA proposes a radical reform based on two guiding principles:

> Nationally created expenditure should be paid for nationally. . . . There are some services which are entirely local in their application, the cost of which is very largely under the control of district and county councils, and which need to be tailored to suit local or county circumstances and conditions. These, we consider, should be paid for locally. Equally, there are other services which are clearly national in design and application.
> Everyone entitled to benefit from the services provided by a local authority should contribute equitably to the cost.[47]

These principles lead to the specific proposals that education in particular should be financed by the central government and that a local income tax should be introduced.

NARAG's position, though similar at first sight, is rather different:

The general consensus of opinion [from a survey conducted by NARAG] is that, nowadays, a national outlook must have preference over a localised attitude. . . . We have therefore looked for a national pattern, with very strong local preferences being catered for, along with local control over matters of local concern.[48]

This position leads to the proposal that whilst 'all Local Authorities should remain Masters in their own Homes, and they should remain free to handle the Finance in the way that they see fit',[49] they should be funded out of central taxation. Local income tax is regarded as being unlikely to increase local control but as having the certain disadvantage that it is administratively expensive.

Unfortunately for NURA and NARAG, the *Layfield Committee*, when it reported in 1976, took up neither of the proposed reforms and suggested a local income tax *in addition* to rates. But even this 'half-way' proposal was too much for the Labour Government. Clearly little impressed by the 'muscle' of NURA or NARAG, it declared itself in favour of various amendments to the rating system but against anything so radical as a local income tax supplement. By 1977–8 even the Conservative Party, which, as we have seen, reacted much more positively to demands for wholesale change, was becoming more cautious. Clearly both parties were increasingly seeing few votes, but not a few problems, in rates reform.

By mid-1978 all the signs were that NARAG was experiencing the sort of difficulties that have long plagued Ratepayers' associations at local level: waning enthusiasm, declining funds and an excessive reliance on the activity of a few. Whilst NURA too was no longer operating at its near-frantic 1974 level it at least had a more permanent base in that it could 'fall back' on its original support: those organisations which, prior to the 'revolt', had attained a measure of permanence by focusing on alternative grievances in their local community. But, with a few exceptions, NARAG's associations were not of this kind. They were new and were formed with a quite specific purpose: to oppose the 1974–5 rate increases. As that issue has become less pressing, many of these groups have withered.

By no means all have disappeared, however, and it would be premature to predict NARAG's imminent demise. Some associations, in an attempt to establish themselves, have broadened out into environmental/community issues. For others electoral success has helped to create political credentials, by providing a focus of activity for supporters and offering avenues for political advancement. In the main, however, continued vigour has been restricted to a few areas and there were clear signs in the 1978 district elections that the tide which had seen sweeping gains in 1975 and 1976, and a slight increase in the 1977 county elections (when many associations chose not to contest), had turned. Thus, in the English districts five seats were gained and twelve were lost: each of the gains was in an area where Ratepayers were already established on the council: Barnsley (2), Wakefield, Walsall (where there was also one loss), and Hartlepool (where there were also three losses).

One year's election results do not, of course, in themselves prove that the Ratepayers are in permanent decline. But when seen in the context of the overall 'nationalisation' of local party politics, discussed earlier, the years 1974–6 do increasingly appear as years of respite rather than as heralding the dawn of a new era. When this long-term decline in 'non-partisan' parties as an electoral force is linked with the general demise of those 1974–5 associations which made no electoral impact even at the height of the revolt – and an account of such associations follows in the next section – then the future of NARAG looks distinctly unpromising.

Tyne and Wear

Differing Ratepayer traditions in the five districts of the metropolitan county of Tyne and Wear helped to determine the nature of Ratepayer activity following the 1974 rises.[50]

In the two districts where there was no recent history of a Ratepayers' movement, new, highly vociferous associations, based on individual membership, appeared: the All South Tyneside Action Group (ASTAG), and the North Tyneside Rates Action Group (NTRAG).

In Sunderland, too, a new association, the Sunderland Ratepayers' and Homebuyers' Association (SRHA), was formed, but in different circumstances in that a Ratepayers' group already existed in the town. It had, however, become virtually dormant in the early 1970s as waning support had seen the workload fall on to the shoulders of a few. In consequence it failed to take any real initiative when the 1974 rises were announced and the new SRHA, as happened in many other areas, was formed almost by accident: a resident wrote to the local newspaper, the *Sunderland Echo*, bemoaning the increases and was subsequently inundated with requests to organise a meeting. What remained of the 'old' association, of which few of the 'new' Ratepayers had heard, proceeded to amalgamate and handed over its records.

In Newcastle associations had existed in some parts of the city since the mid-1960s and in one – Jesmond – had achieved electoral success by winning all three of the ward's district seats plus the county seat in 1973.[51] All, however, had increasingly come to emphasise environmental/community issues, even when they met and lobbied together as the Consortium of Ratepayers' Associations (CORA).[52] In consequence they were rather slow to take up the rates question when it became a pressing matter in 1974. On the other hand, they, as well as the increasing number of residents' associations in the city, were always likely to provide active support for a campaign. Consequently, when moves were set afoot to establish an association with the specific purpose of resisting the increases – subsequently known as the Consortium of Newcastle Rates Action Groups (CONRAG) – it was thought appropriate to try to harness existing energies by creating a coordinating delegate body. In Newcastle no district-based association, to which individuals could directly subscribe, therefore appeared.

In Gateshead no new association appeared at all. Discontent was channelled mainly through the Rent and Ratepayers who, after providing the main opposition to Labour on the council before reorganisation (see above), found themselves from 1973 being forced back by the Conservatives into one area of the new district.

On top of this district structure there was also activity at the county level with the formation in July 1974 of a delegate body from the 'new' associations: the Tyne and Wear Rates Action Groups (TAWRAG). Like CONRAG, it had no individual membership and its purpose was quite specifically limited to coordinating the various campaigns so as to ensure that the county precept in 1975 was kept to a minimum.

The different backgrounds of the five districts also helps to explain the varied strategies of Ratepayer campaigns in Tyne and Wear. Where there had previously been active Ratepayer involvement, i.e. in Newcastle and Gateshead, there tended to be a greater reluctance to engage in brash, publicity-seeking exercises. There was a willingness to make militant noises, but when it came to action traditional lobbying procedures usually prevailed. Thus a proposal in CONRAG to heckle council meetings met with little enthusiasm, most delegates feeling that they would make themselves ridiculous and run the risk of damaging such relations as they enjoyed with councillors and officials. In the event a protest was held in the public gallery of the council chamber but it consisted merely of a few highly disgruntled 'hardliners' throwing leftover car stickers – with the caption 'Cut Spending. Reduce Council Rates. Now' – onto sitting members.

Where there was little or no history of Ratepayer activity there were less inhibitions, and public meetings, demonstrations, petitions, interruptions of council meetings, etc. were common from mid-1974 to the end of 1975. South Tyneside, where the rate increases, at an average 82 per cent, were significantly higher than the 45–55 per cent average in the rest of the county, witnessed the most strident campaign. Apart from demonstrations and marches, activities included the submission to Downing Street of a petition signed by about 40,000, the distribution of questionnaires on rates matters to candidates before the 1975 and 1976 elections, the engaging of an accountant 'to scour the council's annual estimates for evidence of any unnecessary spending', and the holding of a number of public meetings throughout the district, some of which appear to have got almost out of hand (see below).

As for contesting elections, the pattern, as in other parts of the country, varied according to local circumstances. In South Tyneside, where Ratepayers' candidates might have been most expected, given the size of the 1974 increases, ASTAG contented itself with publicising the results of its questionnaires. Inevitably this favoured the Progressive/Conservative group more than Labour (which doubtless did not displease many ASTAG officials), but that should not necessarily be seen as the prime motivation. The 'non-political' stance, as much a feature of the 'ratepayers in revolt' as of the pre-1974 activists, led many to the view that electoral activity was precluded.

In other districts this argument did not always hold sway. Gateshead's Rent and Ratepayers continued to contest, though with reduced success as Conservative opposition increased. In Newcastle too the established Jesmond Ratepayers continued to put forward candidates, though, interestingly, and this perhaps says much about the role of rates in their appeal, they lost a seat in 1975 – the year of the major national Ratepayer gains – but won one in both 1976 and 1978. Elsewhere in Newcastle, as in North Tyneside, there was a great deal of discussion for much of 1974 of putting forward candidates in 1975 but, with two exceptions, nothing came of it. Flagging campaigns as much as 'doctrinal' objections determined the decision not to fight.

Only in Sunderland did a 'new' association run a large number of candidates, and this followed a bitter row and division in the SRHA. Some committee members felt strongly that electoral activity was the only way to make an impact and further believed that such an impact was possible given the sentiments expressed at its public meetings. Others, however, for the traditional reasons, were more wary. The outcome was a split in which the SRHA contented itself with attempting to persuade the main parties that such high rate increases were both avoidable and undesirable, whilst the new association, which called itself the All Sunderland District Action Group (ASDAG), proceeded to enter the electoral fray. Somewhat rashly the Action Group announced, early in 1975, the intention of contesting the seats of all district councillors who claimed full attendance allowance for committee meetings. The not altogether unsurprising result of this promise was that six of their eventual nine candidates found themselves in safe Labour wards, in three of which the Conservatives had not even bothered to put up a full list of candidates at the previous elections in 1973. In what proved to be the Action Group's only year of electoral activity all candidates were sunk, virtually without trace, and none managed to acquire a higher vote than any of the three major parties.

This spasmodic electoral activity in Tyne and Wear rules out the possibility of usefully correlating support for the 'ratepayers' revolt' with social, economic, or political variables. There seems, however, no reason to assume that it was significantly different from the essentially property owning/non-manual base observed in Wakefield and Walsall. Certainly committee members of the various associations were overwhelmingly from such a background and they clearly saw themselves as representing what, in interviews, they frequently described as 'the middle income bracket'. ASTAG indeed constantly stressed its concern for 'those whose incomes are too high to claim government subsidies and too low to absorb rate increases'.[53] (To those familiar with the language, 'government subsidies' is taken to include subsidising the 'artificially low' level of council rents.)

The outstanding feature of the support for the 'revolt' in Tyne and Wear is not its social base, however cohesive that may have been, but its remarkable ephemerality. Most of the associations were still in existence in mid-1978 but had long ceased to attract any popular support. A decline set in as early as January/February 1975 when it became clear that the new rises would be, if still high, by no means as dramatic: on average they were slightly below the Government's recommended 25 per cent maximum, with South Tyneside, where activity had been greatest, having one of the lowest increases in the region – 17 per cent. The local press, by continuing to publicise the statements and views of the associations, perhaps gave the impression of continued watchfulness and vigilance, but the reality was the familiar pattern of responsibilities falling to an ever decreasing number of activists. The expectation of sudden, dramatic successes had died and the demands and realities of maintaining a sustained campaign had become apparent. The former chairman of NTRAG captures what happened perfectly:

We started off with a bang, but it was like a packet of cigarettes going up from 30p to 50p: open rebellion for about a month and then everyone pays the 50p. When it came to doing anything people found an excuse.[54]

Only seventeen people attended NTRAG's 1976 annual general meeting. In 1977, when a similar number attended, disbandment was considered, not least because no one was willing to take on the job of chairman. After much discussion NTRAG decided to continue but was reduced to advertising in the local press for someone with 'time and energy' to fill the post. Similar situations occurred in South Tyneside, Newcastle and Sunderland where the associations, which at one time had attracted hundreds of people to public meetings, and which were going to hold 'mass rates strikes', gradually faded. CONRAG did not formally wind itself up but non-attendance at meetings resulted in its simply ceasing to operate from late 1976. ASTAG folded in March 1977, partly because the secretary, who had come to shoulder an increasing burden, had a heart attack. As for Sunderland, both associations have continued to exist but with virtually no active support. An ASDAG meeting in January 1976, called 'to oppose soaring local government expenditure and the threat of another substantial rise in rates', had a turnout of only thirty.[55] Still not deterred, in public at least, a year later, when it was announced that a proposed 26 per cent rise in Sunderland was being reduced to 17 per cent, ASDAG continued to use the language of the all-powerful: 'We are still furious. A protest meeting is likely to be called, and the ratepayers are talking about paying only a 15 per cent rise and not a penny more. . . . The people of Sunderland cannot afford this increase.'[56] To judge from the subsequent lack of activity, the people of Sunderland, however furious they may have been, concluded that they had no choice but to pay the increase.

With only the 'old' Ratepayers' associations of Gateshead and Jesmond retaining any vigour by 1978[57] – and they, once again, had gone back to emphasising community/environmental matters rather than rates – the 'revolt' was well and truly over. Those who had attended the mass meetings and demonstrations had long since ceased to be involved. A few of the 'hard core' continued to try and breathe life into virtually defunct organisations but most had withdrawn, for the most part dispirited and disillusioned. In the words of the former secretary of CONRAG, 'In a nutshell it was a complete fiasco. . . . We soon met apathy everywhere. . . . We tried to do something but it was the same old story of just being fobbed off by the bureaucrats.'[58]

Nevertheless it would be a mistake to dismiss the 'revolt' as having no effect. Clear relationships are difficult to prove, if only because decision makers are generally reluctant to admit that they have been successfully 'pressurised'. It is true that the Conservative Party in the five districts made sympathetic noises from the onset of the protests but then in each case, as well as naturally being more ideologically sympathetic to demands for retrenchment, they were in opposition and therefore did not have to identify the points at which they would cut expenditure. By and large the Labour Party kept its distance, for which it could hardly be blamed given the reception it received when it did attempt to engage in public discussions, as in South Tyneside. At a meeting in June 1974, called by ASTAG, and attended by over 1,000 people, explanations of the increase offered by Labour MPs and councillors were shouted down, police had to be called in to restrain passions, and ASTAG's chairman stated from the platform, 'We have heard a load of complete waffle'. A general slanging match ensued as, amidst calls for rates strikes, Labour councillors cried 'Send them to jail', 'That's a conspiracy charge', and 'You are recommending illegal action'.[59] Be that as it may, in 1975 the increases in South Tyneside, at 17 per cent, were the lowest in the region; in 1976 they actually fell by 0·5 per cent; and in 1977 they increased by only 7·3 per cent.

Rate increases in Tyne and Wear since 1975 have, on average, been below the Government's guidelines, whilst throughout the country as a whole they have, on average, been slightly above. A simple cause and effect relationship between this and the 'revolt' in Tyne and Wear cannot be drawn, since many other factors have intervened. For example, the increasing local Conservative electoral threat since 1975 has doubtless concentrated many Labour minds in the direction of economic stringency. In addition, changes in the distribution of Rate Support Grant has had differential effects on councils. What can be said, at the least, is that the protests in Tyne and Wear played their part, along with those in other areas, in creating the situation in which the Government felt obliged to intervene in 1975 to hold down rate increases.

Conclusions

The Ratepayers' associations formed in 1974–5, as part of the so-called 'rates revolt', bore all the characteristics of what Dowse and Hughes have called 'sporadic interventionists': their activity was generally of a short-term nature; much of their support was drawn from sections of the population who had not previously been involved in 'established' political activity; and many were founded with a naive set of expectations which, when not realised, produced disillusionment, cynicism and eventually withdrawal from the political arena.[60]

Despite the essentially ephemeral nature of the 'revolt', however, it had, as has been shown, significant effects on both national and local policies. At Westminster, the Government was forced to take emergency action and greatly increased its grants to local authorities, while the Opposition significantly altered its position on the rating system. At local level the numbers involved were such that, for a while at least, even in safe Conservative and Labour areas Ratepayers entered the politicians' calculations in making decisions.

Whether there will be any long-term consequences it is too early to say. Where Ratepayers have gained influential positions on councils – as at Havering and Walsall where they have held the balance of power between the two main parties[61] – they have kept the Conservatives in power. Attempts to measure Ratepayer influence, however, as was suggested early in the chapter, should not necessarily be restricted to such 'observable' situations. It may well be that the greatest impact of the 'revolt' has been, and will continue to be, its effect on the general climate of political opinion and the perceptions of politicians as to what determines the electorate's choice. In this connection it can reasonably be assumed that the greater cost-consciousness of politicians with regard to local spending since 1975, which in South Tyneside, for example, has seen the shelving of a £2m extension to the town hall, has been in no small part a consequence of the 'revolt'.

NOTES

1 For the Committee's findings see *Report of the Committee of Inquiry into the Impact of Rates on Households*, Cmnd 2582, HMSO, 1965. Rate rebates were subsequently introduced as a means of defusing the situation.
2 A study of councillors' perceptions of issues is contained in Newton, K., *Second City Politics: Democratic Processes and Decision Making in Birmingham*, Oxford University Press, 1976.
3 Gregory, R., 'Local Elections and the "Rule of Anticipated Reactions"', *Political Studies*, Vol. XVII, No. 1 (1969).
4 *Report of the Committee of Inquiry on Local Government Finance (Layfield Committee)*, Cmnd 6453, HMSO, 1976, Appendix 6, p. 99.
5 *Layfield Report*, p. 384. It should be added that these figures do conceal considerable local variations.
6 Ibid, p. 159.
7 Ibid, p. 366.
8 See, for example, Steed, M., 'Ratepayers' Associations and Local Politics', Parts 1 and 2, *Insight*, June and July 1965.
9 Stacey, M., *et al.*, *Power, Persistence and Change*, Routledge, 1975, p. 66.
10 King, R., and Nugent, N., 'Ratepayers' Associations in Newcastle and Wakefield', in Garrard, J., *et al.* (eds), *The Middle Class in Politics*, Teakfield, 1978.
11 Grant, W., *Independent Local Politics in England and Wales*, Saxon House, 1977, Ch. 2. Also Grant, W., '"Local" Parties in British Local Politics: A Framework for Empirical Analysis', *Political Studies*, Vol. XIX, No. 2 (1971), p. 204.
12 Stanyer, J., 'Exeter', in Sharpe, L. J. (ed.), *Voting in Cities*, Macmillan, 1967, pp. 112–31.
13 Election broadsheet, *The Jesmond News*, April 1973.
14 Richards, P. G., 'Southampton', in Sharpe, L. J., op. cit., p. 192.
15 *Newcastle Evening Chronicle*, 9 May 1973.
16 Bulpitt, J. G., *Party Politics in English Local Government*, Longmans, 1967, p. 75.
17 Grant, W., op. cit. (1977), pp. 77–83.
18 Ibid, p. 79.
19 For a discussion of the reasons for this commitment, and also an analysis of support for 'non-partisanship' amongst the electorate, see Grant, W., 'Non-Partisanship in British Local Politics', *Policy and Politics*, Vol. 1, No. 3 (March 1973), pp. 241–254.
20 *Royal Commission on Local Government in England (Redcliffe-Maud Report): Written Evidence of Private Citizens, Amenity, Ratepayers' and Residents Organisations and other Witnesses*, HMSO, 1969, p. 319.
21 Ibid, p. 433.
22 For an example of a leadership study see Grant, W., op. cit. (1977), p. 80. Personal, unpublished, material from Newcastle confirms his findings.
23 Grant, W., op. cit. (1977), p. 44.
24 Redcliffe-Maud, Lord, and Wood, B., *English Local Government Reformed*, Oxford University Press, 1974, p. 63. For further discussion of the 'nationalisation' see Schofield, M., 'The Nationalisation of Local Politics', *New Society*, 28 April 1977.
25 Scotland, where events took a different turn, partly because reorganisation was not introduced until a year later, is not being considered here.
26 *Layfield Report*, p. 356.
27 *Newcastle Evening Chronicle*, 7 June 1974.
28 King, R., and Nugent, N., op. cit.
29 *Newcastle Evening Chronicle*, 7 June 1974.
30 King, R., and Nugent, N., op. cit.; Grant, W., op. cit. (1977).
31 King, R., and Nugent, N., op. cit.
32 *Shields Gazette*, 16 July 1975.
33 King, R., and Nugent, N., op. cit.

34 For a review of ratepayers' criticisms of allowances see NURA *Bulletin*, October 1977.
35 *Newcastle Evening Chronicle*, 26 June 1974.
36 Interview with Mrs Hobbs, secretary of NURA, 5 January 1978.
37 Interview with Ian Scott, 18 February 1978.
38 Interview with Mrs Hobbs, op. cit.
39 For further details of the relief, and its estimated effect, see *Layfield Report*, pp. 359, 360, 364.
40 Conservative Election Manifesto, October 1974. Printed in Craig, F. W. S., *British General Election Manifestos 1900–1974*, Macmillan, 1975, p. 436.
41 *The Times*, 8 July 1975.
42 *The Daily Telegraph*, 15 July 1975.
43 Ibid, 7 October 1975.
44 Ibid.
45 See, for example, *Manchester Evening News*, 3 May 1974, for militant resolutions passed at a meeting attended by over 800 people.
46 Interview with Ian Scott, op. cit.
47 *Layfield Report*. Evidence submitted by NURA, pp. 102–3.
48 *Layfield Report*. Evidence submitted by NARAG, p. 97.
49 Ibid, p. 100.
50 The five district authorities are: Newcastle, Sunderland, Gateshead, South Tyneside, North Tyneside.
51 Strictly speaking, the association from 1973 was entitled The Jesmond Residents' Association and its candidates were elected as 'Independents'. In practice, however, they were still generally known as 'Ratepayers' and their monthly newsletter was still *The Jesmond Ratepayer*.
52 For a more detailed discussion of the pre-1974 situation in Newcastle see King, R., and Nugent, N., op. cit.
53 *Shields Gazette*, 21 March 1975.
54 Interview with T. Peart, 11 April 1978.
55 *Sunderland Echo*, 24 January 1976.
56 *Newcastle Evening Chronicle*, 23 February 1977.
57 In the 1978 local elections the Jesmond 'Independents' successfully defended a seat, thus retaining two seats on the city council. The Gateshead Rent and Ratepayers contested three Labour-controlled seats and pushed the Conservatives into third place in two of these. This meant they continued to have one district seat and one county seat.
58 Interview with G. H. Alexander, 14 April 1978.
59 *Newcastle Journal*, 6 June 1974.
60 Dowse, R. E., and Hughes, J. A., 'Sporadic Interventionists', *Political Studies*, Vol. 25, No. 1 (March 1977), pp. 84–92.
61 In 1978 the Conservatives gained overall control at Havering.

John McHugh

3.   The self-employed and the small independent entrepreneur

Introduction

The context of contemporary British politics has been substantially formed by the triumph of collectivism in the post-war period and the parallel development of a formalised and increasingly institutionalised lobby system. The widening role of the State in matters of social and economic policy has been accompanied by the tendency towards the concentration of resources into large units in the private economic sector and the emergence of a politically and economically powerful trade union movement. These developments form the basic elements in the collectivist system symbolised by the special tripartite relationship between government, CBI and TUC and operating through the highly developed Committee system in Whitehall and a host of *ad hoc* agencies.

This collectivist trend has clearly accelerated in recent years with State involvement taking on a variety of guises in industries such as steel and car manufacturing, aircraft and shipbuilding and even the exploration and exploitation of North Sea oil. In an era increasingly dominated by 'big' business, interventionist government and powerful trade unionism, the small independent entrepreneur, the typical representative of the petits-bourgeois has become a marginal social and economic category threatened by powerful political and economic forces. The emergence of various groups over the past few years purporting to represent the small entrepreneur and the self-employed in an aggressive, radical fashion can be seen as a reaction to these forces and an attempt to exercise some control over them. It is the rapid growth in the support of the largest of these radical groups which has given most credence to the notion of a middle class backlash or revolt. This study is predominantly concerned to describe the origins, development and organisation of the three most significant of these new groups, the National Federation of the Self-Employed (NFSE), the National Association of the Self-Employed (NASE), and the Association of Self-Employed People (ASP) and to analyse their ideologies, strategies and general impact.

The background of small business representation before 1974

A useful starting point is the *Bolton Committee* report on small firms which presented its findings in 1971. *Bolton* was engaged in a pioneering study of the role of small firms in the economy and collected much statistical data not previously published in Britain. The Committee tackled the complex question of defining the small firm by utilising both economic and statistical criteria to provide a basis of definition which has become widely accepted. *Bolton* held that the small firm must satisfy three economic criteria. First, a small firm was one that held a relatively small share of its market. Second, it was managed by its owner or part-owner in a personal way and not through a formal management structure. Third, it had to be independent and not part of a larger enterprise, and its owner-managers were to be free from outside control in taking their principal decisions.[1] In addition to the economic criteria, a statistical definition was introduced to take account of the varying shape and size of small firms in different parts of the economy (Table 1).[2]

TABLE 1

The *Bolton Committee*'s assessment of the significance of small firms.

Industry	Statistical definition of small firms adopted by the Bolton Committee	Small firms as % of all firms in the industry in 1963	Proportion of total employment in small firms in 1963 (%)	Average employment per small firm in 1963
Manufacturing	200 employees or less	94	20	25
Retailing	Turnover £50,000 p.a. or less	96	49	3
Wholesale trades	Turnover £200,000 p.a. or less	77	25	7
Construction	25 employees or less	89	33	6
Mining/ Quarrying	25 employees or less	77	20	11
Motor trades	Turnover £100,000 p.a. or less	87	32	3
Miscellaneous services	Turnover £50,000 p.a. or less	90	82	4
Road transport	5 vehicles or less	85	36	4
Catering	All, excluding multiples and brewery-managed public houses	96	75	3

Within this overall definition of the small firm the *Bolton Committee* pointed out that a substantial proportion of those so defined were in essence forms of self-employment. The Committee's sample survey of small firms indicated that 60 per cent of respondents were either in partnership or were sole traders.[3] The most recent government statistics on the numbers of employers and self-employed estimated that they comprised approximately 1·9 million people out of a working population of 25·6 million.[4] Of the 1·9 million employers and self-employed approximately 1·1 million were estimated to be sole traders without employees. Over the period 1966–73 the number of employers and self-employed rose by an estimated 255,000 at a time when the number of male employees fell by over a million. The increase was most marked between 1966 and 1970, but since then any further increase is probably accounted for by the growth of self-employment in the construction industry while in other sectors of the economy the numbers of employer/self-employed may have fallen significantly. Indeed in manufacturing industry the number of establishments with ten employees or less, including small units owned by larger companies, have been in a long-term decline; from about 93,000 in 1930 to approximately 38,000 in 1972.[5]

Although the *Bolton Committee* was not primarily concerned with the role of small businesses as a pressure group it did observe that the general failure of small businesses to impress their problems on government was 'in large part the fault of small businessmen themselves who, in spite of their numbers, have been extremely ineffective as a pressure group'.[6] This ineffectiveness was explained in terms of the wide diversity of small business organisations representing specific trades or professions which thereby diluted and weakened the impact of small businesses on government policy making. It was also apparent that large numbers of small entrepreneurs were unwilling or unable to join any of the various available organisations claiming to represent their interests. This was explained in terms of the lack of time available to the small entrepreneur to join such groups and a general independence of outlook which militated against the ability to conform to a group norm. More interestingly, *Bolton* felt that the perceived political prejudices of the small business community acted as an obstacle to successful pressure group activity. A generally hostile attitude to the Labour Party and Governments as enemies of the independent operator was emphasised by an almost unquestioning loyalty to the Conservative Party. This was felt to have produced a situation where 'unqualified loyalty to one party may result in the small firm vote being taken for granted by one side and being written off by the other'.[7] It is significant that the rise of the new groups after 1974 was linked to a change in this situation with sections of the self-employed in particular becoming progressively disenchanted with the Conservative Party.

Shortly before *Bolton* reported in late 1971, the CBI and the Association of British Chambers of Commerce (ABCC) jointly commissioned an inquiry into industrial and commercial representation under Lord Devlin. *The Devlin Inquiry* sat from January 1971 to November 1972 and produced an interesting picture of industrial and commercial representation. On the question of small business representation *Devlin* suggested that the viable outlets for the small entrepreneur were the CBI, the Chamber of Commerce or a relevant trade association. (Trade associations are based on particular industries or parts of industries and are concerned with the broad economic interests of the industry or trade. They are generally paralleled by employers' organisations which carry out the specific function of national bargaining over pay and conditions of work. The situation is complicated by the existence of bodies like the National Farmers Union which provide the functions of both trade association and employers' organisation.)

Despite this trend towards a rationalisation of function it remains the case that in most industries a multiplicity of trade associations, employers' organisations or some combination of both exists. *Devlin* constructed a table to illustrate this point, indicating that in the distributive trades, for example, 269 such organisations are operative. In total it is probable that about 2,500 trade associations, employers' organisations or combinations exist in Britain. *The Devlin Committee* located 2,484 organisations and received replies from 865 major bodies and a further 815 smaller organisations linked to the major respondents. Of the 865 major bodies, 606 were trade associations, 75 were employers' organisations and 174 were combinations of both. Some indication of the general quality of service provided by the 865 major bodies is the fact that only 231 employed a full-time staff of more than one while more than 500 relied on either part-time assistance or the services of a solicitor or accountant.[8]

Almost all trade associations and related bodies are affiliated to the CBI at national level and provide the CBI with a major source of membership. While the CBI is popularly associated with big business it is increasingly at pains to point out that over a third of its membership comes from smaller firms, and when affiliated organisations like trade associations are taken into account the CBI claims to represent about 200,000 small businessmen. It might appear that the small entrepreneur has an important source of influence on policy-making, given the fact that the CBI is seen by government as the authoritative representative of the industrial, commercial and business interest. Moreover, the CBI has a Small Firms Council composed of sixty-five members which meets monthly to consider the problems of small businesses. The members of the Council are all required to be the owner-managers of small firms, all of which theoretically strengthens the position of the small entrepreneur and offers him access to the Whitehall governmental machine.

However, it is commonly argued that the constitutional structure of the CBI weakens the effective role of the Small Firms Council since only the CBI Grand Council is authorised to determine policy and it is held to be dominated by the concerns of big business. Whatever the reality of the situation, the CBI has faced and continues to face the problem of proving its genuine commitment to small business. Indeed one organisation, the Small Businesses Association, subsequently renamed the Association of Independent Businesses (AIB/SBA), came into existence precisely because of small business dissatisfaction over the creation of the CBI. Prior to the creation of the CBI there were two central bodies representing the trade associations, one of which, the National Association of British Manufacturers (NABM), was composed largely of smaller businesses. A minority element in the NABM remained unconvinced that the proposed CBI would be able to represent adequately the particular problems facing the small business sector, and so set up the Small Businesses Association in 1968.[9] The problem of small business representation is likewise important to the Association of British Chambers of Commerce which derives its membership from approximately ninety affiliated local Chambers. While the local Chambers of Commerce retain an important degree of autonomy within the overall ABCC structure, they are increasingly concerned to follow a collective line under the ABCC.[10]

Despite the importance of small firms for the CBI and the ABCC, the *Devlin Committee* did not pay specific attention to their representation but was concerned to look for a more rational system of business representation in general. Moreover *Devlin* did not investigate in any detail the representation of retail interests, especially the small retailer. Yet to understand the emergence of the more militant forms of small business representation required an examination of the small retailer, and such academic literature as exists on political militancy and small business in Britain focuses heavily on the small shopkeeper.[11] In a comparative context the small shopkeeper is also seen as providing the grass-roots support for petite-bourgeois populist movements. Poujadism in France during the 1950s remains the most obvious example of such a social and political movement.[12]

In Britain the main orthodox representative institutions of the small retailer are the local Chamber of Trade and/or the appropriate trade association. There are more than 830 Chambers of Trade throughout the country and they are represented at the national level by the National Chamber of Trade along with more than thirty affiliated trade associations. The National Chamber of Trade (NCT) claims to speak on behalf of 350,000 businesses and has a regional structure based on twelve Administrative Area Councils which are proportionally represented on the national Board of Management, as are the trade associations with six seats.[13] The NCT in turn is part of the Retail Consortium, which attempts to act as a general representative organisation for the retail trade by bringing together in a confederal structure bodies like the Co-Operative Union, the Retail Distributors Association, the Retail Alliance and other retail bodies. The NCT is principally concerned with the small retailer and sees the Retail Consortium as a means of strengthening his voice in negotiation with government, particularly on issues such as prices and incomes policy.

The emergence of the new groups, 1974–6

This whole system of what might be termed orthodox institutionalised business representation was challenged after 1974 by the newly formed National Federation of the Self-Employed (NFSE). The NFSE was initiated by Mr Norman Small who was a retired army captain and one-time Yorkshire regional organiser for the National Union of Shopkeepers. Small wrote a letter to the *Guardian* on 31 August 1974 in which he proposed setting up a self-employed union:

> I, and many others, regard this huge section of the population as the only real free-thinking individualists in our society today. Welded together they could be a real influence in saving Britain from the slow Hari-Kari she is now intent on committing.[14]

Within six months Small's Federation had recruited more than 30,000 members at a membership fee of £12 per head. It is generally accepted that this phenomenal growth was a consequence of the Social Security Amendment Act 1974 which contained a clause whereby the self-employed would be required to pay a Class 4 graduated National Insurance contribution rate of 8 per cent on gross profits between £1,600 and £3,600 per annum. The payment was additional to the existing flat-rate contribution of £2·41 per week. The new Class 4 contribution was due to come into force in April 1975 and became the *cause célèbre* for the Federation.[15]

Ironically, the rapid growth of NFSE membership in the first six months of its existence threatened to overwhelm its rather fragile administrative structure. While the Federation was attempting to develop an organisation to handle its growing membership and construct a system of local branches, the newly recruited rank and file were reported to be 'screaming for action'.[16] In March 1975 Small urged the Minister of State for Health and Social Security, Mr Brian O'Malley, to back the Federation's plan for the self-employed to receive social security benefits to match the increased Class 4 levy. The Federation was demanding unemployment and industrial injury benefits as part of the more general list of demands sent to the Department of Health. It also argued for a separate insurance fund to be set up to provide the self-employed with the same pension rights as ordinary employees. According to Small, the rank and file members of the Federation were so incensed that it was possible that they might go as far as breaking the law to gain some form of redress.[17] In fact the Department did subsequently agree to set up a commission to investigate the possibility of constructing a comprehensive system of earnings-related contributions and benefits whcih would accommodate the self-employed. However, the result of the commission's findings was a ministerial statement that the cost of such a system, in terms of the additional civil servants required to operate it, made it prohibitive.[18]

While the Class 4 levy payment stimulated the initial growth of the NFSE and remained a constant focus for discontent, the issues surrounding Value Added Tax (VAT) probably provoked the most militant rhetoric and most serious threat of direct action. VAT had originally been introduced in 1973 and extolled as a straightforward flat-rate system of tax collection. However, almost immediately following its introduction VAT had operated at different rates. For small entrepreneurs and particularly the self-employed, VAT was a bitter grievance and the NFSE attacked it on the grounds that it placed the businessman in the position of unpaid tax collector. The general expectation that the Labour Budget of April 1975 would initiate a multi-tier system of VAT and thereby intensify the grievance of the small entrepreneur prompted the NFSE to send a memorandum to the Treasury. The thrust of the NFSE's argument was the simple claim that the VAT system was already 'too complicated and time consuming for the self-employed to be able to contemplate any further changes'.[19]

The Federation's memorandum had no discernible impact on the Budget proposals since the 25 per cent levy which had previously operated on petrol was now extended to include a wide range of domestic electrical appliances. The new differential rates were intended to operate from 1 May and their imposition prompted the 32-man National Executive of the NFSE to meet and agree to advise their membership to withhold VAT payments to the Customs and Excise after 1 July.[20] This move was prompted by a groundswell of grassroots opinion demanding action, and this groundswell was felt by the National Chamber of Trade which faced the possibility of being outflanked by its more aggressive rival. The NCT leadership was clearly alarmed by the Federation's apparent willingness to initiate and condone the illegal act of an organised VAT strike. The NCT publicly deplored the Federation's proposal as a threat to democracy and the leadership was relieved when a motion calling for non-cooperation with the government over the proposed VAT changes was overwhelmingly rejected at their annual conference in May.

The NCT leaders had already been warned by the Government that since the NCT was not a trade union any attempt to organise a VAT strike or the like could open the National Chamber to a charge of conspiracy.[21] Despite the unlikelihood of such a charge, NCT leaders were believed to have taken the possibility very seriously. Their relief that the annual conference had avoided a potential confrontation with the government over VAT was further increased by the belief that the wave of militancy had passed. Leslie Seeney, a leading NCT official, echoed this feeling, arguing: 'The responsible people have seen that normal negotiations are better . . . I am quite relieved that things have settled down a bit.'[22]

While the NCT appeared to agonise over the question of direct action, the NFSE gained much publicity and a certain amount of kudos within the self-employed and small business sector from its more militant stance. Recruitment was claimed to be increasing by several hundred a day and the Federation's growth raised the question of whether it was on the point of leading the loose coalition of self-employed, small entrepreneurs and middle class militants in a British Poujadist-type movement.[23] In fact the threat of militant action over VAT was quickly withdrawn following a promise by a Junior Minister at the Treasury, Dr Mark Hughes, that a delegation from the Federation would be able to meet the Financial Secretary to the Treasury and senior officials at the Customs and Excise to explain their case and outline their grievances. The Federation leaders tended to see this as an important breakthrough in establishing their position with the Government as the authoritative body representing the self-employed. At the same time elements within the Federation and even at the leadership level may have seen this development as the first stage in a Government strategy of drawing the Federation's teeth by enveloping it in the Whitehall web of committees.

The Federation's attempts to establish a relationship with the Government took place against a background of growing internal unrest which produced a major upheaval in the autumn of 1975. As early as February, Frank Thornton, Chairman of the Solihull branch, issued a statement claiming that members of the Federation's National Executive had voted themselves large salary contracts and raised more general doubts about the Federation's financial management.[24] The implication of financial mismanagement was rejected by the Chief Executive, Keith Shouls, who declared that the National Executive were prepared to welcome any inquiry since they had nothing to hide.[25] Thornton's dissatisfaction with the Federation's leadership was more than an individual gripe since rumours of internal wrangling on the Executive over policy and bitter personality clashes were widespread throughout the Federation. Norman Small, who had founded the Federation and undertaken a vigorous round of public engagements to recruit more support, had already resigned in July through ill-health, and Edwin Gornall, a former Honorary Secretary, was seeking compensation for wrongful dismissal. The most serious internal disagreement emerged in September when the activities of a reform group challenged the positions of a number of national leaders.

The reform group was led by Gerry Parker-Brown and Daphne Macara who were respectively the Vice-President and Regional Secretary of the London area NFSE. They made a number of charges against the leadership, claiming the existence of a power clique, the absence of any democratic involvement of the rank and file in policy formulation, and financial mismanagement. They demanded the adoption of a democratic constitution, an inquiry into the Federation's financial accounts and the resignation of three executive officers including the Chief Executive, Keith Shouls.[26]

The Honorary Treasurer and Secretary, Richard Graves and John Kelly, who bore the main brunt of the charges of financial waste and mismanagement, both resigned following the reform group's charges at the annual meeting in September. Graves claimed that £220,000 remained of the £470,000 collected in membership subscriptions during the Federation's first year of operations. He further claimed that the bulk of the organisation's expenditure was incurred by financial commitments to the Federation's 300 local branches which amounted to an estimated £20,000 per month. Graves argued that the Federation had no future. He claimed that with recruitment dropping from over 1,000 new members a week to less than 250 and the financial commitment to the branches growing, the Federation was losing £7,000 a week.[27] Keith Shouls narrowly survived one motion calling for his removal, but it proved to be a temporary reprieve as the reform group secured his dismissal within a few days.[28] Shouls, together with a number of the former Federation officials who resigned or were replaced, set up a rival body in Preston.[29] However, this new group, the Society of Independent Businesses, failed to make any serious impact in terms of replacing the Federation and remained a localised affair. This was only one of a number of splinter groups which emerged as a result of disagreements within the NFSE. The Scottish Association of the Self-Employed and Daphne Macara's Independent Business Persons Association were two early examples. Like Keith Shouls's group they failed to attract much support.

Norman Small subsequently emphasised that the problems of the Federation, which culminated in the September upheaval, were solely administrative. Small issued a press statement which stated:

> During my inevitably prolonged absences from the Federation Head Office the administration fell into the hands of enthusiastic but totally unsuitable officers who were subsequently removed by the National Executive or who voluntarily resigned.[30]

He accepted that many members were frustrated by the lack of communication from the Federation's headquarters at Lytham St Annes and the apparent lack of impact on government departments, but implied that such criticisms were unfair given the largely amateur nature of the Federation's staff and their relative inexperience of lobby politics. Nevertheless Small was still optimistic that the NFSE would become the 'largest and most powerful non-political force in the United Kingdom'.[31] David Kelly, who emerged from the September coup as a major Federation spokesman, felt that the whole episode had inevitably damaged the Federation's credibility but that it was justified: 'We had to take what we knew could be the most potentially damaging steps. But we took them to ensure the long term future of the Federation.' Kelly went on to declare that the Federation aimed to achieve a membership in 1976 of 100,000.[32]

On 16 October 1975 the new management committee, which had replaced the old executive committee and contained the chairman of each of the thirty-five regional committees, held a press conference to outline the NFSE's future strategy. They announced that the Federation would spend £15,000 on a recruitment drive and undertake a search to find a 'thoroughly professional' chief executive officer who had experience of negotiating with government departments. Along with the intention to strengthen the membership and administrative capacity of the Federation, the management committee advised their members to withhold the additional Class 4 National Insurance levy unless the Government agreed to grant tax relief on the payment. David Kelly warned that they would operate a system of 'dirty tricks' short of law-breaking to create bureaucratic confusion and general chaos.[33]

At the end of its first year the NFSE had survived the constant personality clashes and arguments over financial spending, albeit somewhat shakily. It had established its position as the largest of the new groups with a membership of about 43,000 organised in a system of 35 regions and 300 local branches. Despite this large membership, the Federation was not without rivals, although the majority remained small and often localised.

The most significant of the groups that emerged in 1975 was the National Association of the Self-Employed (NASE). The NASE was formed shortly after the Federation as a loosely organised amalgamation of a host of local groups which had emerged spontaneously in the wake of the Social Security Amendment Act 1974. The actual amalgamation was effected through a newspaper advertisement placed in the *Daily Mail* by an Essex builder, Gordon Bridgman.[34] At its peak the NASE claimed to speak for an associated membership of 27,000, although this figure may be an optimistic view of its popular support. In many ways the NASE represented a reaction against the financial wrangles taking place within the NFSE and more specifically against the Federation's annual subscription of £12. It appears that many self-employed and small entrepreneurs considered this sum to be excessive, and the NASE never charged more than £3. Moreover, the looser organisation of the NASE allowed more autonomy to the local NASE action groups and this suited sections of the active self-employed who were suspicious of the more structured, centralised and potentially bureaucratic NFSE. The NASE was strongest around Essex, East Anglia, parts of the West Midlands and particularly the areas on the Anglo-Welsh border.[35]

The other significant self-employed group which emerged out of dissatisfaction with the conduct of the NFSE's affairs and its lack of a firm ideological line was the Association of Self-Employed People (ASP). ASP was founded by Mrs Teresa Gorman following advertisements in the *Daily Mail* and *Daily Express*. Mrs Gorman was an active member of the NFSE and remained so for some time after the formation of ASP. Her dissatisfaction with the NFSE has been directed against the failure of successive leadership groups to firmly grasp and operate the system of liberal–conservative ideology which Mrs Gorman believes to be the central requirement for a group purporting to represent small independent entrepreneurs and especially the self-employed. She has always been concerned to differentiate between NFSE leaders and the rank and file activist who she believes to be broadly sympathetic to her position but loyal to a leadership which fails to provide the correct ideological direction.

In an important sense ASP has never been solely concerned to present itself as the champion of the self-employed or even small business, but is engaged in a crusade on behalf of the extreme libertarian ideology espoused by Mrs Gorman and her close associates, Professor Harry Ferns and Terry Arthur. This ideology is based on the primacy of market forces in the allocation of resources and envisages a strictly limited role for the State which strongly resembles the classic model of nineteenth-century *laissez-faire* liberalism. ASP draws its historical inspiration from the Manchester School, Cobden and Bright, and the French economist Bastiat. In the contemporary period ASP looks to Milton Friedman and F. A. Hayek for guidance and inspiration, and, closer at hand, to the Institute of Economic Affairs.

Teresa Gorman corresponds with a wide variety of trade associations attacking the imposition of professional qualifications or craft regulations as barriers on entry to trades, but emphasises that her commitment to liberal values is not restricted to questions of economics but has a broader sweep. She is concerned to maximise individual liberty in a way which would leave her close to the 'newer liberalism' on issues of social morality such as support for legalised abortion, homosexuality and easier divorce. But the economic argument is the basic element in ASP ideology since it emphasises that individual liberty can only be maximised in an economic environment based on market principles. The ASP involvement with the self-employed, and subsequently the small business sector in general, derives from Gorman's belief that they represent the last bedrock of free enterprise values in a society swamped by collectivism and provide the basis for a movement aiming at the general restoration of those values.[36]

Initially Gorman's press advertisement generated about 4,000 replies and produced a membership of 2,000 drawn from a wide range of self-employed occupations. Although ASP has never achieved the numerical support enjoyed by the NFSE, it has defined its role less in terms of mass support and more in terms of propagating libertarian values and exposing the alleged ideological shortcomings of the NFSE. For ASP there are two kinds of self-employed, those faithful to the ethic of rugged individualism and those who 'see the salvation of the self-employed as getting into the pork barrel with everyone else'.[37] ASP was determined to remain in the first category and has refused to build up any formalised branch system or make a pretence of internal democratic decision-making. It seeks quite simply to propagate its ideological line, publish its newspaper, and occasionally seek a mandate from the membership on specific policy issues like VAT.

At the end of 1975 the growth of support for these groups had been so rapid as to create a degree of alarm in Conservative Party circles. The traditionally close relationship between the small independent entrepreneur and the Conservative Party appeared to be less secure. The virtues of the independent entrepreneur, individual effort and initiative, have been consistent elements in Conservative propaganda, and small business has been generally regarded as the electoral property of the Party. At the local level the independent entrepreneur has traditionally played an important political role and provided a significant proportion of activists in local Conservative Associations. Yet while the rise of the militant self-employed groups has been widely interpreted as a reaction to a punitive Labour Government it is explicable, in part at least, in terms of a growing small business disillusion with the Conservative Party, especially in the wake of the Heath Government.

David Kelly, who was closely involved in the early phase of the NFSE's activities, certainly feels that its rise was fundamentally related to Conservative neglect under Heath:

> I consider that history will see the period of the Heath government as one of the most crucial in cementing the acceptance of Socialism in Britain. It was at this time that the self-employed came to feel most abandoned . . . their so-called own kind turned on them, [and] they were greatly disillusioned. Had this not been the case, had they not had VAT thrust on them, local government reorganisation, the abolition of resale price maintenance, entry into the Common Market . . . etc . . ., then when the Class 4 levy came along, it would not have acted as the catalyst it did.[38]

While many self-employed members of the NFSE, NASE and ASP might not have been able to catalogue the 'sins' of the Heath Government in such detail, there can be little doubt that disillusion with the Conservatives as the traditional guardians of the economic interests of the small entrepreneur was quite widespread. In fact, a small number of Conservative backbenchers had already set up a backbench committee to watch over small business affairs in 1973 and it was officially recognised by the Executive of the Party's powerful 1922 Committee the following year.[39] In the aftermath of the self-employed revolt in late 1974 and its apparently rapid growth in 1975 the Conservatives set up a Small Business Bureau (SBB) under the general auspices of the Community Affairs Department in Conservative Central Office. The driving force behind these developments, Paul Dean and David Mitchell, have been anxious to point out that the SBB is not a rival of the existing groups but a complementary organisation.[40] Nevertheless it is the case that Mitchell did see the backbench Conservative Committee and the SBB as providing the basis for the emergence of an umbrella organisation to cover the diverse forces of the self-employed/small business sector.[41]

Such hopes have still not been realised in late 1978. The important groups, the NFSE and ASP, have often collaborated with the SBB by providing information used in Parliamentary Questions or press statements, but both have been concerned to maintain their full independence. While many of the NFSE's leaders might welcome closer relations with the Conservative Party it would almost certainly precipitate a split in the membership. Up to this point in time the NFSE feels that it is a more effective organisation and certainly more united by maintaining a policy of non-party identification.

ASP is likewise suspicious of Conservative intentions and particularly concerned about the reality of the Conservative leadership's commitment to market economics. The presence of Margaret Thatcher as leader has not been sufficient to offset the persistent belief that the Conservatives would do very little to reverse the slide to collectivism. The ASP attitude to the SBB is quite instrumental: they have affiliated for access to literature, platforms, and an ability to reach an influential audience which would be otherwise denied them. However, the Executive of the SBB is identified by ASP with the spirit of the Tory Reform Group rather than the Selsdon Group, with which ASP would be more at home.[42] Although the SBB has not been able to channel the energies and activities of the new self-employed groups into the orbit of the Conservative Party, it has enjoyed significant success. It has established itself as an influential organisation in the field of self-employed/small business representation and enabled the Conservative Party to reach, and possibly gain recruits from, an important section of the electorate.

The re-alignment of the self-employed groups, 1976–7

While the Conservatives tried to respond to the new groups, a number of important changes were taking place between and within the NFSE, NASE and ASP. In early 1976 the NASE approached ASP with a general proposal for establishing a system of liaison which would create a closer organisational relationship and enable both to act in concert on issues affecting the self-employed. Although the NASE had shortly before claimed a membership of about 27,000, subsequent events would seem to show that its position must have waned dramatically and that its overture to ASP was made from a position of weakness rather than strength. The NASE's loose organisational structure and fragile financial situation, due to its policy of low subscription, were at the root of its weakness. Part of the NASE/ASP relationship concerned the desire to collaborate on the newspaper, *Counterattack*, and involved the NASE in placing a firm order for 10,000 copies to be distributed among its members.[43]

In the event this arrangement lasted for only three issues before the NASE was forced to cry off because it could no longer guarantee payment. A subsequent attempt by the NASE to generate a firm financial base through the creation of a joint fund based on a per capita subscription was aborted by the failure of local action groups to contribute. It is apparent that by early 1976 the NASE was already on the point of disintegration, with local action groups surviving only where the members were most enthusiastic and energetic. At the point of establishing a working relationship with ASP it is probable that the NASE membership had fallen from an estimated peak of 27,000 to less than 10,000. Moreover, not all sections of the NASE were content to associate with ASP and the active East Anglia branch was already moving towards affiliation with the NFSE.[44]

The NFSE was itself undergoing internal organisational changes in the light of the September leadership changes but more importantly was becoming more cautious and moderate in its general political approach. One consequence of the September changes was an approach to a number of established political leaders for advice about the future role of the NFSE. An important criticism of it under the Shouls leadership had been precisely the quality of the leading personnel. Now figures like Peter Walker, ironically a leading Heathite and former Cabinet Minister, were asked for guidance. It appears that the NFSE was told of the importance of establishing a responsible and credible image as the necessary prelude to acceptance by the governmental machine for the purposes of negotiation. Certainly it can be argued that the NFSE was much less vociferous in its public outbursts and was moving away from an emphasis on a publicity-conscious propagandist role, which had characterised its early days, and towards 'a more conventional pressure group role'.

The essential argument within the NFSE about its role was, and is, between those concerned to transform it from an 'outsider' group, denied legitimacy by government, to an 'insider' group which would gain access to the governmental decision-making process. This argument was often ill-defined and perhaps not clearly understood by the majority of members, but it established the lines of debate at the leadership level and lies at the heart of the NFSE's continuing problem of identity. The argument has never been decisively resolved but at different points in the Federation's development one tendency or the other has been more in evidence. It manifests itself in terms of the various approaches to individual issues, like the Class 4 levy or VAT reform, and inevitably on questions concerning the organisation and structure of the Federation.

The evidence suggests that in 1976 the tendency towards conventional pressure group politics was pre-eminent with its consequent emphasis on caution, willingness to compromise and desire for recognition by Whitehall. The 'dirty tricks' campaign, designed to create administrative chaos, which David Kelly had threatened would begin in January, never seriously materialised, and in March the threat of some form of direct action over the Class 4 levy was officially lifted by the Federation. The decision to call off the threatened action was brought about by a further promise of discussions with the Treasury.[45] In June the position of Chief Administrative Officer, which had remained unfilled, became an issue within the Federation. It appeared that David Kelly, a leading opponent of any compromise with government and critic of the lack of free-enterprise commitment within the Federation leadership, was to be given the position.[46]

In fact the position went to an outsider, Mr Michael Norton, in confusing circumstances. Press reports indicate that David Kelly turned the position down, but the reasons for his alleged refusal are unclear. It is possible that Kelly's ideas on the future of the Federation were unacceptable to a majority on the management committee. Certainly Kelly was out of sympathy with many of its members and envisaged the creation of a smaller power house at the centre of the Federation which would direct its activities and substantially shape its policies. It has been suggested by some NFSE activists that the terms offered Kelly were such as to make the job unacceptable to him, given his attitudes and views on the way the Federation should be going. Whatever the actual circumstances, Norton's appointment was a further indication of the Federation's movement towards orthodox pressure group politics. The NFSE was not engaged in a crusade to change the nature of British society, as was the ASP/NASE group, but to negotiate improvements in the position of the self-employed within the existing context. Kelly remained in the Federation for a further six months before resigning in protest at its alleged departure from the aggressive individualist and free-enterprise stance which had led to its formation.

It is ironic that the NFSE's movement towards a more accommodating position took place at a time when the Labour Government implemented a number of important Acts which were seen to be antagonistic to small employers. Although the legislation was not specifically directed at small business, the small entrepreneurs still interpreted it as an attack on their existence and a further stage in the drift towards full socialism. Most contentious among this legislation were the Trade Union and Labour Relations Act and the Employment Protection Act. The passage of the Trade Union and Labour Relations Act extended the opportunities open to trade unions for increasing union membership through the development of the 100 per cent unionised closed shop. Although the Act did not make the closed shop compulsory on employers, it did require them to consider the imposition of a closed shop when more than half the employees of a firm requested it. ASP was quick to point out that the main impact of the Act would be on small-scale enterprises which were 'previously and mercifully immune from union activity'.[47]

The Employment Protection Act was likewise seen as a threat to the small entrepreneur. Under this Act the Advisory Conciliation and Arbitration Service (ACAS) was given a statutory basis for its considerable powers over the terms and conditions of employment offered by firms. ACAS was empowered to look at the pay and conditions of individual firms and in effect to force an improvement through the operation of the Central Arbitration Committee where they were shown to be inferior to those obtaining in the trade or industry generally. However, the main target for the self-employed groups was the provision which enabled industrial tribunals to impose fines up to a maximum of £12,000 on firms held to have dismissed workers unfairly. These two Acts of Parliament, together with redundancy payments, the legislation concerning equal wages for women and the employment rights of expectant and new mothers, have been consistently attacked as harmful to the small employer and to employment in general by dissuading employers from taking on new employees.[48]

ASP was particularly active in attempting to lead opposition to the Trade Union and Labour Relations and Employment Protection Acts. Both were seen as more than attacks on the economic position of the small entrepreneur. They represented a general attack on individual liberty and were opposed for that above all else. At the same time ASP provided practical guidance to employers on the implications of the Acts and advice on minimising their impact. Rachel Tingle, one of ASP's very capable researchers and lobbyists, published a booklet, *Slow to Hire – Quick to Fire*, which provided a brief, but well-informed account of the main obligations of employers in their dealings with employees as imposed by a number of parliamentary Acts. These included the Redundancy Payments Act 1965, the Equal Pay Act 1970 and the Sex Discrimination Act 1976, but the booklet concentrated on the Employment Protection Act.

The booklet outlined the main legal machinery involved in industrial relations and industrial disputes and the liabilities of employers for breaches of the Acts. Operating a question and answer system, *Slow to Hire – Quick to Fire* outlined the main pitfalls for employers to avoid and argued the case for recruiting additional workers on self-employed contracts.[49] In a double irony for ASP, an NFSE activist, Brian Kelly, uncovered a relatively simple way of avoiding the obligations of the Employment Protection Act which the nationalised Steel Corporation of Wales operated. It involved recruiting employees on a fixed-term contract of twenty-five weeks after which they would sign on as unemployed for two weeks and be subsequently re-engaged by the employer. This device evaded the Employment Protection Act because an employee on a 25-week contract did not count as full-time and the Act's provisions covered only full-time employees.

One of the more significant campaigns mounted in 1976 and one which served to illustrate the differences between the Federation and ASP concerned the Petre Constantinescu case. This was seen by ASP as a glorious opportunity to publicise the powers of the VAT inspectorate to search private premises and homes with a search warrant for suspected VAT evasion. Moreover, it was a means of publicising the fact that similar powers had been given to the Inland Revenue under the 1976 Finance Act. The operation of the VAT inspectorate's powers has been the subject of repeated criticism by both the NFSE and ASP. It has also provided a constant source of irritation between the Customs and Excise and the various self-employed groups. The VAT inspectorate has been under attack from the self-employed for employing vindictive methods and for excessive recourse to the use of search warrants despite the fact that warrants are issued by magistrates only where *prima facie* evidence of evasion exists. In July 1976 the General Secretary of the Customs and Excise Group of the Society of Civil and Public Servants, Mr C. Christie, wrote a letter to the *Guardian* defending his members and attacking VAT evasion.[50] He argued that since 1 April 1973 some 343 search warrants had been issued for 152 investigations of suspected tax fraud of which 326 produced evidence of offences leading to the recovery of more than £3m. He went on to argue that VAT evasion was a direct form of stealing from the consumer and that exceptional but tightly regulated procedures were necessary to combat that evasion, which he estimated was running at £134m a year. Mr Christie's defence of the search powers open to the VAT inspectorate came in the immediate aftermath of a demonstration outside the Customs and Excise headquarters in London to gain publicity for the Constantinescu case.

Mr Petre Constantinescu committed suicide shortly after a lengthy search of his home by VAT men. The case was reported in the *Daily Mail*[51] and prompted members of the NASE action group in Shropshire to demand some demonstration in protest. As a result of their indignation the ASP/NASE leadership organised a demonstration which also involved members of the NFSE in south-east England. The demonstration involved about 150 people and was followed by a group proceeding to Parliament to lobby MPs about the proposed extension of the search powers to the Inland Revenue.[52] Although the demonstration and lobby were reported in some of the national daily press, they received scant attention in the NFSE's newspaper, *First Voice*, Teresa Gorman, who was still a paid-up member of the Federation, protested to the editor pointing out that the demonstration had been attended by many Federation members, including Jim Walters, a NFSE vice-president and London regional chairman, as well as the Federation's national spokesman, Tony Armstrong.[53]

In an exchange of letters with *First Voice*'s editor, Zena Brown, it was apparent that certain elements in the Constantinescu case had largely invalidated its value as an illustration of the tyranny of the VAT regulations. Brown argued that the Federation's concern was with the powers themselves and felt that attachment to a dubious case might result in the Federation getting 'its fingers burned'.[54] Gorman saw this as further evidence of Federation temporising and suggested that 'our enemies are not just outside the Federation but, much more dangerous, within it'.[55] However, the cautious attitude of the Federation is understandable in the light of its desire to establish a responsible and credible image. This cautious approach inevitably led to a more selective use of evidence, and particular cases, to illustrate and publicise more general grievances.

Despite the differences between the ASP/NASE block and the Federation over the Constantinescu case and ideological questions, the idea of an amalgamation between all three was informally discussed. The Federation was seeking an amalgamation as part of a 'determined effort to present a united front against the increasing pressures on the self-employed'.[56] The ASP/NASE organisation was prompted towards discussion of amalgamation by the unilateral decision of the East Anglia NASE group to seek an agreement with the NFSE.[57] At the same time the Federation was attempting to initiate an important new development, an Alliance of Independent Workers and Enterprises which would become a 'TUC of the middle class'[58] and square the triangle of Government, CBI and TUC.

Hopes for the alliance were not enhanced by the failure of the NFSE/ASP/NASE amalgamation. It failed to materialise because the Federation was not prepared to meet the conditions of the ASP/NASE groups which included a new name, significant representation on a new Executive and the continued existence of the ASP London office with its small but energetic political lobby and research staff. The Federation's counter-offer was rejected by ASP/NASE following a mandate conducted through *Counterattack*, and the terms were described by ASP as derisory; 'the NFSE Executive is not interested in amalgamation but only in total takeover with the obliteration of all other groups'.[59]

In fact ASP/NASE had little to offer the NFSE in return for significant concessions within an amalgamated structure. ASP was a relatively small organisation in terms of numbers and its penchant for creating occasional publicity owed much to the energy and personality of its driving force, Teresa Gorman. However, it is doubtful whether the Federation's Executive would have looked forward with much sympathy to her inclusion in a position of eminence in a new organisation. The NASE prospects were even poorer than ASP's. The Federation was already assured of absorbing the East Anglia group, with its 3,500 members, and the remainder was in a weak financial state. Indeed, following the failure of the amalgamation discussions the NASE simply disintegrated. The East Anglia group joined the Federation and the Essex group, with about 900 members, was absorbed into ASP. At the point of its collapse the NASE had reached a point where it could not afford to send out reminders to its members to renew subscriptions.

The initial preliminary meeting to explore the possibility of establishing an Alliance of Independent Workers and Enterprises took place in Brighton in October 1976. This two-day meeting, sponsored by the Federation, was followed by a further preliminary meeting held in London and attended by representatives of about fifty groups not affiliated to either the CBI or the TUC.[60] From these initial meetings it was apparent that common ground did not really exist between the groups representing interests involved in private industry and those involved in the public sector.

One of the most interesting relationships highlighted by the Alliance conferences and subsequent events was that between the NFSE and the National Association for Freedom (NAFF). NAFF is an overtly political organisation which opposes the growth of collectivism and espouses the values of individualism and the economics of free competition. For NAFF the self-employed/small business sector was, and is, a natural target and NAFF had already established close relations with ASP with which it shared broadly similar economic views. However, the bulk of the active self-employed were to be found within the Federation and there is a significant overlap of membership between the Federation and NAFF.

In December 1976 the rather cloudy relationship between the NFSE and NAFF erupted into a bitter public controversy. Following a series of articles in the *Guardian*, which indicated that a number of NAFF leaders had at some point been sponsored by the American CIA, the Federation issued a public statement that it had informed NAFF of its desire 'to sever all connections "because of the NAFF's political views"'.[61] Further, the Federation instructed NAFF to remove from its literature any suggestion that the groups were linked. Owen Dyer, a member of the Federation's executive, had attended one sitting of the NAFF ruling council, ostensibly as an observer, and it was after Dyer's report that the Federation decided 'to end the relationship because of their political views'.[62] The Federation was also concerned to emphasise that it was not party political, had not subscribed to NAFF and provided it with no other form of financial assistance.

Following this public breach the Federation declared its intention of blocking any attempt by NAFF to become involved in the embryonic Alliance. The first formal meeting was scheduled for February and the Federation was determined to 'recommend that the NAFF should not be invited'. ASP, which was keen to increase the libertarian element in the Alliance by involving NAFF, viewed the Federation's attitude with dismay. It was interpreted as further evidence of 'paranoia' on the part of an organisation described by ASP as a 'bureaucratic blancmange'.[63] In fact, the Alliance has never really developed beyond an idea. The divisions between the groups involved rendered the Alliance impractical, although it still remains a live issue within the NFSE.

Whatever the merits of Gorman's pungent criticism of the Federation, its desire to distance itself from the more extreme views of NAFF was further evidence of its desire for legitimacy through a 'responsible' representation of self-employed interests. Calls for government aid for struggling businesses and training schemes for the self-employed were further indications of the Federation's movement towards orthodox pressure group politics. This trend was recognised by David Kelly who resigned in protest and disgust at the growing 'left-wing influence' within the Federation leadership which produced policy proposals contrary to 'the very principles and ideals on which the federation was formed'.[64] Kelly has subsequently denied a suggestion that he intended to rejoin the NFSE and has joined NAFF, albeit with a consciously low-key commitment.

Although relations between the leaders of the Federation and ASP were constantly strained, a more workable relationship existed at the grassroots level. This relationship operated over the issue of the Building Tax Exemption Certificate, the so-called 714, despite the refusal of the Federation's leadership to collaborate with ASP in a 'Fight the 714 Campaign' initiated by Teresa Gorman and Gordon Bridgman. The 714 issue was specifically concerned with the use of sub-contract labour in the building industry, which has been associated with the notorious system of tax-evasion known as the lump.

The lump derives from the cash payments made to sub-contractors which they are then required to declare to the Inland Revenue each year. In fact the system was wide open to abuse and in 1971 an attempt to tighten up the situation was made. This involved the introduction of a system whereby only sub-contractors with an Inland Revenue approved form could be paid a gross figure by a contractor which would be subsequently submitted as part of an annual tax declaration to the Inland Revenue. The expectation that this would end the lump by providing a means of tracing payments was not realised because forgery and a black market in real and forged forms flourished. The Labour Government replaced the original forms with the 714 Certificate which contained a photograph of the sub-contractor and thereby made forgery or duplication almost impossible.

The use of photographs and certificates was opposed as an attempt at a licensing system of employment in the sub-contracting trades but more generally as an infringement of individual liberty.[65] Evidence was brought forward to argue that the 714 certificate was being withheld from certain builders and sole traders because of alleged tax irregularities in the past. It was claimed that by early 1977 more than 22,000 applications for the 714 had been refused and more than 50,000 referred back to the applicants. As early as June 1976 the Federation had responded to rank and file pressure by campaigning against the certificate.[66] The campaign was organised by the Federation's Freedom to Work Group and in November it was joined in the field by the ASP/NASE inspired 'Fight the 714 Campaign'. In early November Teresa Gorman and Gordon Bridgman met members of the NFSE's 'Freedom to Work Group', who were already working on the issue, and established a tentative agreement to mount a joint campaign. This agreement was not validated by the NFSE's powerful Policy Committee and thus the joint action did not officially materialise.[67] None the less, cooperation between the '714 Campaign' and local NFSE activists did develop in the London area.

Once again ASP was prepared to fight the 714 certificate on straight libertarian grounds while the official NFSE line was more cautious. As in the Constantinescu case, the Federation saw the 714 certificate as a more difficult issue which could backfire on the organisation. The Federation had a much larger membership than ASP and had to take account of the interests of the whole membership. Many of the self-employed builders affected by the 714 were individual bricklayers, carpenters and plasterers who would normally be described as working-class. Moreover, the lump was widely viewed as a straightforward method of tax evasion and a defence of the self-employed builder in regard to the 714 might be interpreted as a defence of the abuse.

The NFSE was careful of its image and therefore cautious of too close an involvement with the 714. The letters to *First Voice* on the 714 issue were also by no means firm in their opposition to the certificate and there were a number who felt it to be justified. In the event the effective campaign against the 714 was carried on by ASP's 'Fight the 714 Campaign' which was supported by a significant number of NFSE activists around London. The most important victory was achieved with the decision of the Conservative Party to devote three hours of its parliamentary allocation to a debate on the 714. Credit for this Conservative move was claimed by both ASP and the NFSE. The latter argued that it had carefully lobbied backbench MPs and provided information on the tax-exemption certificate issue. But nothing was conceded by the Labour Government which remained convinced that only exceptional measures could stamp out tax abuse in the building industry.[68]

The NFSE has remained determined to impress itself on public opinion and government bodies as the legitimate and authoritative spokesman for the interests of the self-employed and small entrepreneurs. It can be argued that the more considered and moderate tone and approach of the Federation was part of this more general drive for official recognition. However, the fact that the Federation was easily the best supported of the new groups, with a membership of about 43,000 at the end of 1976, has to be placed against the existence of a potential membership of about 2,000,000 self-employed and a further 80,000 small independent firms. In fact the total membership of the various self-employed groups probably accounted for less than 5 per cent of the total self-employed population.[69]

It has always been the objective of the NFSE to achieve a mass membership, and with more than 40,000 recruits at the end of its first year this objective appeared capable of achievement. Yet at the end of 1976 the membership figure remained around the 43,000 mark despite efforts to increase it. The Federation leaders were concerned to achieve a rapid membership growth in 1977 which would strengthen its demand for recognition by government for the purposes of consultation and negotiation. To that end a campaign was mounted to stimulate membership and generally increase public awareness of the Federation's existence and purposes.

This campaign was officially launched at the Federation's first annual conference held in February 1977, and lasted until early May when it culminated in a rally and a mass lobby of Parliament. It was the result of months of planning and involved a series of full-page advertisements in the national press and meetings organised and co-ordinated by a London-based Campaign Headquarters supported by the Federation's Lytham St Annes official base. The actual results of the campaign were a major disappointment in that membership remained substantially unaffected and the campaign cost the Federation an estimated £100,000. Its failure was to create a further round of tension and internal struggle which produced a major change of leadership and a possible change in the direction of the Federation's strategy.

The Federation's first annual conference was something of a disappointment from the point of view of the turnout. *First Voice* noted the thin attendance but felt it was offset by the standard and vigour of the debates.[70] The major guest speaker was Lord Alexander Hesketh who had established a public reputation for his pioneering attempt to break into Grand Prix motor racing as an independent operator. Hesketh's initial motor-racing success in conjunction with James Hunt made him an important asset for the Federation and its quest to establish a moderate responsible image in the public mind. Lord Hesketh made the keynote speech to the conference and emphasised the absolute importance of acquiring public credibility which would assist the Federation in securing a more powerful bargaining position. This necessitated the removal of unspecified extremists from the organisation and a campaign to increase membership and remove media misconceptions. Hesketh understood that some members were concerned at the proposed expenditure of £100,000 on a recruitment campaign but felt it was a risk well worth taking if they could get the members: 'We should represent 2·3 million. We may hope to directly represent 300,000 which would then provide us with the mandate of leadership to provide the counterbalance to the trades unions.'[71]

The conference debated a number of issues in a way which highlighted some of the attitudes held by Federation activists. One debate on a motion calling for the Conservative Party to commit itself to protect and promote the interests of the self-employed turned into a general discussion of relations with the political parties. The motion was amended to include 'all other parties' following criticism of the Conservatives and a majority feeling that a non-party political position should be maintained.[72] On the issue of the Class 4 levy the debate was shaped by an argument between those calling for the abolition of the levy and a more moderate line, that the Federation should seek tax relief on the money paid in levy and a commitment from the Department of Health and Social Security to provide fairer treatment for the self-employed in insurance matters.[73] The more moderate line prevailed. One interesting outcome of the conference was the passage of a resolution calling on the Federation to take the case of the Class 4 levy to the European Court at Strasbourg.[74] This was accomplished the following August, but in 1979 their case failed.

The general mood of the conference was pragmatic and hard-headed. While those present were concerned to point out alleged injustices, they tended to take a more realistic short-term approach to their removal. Certainly there was a tendency to argue against collectivism and in favour of free enterprise, but the main concern was less with ideology than with practical issues. Jim Sharpe, a member of the Executive, in answer to a question on relations with NAFF said that although the Federation was concerned with freedom the organisation was not ready 'to get involved in the extremely wide matters of liberty and freedom which NAFF specialise in'.[75] The conference ended with the perennial criticism of the administration which prompted a Federation leader, David Dexter, to appeal for an end to 'this inward criticism. Let the administration have a chance to settle down and work. You get out and fight – outside the Federation, not inside.'[76] Despite this appeal for internal unity, the Federation was soon engaged in a further internal struggle.

At the end of the recruitment campaign the Federation held a meeting at the Central Hall Westminster which was addressed by David Steel and Geraint Howells of the Liberal Party, Bob Cryer, a junior minister at the Department of Trade and Industry in the Labour Government, and Sir Geoffrey Howe and Paul Dean representing the Conservatives. Cryer's presence held a certain significance in that he was the first Labour minister to address a public meeting of the Federation. Despite this, he received a rough ride in presenting the case for the Government's line on small businesses, in contrast to the Conservative speakers who received 'a tumultuous welcome'.[77] This meeting and the lobby of Parliament which followed marked the end of the £100,000 recruitment campaign, and its failure saw the start of an attempt to overturn the dominant NFSE leadership and alter the organisation's approach.

The tendency for Federation activists to react to such failures by demanding changes in leadership, policy and organisational structure reflects a naive approach to the problems of increasing support among the self-employed. It appears that activists and leaders alike had an image of the self-employed as an essentially homogeneous group with common economic interests and broadly similar attitudes and values. Consequently the problem of recruiting the self-employed appeared to be one of establishing a popular identity and formulating a policy likely to activate the massive but still overwhelming passive self-employed population. There is little evidence to suggest that the NFSE ever seriously considered that the differences between the self-employed in terms of occupation, social status and scope of activity required a more sophisticated and varied approach to recruitment. It was apparently assumed that such differences were irrelevant or were offset by the shared experience of self-employment and the common attitudes which it was believed to generate.

The diverse nature of the self-employed population was indicated not only by Government statistics by also by the NFSE's own research. In April 1977 the Federation analysed a random sample of 7,500 members by occupation and produced an interesting profile of its membership. Perhaps the most surprising information, indicated in Table 2,[78] is the prominent contribution made by

TABLE 2

An occupational profile of the NFSE membership

Overall occupational group classification	Numbers	Percentage
Primary	688	9·22
Manufacturing	435	5·83
Construction	1,283	17·19
Distribution	2,391	32·04
Professional	732	9·81
Services	1,933	25·91
Total	7,462	100

Single Group classification (the ten largest groups)	Numbers	Percentage
Farming (all types)	620	8·31
Garage proprietors	429	5·75
General building	360	4·82
Hotels	196	2·62
Catering	195	2·61
Grocers	179	2·40
Variety stores	157	2·10
Confectioners	156	2·09
Road haulage	144	1·93
Licensed victuallers	142	1·90

farmers to the Federation's membership. They provide the largest single occupational block, followed by garage proprietors and general builders. Beyond these three groups no specific occupation comprises more than 3 per cent of the total membership.

The existence of such a variety of occupational groupings, each forming a fractional part of the Federation's total membership, goes some way towards highlighting the difficulty of defining the self-employed as a homogeneous social group. It is just possible to suggest that the nature of self-employment is itself sufficient to offset this apparent diversity, but this argument is not convincing. It is *a priori* difficult to accept that the self-employed artisan such as a bricklayer, plumber or electrician has a readily available identity of interest with the professional groups such as doctors, dentists or lawyers. Indeed it would seem that any consensus in terms of political values and objectives would be difficult to achieve. The self-employed bricklayer is almost inevitably drawn from the traditional working classes, and his work experience, leisure pursuits and social behaviour leave him closer to employed building workers than to doctors or farmers.

Fragmentation of the self-employed class is not restricted to questions of social class and occupational status but includes the economic differences involved in the relative scale of their activities. It is difficult to construct a detailed breakdown of such differences in capital outlay and the amount of plant utilised, but there is an obvious and important distinction to be made between the self-employed who are employers of labour and those who are not. It is the case that some self-employed entrepreneurs employ substantial amounts of labour, in excess of 100 employees, but Government statistics indicate that more than half are sole traders.[79] Clearly recent legislation dealing with employer/employee relationships governing unfair dismissal, equal opportunities for women, redundancy payments and suchlike have a differential impact on the self-employed as a whole. Those without employees are not directly, or at least not immediately, affected and will presumably be less moved to protest than those who are affected. In an important sense the issues of the National Insurance levy and VAT regulations are atypical pieces of legislation in so far as they have a more general application to the self-employed population. Most legislation has a differential impact affecting particular self-employed groups such as employers, or building workers or farmers.

The existence of various differences between the self-employed provides a substantial barrier against the emergence of a self-employed consensus which will unite the fragmentary elements. The annual conference of the NFSE showed evidence of real divisions on policy over issues from the National Insurance levy to relations with the Conservative Party. If no easy consensus exists within the Federation on the major problems confronting the self-employed it is difficult to imagine its existence among the majority of those as yet uncommitted to either ASP or the NFSE.

Whatever the significance of the marked differences within the self-employed sector, there can be no doubt that the failure of the Federation's recruitment campaign in 1977 emphasised that future growth in membership was going to be difficult to achieve. Further, that failure may have had a deeper significance when taken in conjunction with a closer evaluation of the Federation's membership returns for 1976. At a superficial level it achieved a marginal increase in membership from about 40,000 in 1975 to around 43,000 in 1976, but the net improvement obscures an interesting trend. Between 1975 and 1976 the Federation experienced a loss of approximately 7,000 members which was offset by additional recruitment, most notably the 'windfall' afforded by the adhesion of the 3,500 former members of the the the NASE's East Anglia group.[80] Clearly continued wastage of membership on the scale of 1975–6 required substantial fresh recruitment to compensate, and the evidence of early 1977 appeared to suggest that, notwithstanding a substantial financial outlay and a national advertising campaign, such recruitment was not immediately forth-coming.

The Federation's leadership has always recognised the paramount impor-tance of maintaining and expanding its support. It has therefore developed an elaborate administrative and organisational structure which is financed almost entirely by membership subscriptions. This makes it particularly vulnerable to the effects of any significant erosion of its membership, for this would rapidly produce a financial crisis with implications for the Federation's survival. In this context the failure of the recruitment campaign was particularly damaging since it wasted valuable financial resources without producing the vital new membership. Certainly the growing dissatisfaction with the existing policies and leaders which emerged forcefully after May 1977 was prompted by con-cern that the Federation was no longer making a popular impact.

In July the Federation organised a rally in Hyde Park on the issue of the closed shop, but the fact that it took place the day before the mass trade union lobby at Grunwick transformed in into a rally in defence of Mr George Ward. The expected turnout at the Federation's rally of 10,000 did not materialise and only 500 attended. Hopes that major politicians from the Liberal and Conservative parties would attend were likewise unrealised when John Pardoe and Dr Rhodes Boyson did not appear. However, frustration on the part of some Federation members was essentially centred on the refusal of the Execu-tive to countenance a demonstration march rather than a rally.

Mr Shawn Prescott, Chairman of the Kent and East Sussex Region, was so incensed that he circulated regional chairmen throughout Britain calling for an emergency meeting of the national council. He wanted the meeting to imple-ment a resolution passed by his region which demanded the resignation of Mr Owen Dyer and Mr Lex Reid, Federation Vice-Presidents, and the termination of the Federation's contract with Russell Greer and Associates who were public relations advisers. Prescott felt that the failure to march had caused the Federation to lose face on what should have been its most important demon-stration to date.[81] The Executive's explanation was that a march had been called off following advice from the police. In fact the march was the catalyst which produced a revolt building up over the alleged waste of £100,000 on the recruitment campaign, the general failure of leadership and the Federation's lack of public impact.

The emergency meeting of the national council took place in September and resulted in the resignation of the Federation's Chief Administrator, Mr Michael Norton. This resignation followed a vote of no confidence in Norton because of his plans to develop further the Federation's administration at Lytham St Annes beyond its existing full-time staff of about thirty. Mr Brian Kelly, Chairman of the South Wales Region, became Honorary Secretary and temporary head of the Federation pending a further reorganisation.[82] The reorganisation confirmed Mr Kelly in his position and produced a number of leadership changes as well as a renaming of organisational and decision-making structures within the Federation. More significantly it appears to have marked a return to the less restrained politics of the 'outsider' group concerned to create public debate and attract attention through an aggressive approach likely to alienate official opinion. This change has been demonstrated quite clearly in 1978.

In February Brian Kelly declared that as a protest against the Employment Protection Act and Labour's refusal to amend it substantially, the Federation would initiate the sackings of some 250,000 workers in small businesses at the rate of 50,000 a month. Kelly appeared to believe that this threat was credible and was quoted as saying: 'Imagine the impact this would have on Government statistics, dole payments and departmental workloads.'[83] The earlier approach to the Class 4 levy, which had been to seek tax relief and improved benefits, was replaced by a policy calling for its complete abolition. The Federation again captured media headlines in *The Daily Telegraph* and *The Sunday Times* with its accusation that the tax inspectorate questioned the children of those suspected of tax evasion about the amount of pocket money they received for sweets.[84] Publicity for the tax issue, which was an old one, was engineered by the Federation's new lobbyist, John Blundell, who had previously worked for ASP and was largely responsible for organising its 'Fight the 714 Campaign'.

The most recent (in mid-1978) of the Federation's new initiatives is its detailed attack on ACAS.[85] The NFSE has issued a 'research document' claiming that ACAS is politically biased and is completely uninformed about and unsympathetic towards small business despite the fact that well over 80 per cent of the time is spent on trade union recognition disputes involving small firms. To counter ACAS the Federation has set up a body called the Independent Conciliation and Advisory Service, which is non-profit-making and will provide an alternative report to ACAS in any trade union recognition dispute. The Federation appeared to have gone full circle, abandoning any attempt at caution or moderation. It was again operating the strategy of belligerent public statements, perhaps to halt a possible slide in membership, but it certainly indicated a movement away from its middle period when it sought accommodation with the Government. The NFSE had gone back to the initial phase of the clarion call when it sought influence through a capacity to disrupt the administrative process and undermine Government policy.

Conclusions

The idea that the NFSE, NASE and ASP constituted a core element in a wider phenomenon of 'middle-class revolt' had a superficial plausibility when first canvassed but is now open to serious doubt. In 1974–5 the rapid growth in the numerical support for the Federation and the NASE took place against a background of high inflation, a Labour Government and the perceived power of trade unions. This background provided a classic recipe for an emerging middle class discontent to manifest itself in groups such as the NFSE, ratepayers' associations and overtly political organisations like NAFF and the Middle Class Association. The confusion and lack of confidence exhibited by the Conservative Party in the wake of the confrontation with the miners, the three-day week and the electoral defeats of 1974, left the Party ill-equipped to deal with these more radical developments and, indeed, possibly encouraged them. All of this contributed to an atmosphere in which the popular media concentrated considerable attention on the new groups and organisations and put forward the general theme of 'middle-class revolt'.

While the initial growth of NFSE membership was quite spectacular, it has not been sustained. It is doubtful whether the organisation has achieved any significant growth in membership since late 1975 despite the vigorous and expensive recruitment campaign mounted in early 1977. Recent (early 1979) assessments of the Federation's membership place it at about 50,000, but there are grounds for believing the true figure to be much smaller. From the earliest days of its most rapid growth the Federation has experienced a relatively high turnover in support – perhaps as much as 25 per cent during 1975–6. This wastage has always been a source of concern, and much time is spent trying to contact members who have failed to renew their subscriptions. The experience of 1977 seems to indicate that recruits are increasingly less forthcoming and that continued wastage may be producing a net loss in membership. It was noted earlier that the financial implications of any serious drop in membership for the maintenance of the Federation's organisation and administration would be damaging. There are suggestions from rival organisations, notably ASP, that the NFSE has in fact suffered very substantial losses of membership and by 1978 was facing a major financial crisis.[86] It is difficult to substantiate such claims, and rumours of the Federation's imminent collapse have been so frequent that they have to be treated with caution. None the less, the Federation has an elaborate organisational structure and a large professional staff requiring substantial financial support. Moreover, there is the evidence of the failed recruitment campaign in 1977 and the previous history of a high turnover in membership to provide some support for the claim that the Federation is in serious financial difficulties.

These difficulties over membership are complemented by the related problem of fashioning a strategy for dealing with political questions and Government legislation in a way that will maximise rank and file support. The Federation remains beset by a kind of ideological-organisational schizophrenia, unable to establish whether it is a conventional pressure group operating in the context of bargains and compromises or a group content to remain outside the lobby system propagating a return to a society based on the private enterprise model and the individualistic ethic. In the event it has operated as a kind of 'marginal' group vacillating between the two positions. Many critics argue that this is a consequence of leadership failure or a failure of vision, but again it may be a constraint imposed by a large, diverse membership subject to widely different pressures and without the necessary political skill or experience to forge a workable internal alliance. ASP has been able to define and propagate a relatively precise ideological line, but the cost has been a small and reducing membership. Moreover, to talk of an 'ASP line' is also of doubtful utility since ASP views are essentially based on the individual position of Teresa Gorman.

Gorman has been unencumbered by the need to explain the policies to an organisation of branches, since they have not existed; supporters are simply required to support the policies or leave. In May 1978 ASP claimed a membership of 5,126, drawn from a wide range of occupations, of which one third had no employees, while the remainder employed an average workforce of 13·9 employees.[87] This contrasts with the position in early 1976 when ASP claimed a membership of over 12,000, including recruits from the NASE. It clearly appears to have lost members at an alarming rate, which may be significant for its future role.

It is possible that the already close relationship between NAFF and ASP, which sees Teresa Gorman and Gordon Bridgman on NAFF platforms and Gorman on the NAFF Council, will become closer. Already the ASP news-sheet *Counterattack* is being circulated as a supplement to NAFF's *Free Nation* and in Essex, where ASP has substantial support, the NAFF/ASP membership over-laps to a point where NAFF branches may provide ASP with an effective branch structure. It is also the case that the relationship between NAFF and the NFSE is improving. It has always been claimed by NAFF that it has good relations with grassroots Federation branches and shares members in common. The strains have been at the leadership level, but following the most recent changes in the Federation leadership and its return to a more radical line, NAFF has been notably less hostile to the NFSE and *The Free Nation* has recently carried more favourable references to Federation activities.

Although the aspirations of the NFSE and ASP have not been realised they certainly alerted bodies such as the CBI, NCT and Conservative Party to the volatility of small business and self-employed entrepreneurs and they have made efforts to represent these interests in a more vigorous, public fashion. The CBI have made efforts to publicise the activity of the Small Firms Council and their efforts on behalf of the small entrepreneur. In November 1977 the CBI held its first national conference, attended by 1,300 members including a significant representation from the small-firm sector. The NCT has recently emphasised its position as the premier organisation representing 'independents', 'family businesses' and the 'self-employed'. It has made much of its role in a somewhat mysterious body called the National Trade and Kindred Organisations Committee for National Insurance (NATKO). This body, claiming to represent over a million self-employed, is composed of thirty-six constituent bodies, mostly trade associations, has operated for more than fifty years and is recognised by the Department of Health and Social Security for the purposes of negotiating on specialised National Insurance legislation. It claims to have regular, often weekly, meetings at the Department with reasonable access to Ministers.

Both the CBI and NCT have publicised their expertise and specialised knowledge, which, they argue, they can mobilise in negotiations with Government. It is possible that the measures taken by the last Labour Government to assist small business, including the reduction in the Class 4 levy to 5 per cent, the abolition of Capital Transfer Tax on businesses transferred within a family, and relief from VAT on bad debts, have strengthened the CBI's authority as the main national representative of business and industry. The Labour Government's more sympathetic attitude to the small business sector was generally associated with the view that small business offers a reasonable possibility in terms of generating employment. The appointment of Harold Lever and Bob Cryer by the Labour Government to carry out a special investigation of the small-firm sector may have been guided by that view, although it has also been seen as a public relations exercise, and has probably led to the establishment of a more orderly process of negotiation on the problems of small firms. At the same time this process has probably reasserted the premier role of the CBI as the authoritative voice of small business in terms of negotiations with Government.

The whole field of business representation may be on the point of significant changes. Already employers' organisations and trade associations are seeking to redefine their roles in terms of new services and ideas in the wake of the abolition of retail price maintenance and other restrictive practices. The SBA has operated for over ten years and a new organisation, the Union of Independent Companies (UIC), emerged in 1977 as a potentially powerful voice for small firms in the engineering and related trades. In fact the UIC is itself the result of a split within the SBA caused by serious disagreements over tactics, organisation and leadership. The core of the UIC's membership is the old South West Region of the SBA, and its principal architect, Bill Poeton, is a long-time activist in the field of small business representation. The UIC claims to allow maximum autonomy to the local branches, which are based on parliamentary constituencies so as to ensure that pressure may be brought to bear directly on Members of Parliament. Despite its small support, the UIC has an experienced leadership and could well come to represent an important and new development in the field of small business representation.

In conclusion, it may be that the phenomenon of the self-employed groups was a consequence of the existence of a particular set of socio-economic and political circumstances between 1974 and 1976. Since that point the slowing down in the rate of inflation, the revival of morale within the Conservative Party and the more positive attitude of the Labour Government towards small business may have reduced the radical, aggressive appeal of groups like the NFSE and ASP. At the same time the heterogeneous nature of self-employment in terms of occupation, social status and size of plant utilised limits the opportunities of developing a mass organisation on the basis of the simple appeal of shared self-employment. The fact that the self-employed/small business sector is so diverse, coupled with the wider application of government legislation to most forms and sizes of business, commercial and industrial activity, may encourage the development of new and varied forms of business representation. The CBI and the NCT may still remain as the dominant organisations in their field, but they may be increasingly challenged by new groups representing specific interests and viewpoints.

NOTES

1 *Report of the Committee of Inquiry on Small Firms (Bolton Committee)*, HMSO, 1971, Cmnd 4811, pp. 1–2.
2 Ibid, p. 3.
3 Ibid, p. 5.
4 *Department of Employment Gazette*, Vol. LXXXIV, No. 12 (December 1976), pp. 1344–9.
5 Cf. *Enterprise Into the Eighties*, CBI, 1977, p. 10.
6 *Report of the Committee of Inquiry on Small Firms*, op. cit., p. 93.
7 Ibid.
8 Cf. *Report of the Committee of Inquiry Into Industrial and Commercial Representation*. The Association of British Chambers of Commerce/The CBI, November 1972, Appendices VII and IX.
9 Ibid, p. 78.
10 Cf. Hamilton, R. T., 'Government Decisions and Small Firms', unpublished draft manuscript, 1975, p. 14. This piece provides a useful background to the literature on the relationship between government and small business prior to 1975.
11 Cf. Bechhofer, F., *et al.*, 'The Petit Bourgeois in the Class Structure: The Case of the Small Shopkeepers', in Parkin, F. (ed.), *The Social Analysis of Class Structure*, Tavistock Publications, 1974. Also Killingback, N., 'Retail Traders and Co-operative Societies: The Shopocracy and Politics 1931–35', paper given to the BSA/PSA Conference on the Middle Class in Politics, Salford University, 1976.
12 For a brief note on Poujadism see Anderson, M., *Conservative Politics in France*, Allen & Unwin, 1974, pp. 276–80.
13 For an account of its organisation, structure, membership and activities, see *The 79th Annual Report of The National Chamber of Trade 1977*.
14 *Guardian*, 31 August 1974.
15 See, for example, *The Sunday Times*, 8 December 1974, and *The Sunday Telegraph*, 19 January 1975, which carry accounts of the impact of the proposed National Insurance payments on the self-employed; also *Guardian*, 14 November 1974.
16 *Daily Mail*, 28 April 1975.
17 *Daily Mail*, 25 March 1975.
18 In an interview with Paul Ruffley of the NFSE it was made clear that this refusal strengthened the position of those in the Federation who had consistently opposed the levy in principle and were not interested in reciprocal benefits for the extra levy.
19 Ruffley, P. G., 'A Discussion of Some Aspects of the Self-Employed, Small Business and Government', unpublished dissertation, University of Manchester Institute of Science and Technology, 1976.
20 *Guardian*, 17 April 1975.
21 *Guardian*, 27 November 1975.
22 Ibid.
23 For an early attempt to locate the self-employed revolt in the wider context of a more general middle class political movement, see the *Guardian*, 26, 27, 28 November 1975.
24 *Guardian*, 22 February 1975.
25 Ibid.
26 *The Times*, 9 September 1975; also the *Guardian*, 9 September 1975.
27 *Guardian*, 15 September 1975.
28 *Guardian*, 19 September 1975.
29 *The Times*, 19 January 1976.
30 A press release by Norman Small dated 27 January 1976.
31 Ibid.
32 *The Sunday Telegraph*, 2 May 1976.
33 *Daily Mail*, 26 November 1975.

34 The information on the NASE is derived mainly from conversations and written communications with Teresa Gorman, General Secretary of ASP.

35 The NASE had thirteen action groups in late 1976. Nine were based in the Midlands and West, only two in London and the South East, and none in the North East or Scotland. *Counterattack*, Vol. 1, No. 4 (1976), p. 16.

36 This assessment of Gorman's view is drawn from an interview and subsequent communication.

37 *Counterattack*, Vol. 1, No. 4 (1976), p. 2.

38 Quoted from a letter to the author dated 13 May 1978.

39 *Guardian*, 19 May 1975. See also the *Guardian*, 7 July 1978, for an account of the Conservative SBB.

40 *Guardian*, 7 July 1978.

41 *Guardian*, 20 May 1975.

42 A letter from Judith Englander, ASP's Research Officer, dated 23 May 1978.

43 A letter from Teresa Gorman dated 2 May 1978.

44 See *Daily Mail*, 24 August 1978, for evidence of the often confusing nature of the relationships between the various self-employed groups and the proposed alliance between the NASE and the NFSE. In Gorman's letter of 2 May 1978 she points out that 'sometime in 1976 the NASE group in Norfolk decided unilaterally to join the NFSE'.

45 *The Times*, 2 March 1976.

46 *Daily Mail*, 10 June 1976.

47 *Counterattack*, Vol. 1, No. 2 (1976), p. 5.

48 Ibid, pp. 6–7.

49 *Slow to Hire – Quick to Fire*, ASP, 1976.

50 *Guardian*, 15 July 1976.

51 *Daily Mail*, 8 July 1976.

52 For an account of the Constantinescu demonstration, see *Counterattack*, Vol. 1, No. 3 (1976).

53 A letter from Teresa Gorman to the editor of *First Voice*, dated 27 August 1976.

54 A letter from the editor of *First Voice* to Teresa Gorman dated 21 September 1976.

55 Quoted from Gorman's letter to the editor of *First Voice* dated 15 September 1976.

56 *First Voice*, October 1976, p. 4.

57 An account of these negotiations with photocopies of the crucial letters dealing with the terms of the proposed amalgamation is contained in a handout entitled *Lost Voice* published by ASP and obtainable from Teresa Gorman.

58 Cf. *The Observer*, 19 September 1976.

59 *Lost Voice*, op. cit.

60 *Counterattack*, Vol. 1, No. 5 (1977), p. 2.

61 *Guardian*, 23 December 1976.

62 Ibid.

63 *Counterattack*, Vol. 1, No. 5, p. 2.

64 *Daily Mail*, 19 February 1977.

65 Teresa Gorman saw this as the crucial element in the campaign and quoted Labour MPs who proposed to extend the use of certificates to other self-employed professions like law and medicine.

66 Cf. *The Times*, 4 June 1976 and *First Voice*, February 1977 and March 1977.

67 For an account of this development, see *Lost Voice*, op. cit., p. 4.

68 See Alex Lyon's letter reprinted in *First Voice*, June 1978, p. 8, which commented: 'Unfortunately there were so many crooks in the building industry that this was the only way to defeat the lump.'

69 An accurate calculation is impossible to make but it is difficult to find evidence to support the view that the various groups ever accounted for more than 5 per cent of the total self-employed population.

70 *First Voice*, March 1977, p. 3.

71 Ibid, p. 1.

72 Ibid, p. 5.

73 Ibid.
74 Ibid.
75 Ibid, p. 3.
76 Ibid, p. 5.
77 Ibid, June 1977, p. 1.
78 NFSE Head Office Communication No. 115, 25 April 1977.
79 Cf. *Department of Employment Gazette*, op. cit., p. 1344. In 1971 three-fifths of the self-employed had no employees.
80 NFSE Annual Conference Report, February 1977, p. 15.
81 *Daily Mail*, 11 July 1977, reported the rally and *The Times*, 8 August 1977, noted Prescott's concern over the cancellation of the march.
82 *The Times*, 9 September 1977.
83 *Daily Mail*, 27 February 1978.
84 Ibid, 15 February 1978.
85 See *The Daily Telegraph*, 1 June 1978.
86 In an interview with the author Teresa Gorman estimated the NFSE's 1978 membership at 20,000.
87 A letter from Teresa Gorman dated 2 May 1978.

Neill Nugent

4. The National Association for Freedom*

Introduction

The National Association for Freedom (NAFF) may fairly claim to have been one of the more successful pressure groups of recent years. Despite having few initial advantages, such as the guaranteed membership and income of the occupational based groups, it has already achieved much since its formation at the end of 1975: a number of successful court actions have been fought in support of its aims; a regular and well-produced newspaper has been launched; membership has grown and the organisation has developed to a level which few observers would ever have predicted; and finally it has shown a remarkable capacity for attracting attention to itself. The publicity has by no means all been favourable but there can be no doubt that it has resulted in NAFF's name becoming well known in political circles and, in consequence, in its becoming a much-discussed organisation. Indeed, that it has established itself, along with the National Front, as perhaps the principal *bête noire* of the left, is claimed by some NAFF supporters, only half jokingly, to be true proof of its progress.

Much of the attention given to NAFF has arisen from its generally being seen as a new type of organisation in British politics: a non-party political body seeking to create a mass following behind a campaign for the preservation, even restoration, of British freedoms. Freedoms which are seen to be threatened from four sources: 'the excessive power that is wielded by trade union militants'; the fact 'that there are virtually no curbs on what the Government can do on the basis of a transient majority of one in the House of Commons'; that 'we have lacked an effective and articulate defence of the values and traditions on which Britain's past greatness was built'; and, finally, that 'Despite the spread of bureaucracy, we have never had as much government as we now have in Britain – and yet we are not being properly protected against the menace of Soviet military expansion or, for that matter, against terrorists inside our own frontiers.'[1]

Collectivism, the ever-encroaching state, increasingly powerful and irresponsible trade unions, and communists are thus seen as the principal subverters of liberty. If freedoms are to be preserved, these forces must be challenged by whatever legal means are available. The message from NAFF thus rings loud and clear: the best society is the least governed society – except, significantly, in the areas of law enforcement, defence and alleged abuse of trade union power.

* In January 1979, NAFF changed its name to The Freedom Association. One reason for making this change was to distinguish the Association more clearly from the National Front.

But though there are new and distinctive features about NAFF it is not as innovative as might appear to be the case at first sight. For there have long been active in British politics organisations which have taken as their central aim the making of 'non-partisan' appeals for the defence of freedom against state interventionism and the stranglehold of trade unionism. Certainly they have differed from NAFF in terms of specific policies and tactics but the similarities are nevertheless striking. These organisations thus need to be considered in examining the background to the emergence of NAFF and in discussing the extent to which it really is a new phenomenon.

The freedom groups

All the 'freedom groups' have taken as their starting point the view that collectivism is both economically unsound and morally undesirable. Only by the strictest limitation on governmental activity can material wealth be increased and individual liberties safeguarded. There has then been agreement on basics. This has not, however, led to duplication, for each of the organisations has sought to play a specific role and to appeal to a distinct audience.

In identifying these roles and audiences a broad distinction may be made. On the one hand there are what may be called the 'economic' freedom groups. Based principally on institutional affiliation and financed largely by business contributions, their main role is to act as the spokesmen of unfettered capitalism. The case for market mechanisms is boldly stated, the dangers of nationalisation and creeping state controls are emphasised, and growing left-wing infiltration on the shop floor is highlighted. On the other hand there are those organisations which, though equally firm advocates of economic *laissez-faire*, go beyond an interest in the structure of the economy to take up threats to civil and judicial freedoms. In so doing they seek to recruit a popular base, and thus they tend to be less dependent on industry for finance.

Of the economic freedom groups, four are of particular importance: Aims for Freedom and Enterprise, the British United Industrialists, the Economic League, and the Institute of Economic Affairs. Their potential influence may be gauged from their combined annual income which probably approaches £2,000,000. The exact source of these funds is to some extent conjectural as contributors are able to avoid the 1967 Companies Act, which requires businesses to reveal political donations over £50, by simply choosing to regard such donations as not being political. It is, however, known that most contributions are from firms with strong individualistic or family traditions – breweries and insurance companies are prominent – rather than the larger international companies which tend to avoid the risk of overt political activities.[2]

Aims for Freedom and Enterprise (AIMS), the best known of the four, was established in 1942 as Aims of Industry. Since making its name with the 'Mr Cube' campaign in the late 1940s, when, on behalf of Tate & Lyle, it successfully fought against the nationalisation of the sugar industry, it has acted both on behalf of individual clients and as a general free enterprise pressure group.

In its latter role it promotes its principles in three ways. Firstly, it directly lobbies decision makers – both political and administrative – through the submission of evidence and memoranda and also through the many personal contacts it enjoys, especially with prominent figures in the Conservative Party. Secondly, it seeks to change the climate of influential opinion by the publication of pamphlets and booklets. Most of these are concerned, one way or another, with highlighting the advantages of free enterprise and the evils of socialism, though it should be said that the latter is given an extremely broad interpretation. Thus, the first in its series 'Studies of the Left', which was launched in 1977, was entitled *The National Front is a Socialist Front*. (The author of this booklet, Stephen Eyres, later in 1977 became editor of NAFF's newspaper, *The Free Nation*.) Thirdly, appeals are made to the general public through the placement of large, and therefore expensive, advertisements in the national press.

Like all the freedom groups, AIMS claims to be 'entirely independent of any political party, both ideologically and financially' and in support of this it stresses that it has 'never supported any political party or given money to, or received money from, any political party'. It also points to the breadth of its support, claiming that over 2,000 industrial organisations are members of AIMS and that this includes associations and federations which in turn represent 36,000 companies. There are also said to be 'several thousand individual members'.[3]

But though the claim to be non-party-political is justified in the formal sense, in practice, because of its principles and its base of support, there are inevitably areas of 'overlap' with the Conservative Party. For example, many of AIMS's booklets have been written by prominent Conservative figures such as Rhodes Boyson MP, Nicholas Ridley MP, Sir John Foster QC, and Russell Lewis (former director of the Conservative Political Centre). More significantly, AIMS invariably increases its activities in pre-election periods. So, in the run-up to the February 1974 election a series of advertisements appeared in the national press which, by attacking militants and extremists in society, implicitly advocated a Conservative vote. One headline queried 'The end of freedom in Britain?' and portrayed a 'moderate' family tied in tape; another was headed 'Don't be fooled out of your freedom' and showed a picture of Stalin lurking behind a jester's mask. Pamphlets were equally forthright. One, shaped as a coffin, asked if this was the fate which awaited free enterprise. It stated that the threats facing Britain included the Communist Party's intention of taking over the unions, 'and thus in the near future, the Labour Party'; the 'massive programme of State ownership from the Labour Party'; and the 'major threat to politicise industry . . . contained in the Labour Party's plans to put socialists in "key influence" positions on the boards of the 100 companies to be controlled by the National Enterprise Board'.[4] The main slogan for the autumn election campaign was 'Say no to the Elephants', the two elephants being 'Nationalisation' and 'State Control'.

The Economic League was established in 1919 by coal and steel owners with the following object:

> To promote and improve the knowledge and study of economics and of other industrial and social subjects affecting the interests of the community and of members thereof, from the standpoint that –
>
> (1) The preservation of personal freedom and free enterprise is essential to national well-being.
>
> (2) While maintaining its complete independence of any political party the League must actively oppose all subversive forces – whatever their origin and inspiration –

that seek to undermine the security of Britain in general and of British industry in particular.[5]

In seeking to propagate these views the League moves on a narrower front than AIMS in that although it too aims to influence the general public – by, for example, mass leafleting campaigns – its main forum is industry. Much of its income – claimed to be £660,000 in 1977 – is spent on a range of 'in company training courses' to which member firms send employees (3,317 courses and lectures in 1977) and on producing a number of publications 'covering reader-ships at shop floor level, among apprentices and supervisory, middle and top management'. (Almost 20 million leaflets, pamphlets and newsletters are claimed to have been distributed in 1977.)[6]

A particular concern is the exposure of left-wing influence in the workplace. Allegations have been made that the League's activities in this direction include the compilation of blacklists of workers which are made available to employers. Thus a report in *The Observer* in 1969 stated that 'One very large company which makes a four-figure donation says flatly that the League "does a hell of a lot of security vetting for us on political grounds. This is their sole use to us, and for X pounds a year, it's good value for money".'[7] The League itself denies having blacklists but admits to having at its disposal a fund of information about subversive/revolutionary bodies.

British United Industrialists (BUI) is by far the most secretive group. Formed in 1959 following a merger between the Home Counties Industrialists Association and the British Industrialists Association, it is not prepared to reveal where its money goes other than to state: 'Our activities are many and various but all entirely in the interests of freedom of industry and opposition to all forms of interference and control by *any* Government'.[8] The secrecy is even seen as a positive merit, Colonel J. B. Hobbs, BUI's Director, having asserted that 'A great deal of the value of the organisation to my mind is that most people do not know exactly how we function.'[9] Not surprisingly, this attitude has given rise to much speculation as to BUI's activities, particularly since Hobbs has admitted that it 'supports a certain number of things which the Conservative Party wouldn't, or shouldn't do'.[10] The general consensus amongst informed observers is that, apart from anonymously sponsoring the publication of a number of pamphlets, which doubtless reflects Hobbs's asser-tion that 'Demands for nationalisation spring from subversion on the shop floor',[11] the main function is to act as a collecting agency for 'free enteprise funds', most of which are passed on to the Conservative Party. BUI admits some contributions are made to the Tories but dismisses the general 'fundrais-ing' charge as a fallacy propagated by the extreme left. At the same time, BUI makes no attempt to shed further light on the question by, for example, publishing a list of alternative activities or attempting to explain why com-panies which do make 'political' contributions usually give something to the Economic League but only to one or other of the BUI and the Conservatives.

The fourth freedom group, the Institute of Economic Affairs (IEA), describes itself as a 'research and educational trust that specialises in the study of markets and pricing systems as technical devices for registering preferences and apportioning resources'.[12] Its principles are thus much the same as those of the organisations discussed above. It is also equally dependent on business for its income. Nevertheless it does stand apart in that it is a genuinely scholarly body whose whole approach is quite different from the rather crude propagandist emphasis of AIMS and the Economic League. Since its establishment in 1957 the Institute has concentrated on the publication of 'in-depth' booklets and pamphlets, many of which have been written by distinguished economists. Their general theme is that, except for the provision of a minimum, state services should be taken over by the private sector. Vouchers and credits for educational and health services are among the more controversial proposals that have been advanced.[13]

The most prominent of the 'non-economic' freedom groups in the post-war period, and in many ways the most similar to NAFF, have been those associated with Edward Martell. From 1955 he established a number of organisations, each of which reflected his many diverse opinions – from the need for decimalisation to the demand for the abolition of capital punishment – and each of which had a distinct role. Thus the Free Press Society offered printing facilities to the public during strikes; the People's League for the Defence of Freedom circulated literature 'exposing' threats to liberty; and the National Fellowship sought to influence government and church by relating Christian principles to a national morality.

But though moving on a broad front, the organisations, which were federated in 1963 into the Freedom Group, continually emphasised three central themes: the level of state activity should be severely reduced; all efforts should be made to ensure that the Labour Party was not elected to office; strict controls should be exercised over the trade unions. In Martell's view, unions stood 'between us and sane government and a national morality based on Christian principles'. Legislation should be introduced restricting the power of picketing, making the deliberate fostering of strikes illegal and liable to charges of conspiracy, and banning the closed shop.

Martell sought to spread his message in three ways.

Firstly, he sought to recruit a mass membership directly. Reliable figures are not available, though an estimate in the *Spectator* at the peak of Freedom Group activity, in 1964, that there were 160,000 'acknowledged supporters' seems to have had little substance. Even Martell's more conservative claims, to have had 100,000 supporters in 1963 and an active manpower of 30,000 in 1964, seem on the high side.[14] More probably there was in many right-wing circles a general fund of goodwill for his ideals, but only a small hard core, numbering perhaps 5,000, who could be called upon to give active assistance.

Secondly, literature was distributed on a mass basis. Throughout the late 1950s and early 1960s leaflets and pamphlets outlining the anti-socialist case, but also emphasising Martell's other diverse interests, were widely circulated. In addition a newspaper, the *New Daily*, was printed and for a while attracted a large audience. Indeed in the early 1960s it claimed a daily average circulation of 45,000, with peaks of up to 90,000.

Thirdly, attempts were made to influence the Conservative Party. As a Labour victory looked increasingly likely in 1964, links with many local Conservative associations were established, and after Huyton accepted an offer to try and unseat Harold Wilson all constituency chairmen and prospective candidates were circulated with offers of help. The situation was both awkward and embarrassing for Conservative Central Office, not only because of Martell's radical policies and known opposition to such liberals and 'creeping socialists' as Macleod, Boyd, Heath and Maudling, but also because many active Tories were known to be sympathetic to Freedom Group ideals. Such was the concern that a circular was issued advising local parties to accept Freedom Group assistance only on an individual basis. In the event, a large number of constituencies still went ahead and accepted assistance of various kinds.

But the 1964 campaign proved to be the peak of Freedom Group activity. Financial problems were soon pressing and the *New Daily* began to appear only spasmodically. Overspending during the campaign had emptied the coffers, though the proposal of the Labour Government to make companies declare their donations to political organisations was, according to Martell, a contributory factor. He declared that the consequences of the legislation were such that 'a lot of our income disappeared overnight'.[15]

However, activities did not completely cease. In 1966 a group of Midland businessmen put up the necessary finance to allow the *New Daily* to resume regular publication for a while. In the same year the National Party was formed by Martell and in 1967 it unsuccessfully contested a by-election at Nuneaton. The candidate, interestingly, was Air Vice-Marshal Donald Bennett, a distinguished war hero and former Liberal MP, who has since become involved with a number of organisations on the far right. He has also been reported as having been prepared to make available substantial sums of money to parliamentary candidates standing on an anti-Common-Market platform.

The revival of activity was, however, only temporary. Further resources were not forthcoming and in December 1967, with debts of £179,000, Martell was declared bankrupt. Following this he and his organisations virtually disappeared from public view. (For his later re-emergence, see below.)

Another 'non-economic' freedom group is the Society for Individual Freedom (SIF). Formed in 1942 by the amalgamation of the Society of Individualists and the National League for Freedom, its view is that 'Every time the government assumes responsibility for an area of your life, your freedom of choice and action is curtailed.' Members, who number around 1,000 – including a parliamentary group of 20 or so Conservative MPs – use the Society as a forum for the exchange of ideas. This takes place through the occasional dinner, usually in the Palace of Westminster, and through the quarterly journal *Freedom First*. As with other 'non-economic' groups, much time is spent eulogising free enterprise, but the Society has also ventured into other areas such as championing individual cases of alleged maladministration by public bodies, opposing the Automobile Association's campaign to make the wearing of seat belts compulsory, advocating an ombudsman (the creation of which it sees as one of its successes) and the drawing up of a Bill of Rights.

Finally, reference must be made to the activities and organisations with which the late Ross McWhirter was associated. McWhirter saw himself as a libertarian and a defender of the supremacy of law. Armed with a legal background and private funds, which were mainly derived from his co-editorship with his brother Norris of *The Guinness Book of Records*, he sought to defend his values by bringing a series of individual actions in the courts, e.g. against

Britain's entry into the Common Market, against the introduction of comprehensive education in England, and against subliminal advertising on television. But, apart from the occasional legal judgment in his favour, little headway was made and by the mid-1970s, affected by the mood of revolt, especially amongst the ratepayers, he began to think in terms of seeking popular support for his campaigns. Referring to the anger and indignation in the country, he said, 'It's something the press are altogether missing. You haven't tapped it yet. People are beginning to see there is no end in sight, and they are very, very angry.'[16]

The outcome was the setting up of 'an organisation [that] has come into being for the express purpose of standing up to the unions':[17] the Current Affairs Press. Claiming a working capital of £100,000 and the ability to be able to print 3,000,000 newspapers a day in the event of a national newspaper strike, a fortnightly news-sheet, *Majority*, was launched, the contents of which are indicated by its two sub-titles: *The Organ of the Radical Right*, and *Journal of Free Enterprise and Self-Help*. The 'free' economy was defended, socialist interventionism was bitterly attacked. The establishment of 'Self-Help' organisations was advocated and advice was given on how to set up 'Generator Clubs', how to be more self-reliant in foodstuffs, how to pool private transport resources, etc.[18] The drafting of a written constitution, which would restore the full sovereignty of Parliament, was also regarded as a priority. McWhirter added, however, somewhat ambiguously, 'Parliamentary Sovereignty is entirely acceptable, and only acceptable, so long as it is not manipulated, so long as it is decently and honestly run.'[19]

As for relations with the established parties, there was the usual 'non-political' stance accompanied by a general, and frequently warm, support for right-wing Conservatism. This led in turn, as it has done with NAFF, to encouragement and praise for the post-Heath Conservative leadership:

> Mrs Margaret Thatcher deserves, and must be given, the wholehearted support not only of the Conservative Party but of anti-Socialists everywhere. . . .
> The country will give her that chance. The rank-and-file of the Tory Party will also do so. It is the Old Gang of the Tory Party, Heath, Whitelaw, Prior, Carr, Walker, Gilmour and their hangers-on who are standing in the way, and apparently do not want to see her succeed. . . .
> A bunch of political failures, has beens who never were, must not be allowed to stand in the way.[20]

But though the Current Affairs Press, or Self-Help as it called itself from November 1975, forms, with the other freedom groups, part of the background to the emergence of NAFF, its significance should not be exaggerated. Self-Help sympathisers certainly provided some of the initial support for NAFF – John Gouriet, NAFF's first Director, is a notable example – but its total membership was small and its public impact limited. It was too dependent on McWhirter and he, despite having a 'respectable' background – having been both a former Conservative parliamentary candidate and an executive committee member of the SIF – was regarded with misgivings by many fellow 'libertarians'. He was thought to be too much of a cavalier and to sail too close to figures who were involved with the 'disreputable' far right. So at the time of McWhirter's murder in November 1975, following his publication of a pamphlet, *How to Stop the Bombers*, NAFF – which to all appearances had identical aims – was already being set up.

Self-Help still exists but is now even more narrowly focused on its strike-breaking role. Its aim is to build a national network of Self-Help Associations 'which would go far towards making trade union strikes impotent, so curbing excessive union power'.[21] Headed by Lady Jane Birdwood (who has long been associated with various anti-immigration campaigns) and the newly re-emerged Edward Martell, its size, resources and activities are shrouded in secrecy. One may, however, doubt both its claim to have nearly 8,000 suppor-ters[22] and its boasts of its potential political muscle: of being able to put thousands of people onto the streets to break strikes; of having been in a position to offer the use of 2,000 vehicles, with drivers, to George Ward at Grunwick; and of being capable of printing daily 3,000,000 copies of a news-paper in the event of a national newspaper stoppage.

The fancifulness and delusions of grandeur embodied in Self-Help's cam-paign may be gauged from a leaflet it distributed, under the aegis of 'The Anti-Strike Union', during the 1977 firemen's dispute. It stated: 'The time has come for the public to deal with the minority in the country who use their trade union power to intimidate and blackmail their fellow citizens.' The ten-point programme to counteract the threat included:

> If you are a shopkeeper, refuse any strikers who may use your shop.
> At every opportunity lobby every trade unionist you meet and tell them that if half a million or so trade union members would threaten to tear up their cards if such excesses continue, sanity would be very quickly restored.
> Challenge the leader of the Firemen's Union at your nearest Fire Station to a public debate on the ethics of risking lives to obtain a financial gain. . . .[23]

In fact on those occasions when Self-Help has attempted to intervene directly in a dispute, for example at Grunwick and at the Trust House Forte union recognition case at Oxford, its role has been minimal. Indeed it appears to have done little more than incur the hostility of NAFF which has seen a danger of being associated with racialism as well as a bid to steal its glory.[24]

By the mid-1970s there was thus no shortage of proponents of the freedom/non-interventionist cause. AIMS, IEA, SIF and Self-Help may have differed in emphasis, approach and strategy, but they were agreed on essentials and all were concerned with advancing basically the same viewpoint.

Despite this crowded field, a number of people, including businessmen, politicians and representatives of the main 'freedom groups', felt the need for a new body – one which would be similar in ideas to AIMS and the IEA but broader in that it would aim for a popular base by attempting to build up a grassroots organisation. It would also seek to effect communications and coordinate activities between like-minded groups: the self-employed, the ratepayers, the freedom associations, etc.

Accordingly, in the summer of 1975, a new organisation was planned.

Formation and aims of NAFF

NAFF was formally launched on 2 December 1975 at a news conference chaired by the former Governor-General of Australia, Lord De l'Isle. The meeting, which received widespread publicity since it took place, quite coincidentally, only a week after Ross McWhirter's murder, heard Norris McWhirter explain why he felt that the people of Britain should not 'bow to the threats of intimidators who seek to destroy us'. Taking the same theme, De l'Isle spoke of there being four recognisable threats to freedom in Britain: a failure to see that the country was drifting towards drab collectivism; inflation; the growing machinery of government; and the extra-parliamentary power of the leaders of organised labour. NAFF's aim, he said, would be to defend freedom and in so doing it would base itself on a fifteen-point *Charter of Rights and Liberties*:

1. The Right to be defended against the country's enemies.
2. The Right to live under the Queen's peace.
3. Freedom of movement within the country and in leaving or re-entering it.
4. Freedom of religion and worship.
5. Freedom of speech and publication.
6. Freedom of assembly and association for a lawful purpose.
7. Freedom to withdraw one's labour, other than contrary to public safety.
8. Freedom to belong or not to belong to a trade union or employer's association.
9. The Right to private ownership.
10. The Right to dispose or convey property by deed or will.
11. Freedom to exercise choice or personal priority in spending, and from oppressive, unnecessary or confiscatory taxation.
12. Freedom from all coercive monopolies.
13. Freedom to engage in private enterprise and pursue the trade or profession of one's choice without harassment.
14. Freedom of choice in the use of State and private services (including education and medicine).
15. The Right to protection from invasion of privacy.

Many of these rights, particularly in the upper half of the Charter, are straightforward and uncontroversial. The importance of 'freedom' and 'privacy', the two key concepts of the Charter, would be denied by few political organisations seeking a popular base. Few would dissent from demands 'to be defended against the country's enemies' or for the basic freedoms of speech, worship, publication and association to be preserved.

Some clauses, however, on reflection, are ambiguous, begging almost as many questions as they answer. Phrases such as 'Freedom . . . from oppressive, unnecessary or confiscatory taxation', 'Freedom to engage in private enterprise . . . without harassment', 'The Right to protection from invasion of privacy', are open to differing interpretations. NAFF's true nature must therefore be gauged not by analysing the contents of its Charter but by observing the issues it takes up and the causes it defends. As might be expected, such an examination shows NAFF to be particularly interested in those infringements of liberty which stem from trade union power and the closed shop. Its philosophy and perspective are thus wholly different from those of an organisation such as the National Council for Civil Liberties which claims to be equally interested in freedom. As Gerald Hartup, National Branch Organiser of NAFF, states, in comparing the two,

> Most of our members would not consider that police harassment will lead to a police state. If there was evidence of corrupt policemen we would push for an enquiry as this sort of thing would clearly undermine confidence in the police, but it is hardly

the essential law and order problem today. The major problem is the lack of support the police are getting. Civil liberties are much more likely to be infringed by the police being unable to enforce law than by individual corrupt policemen. NCCL sometimes give the impression we are already living in a police state.[25]

NAFF's campaign has thus tended to focus on the bottom half of the Charter – attempting to counteract and challenge the threats it sees as being posed to the British way of life by the forces of collectivism, the all-embracing state, the monopoly power of the trade unions, and the unwillingness of most 'moderates' and 'non-socialists' to stand up and resist the onslaught. A selection of leading headlines from NAFF's fortnightly newspaper, *The Free Nation*, gives a flavour of the way in which the campaign has been conducted: 'Commissar Jones's orders' (claiming that 'the most powerful union leader in Britain interprets the Government's closed shop legislation as a licence to enforce 100 per cent compulsory unionisation'); 'We Launch Another Vital Campaign – Stop The Scroungers' (alleging that there is a 'great official cover up of the benefits racket'); 'Another Free Nation Scoop: Revealed: Labour Plan to Nationalise Football'; 'Set The Unions Free!' (from the likes of 'a Marxist leader' such as Hugh Scanlon who has 'long ceased to represent the interests of the man on the factory floor'); 'Labour Goes Leninist' (drawing attention to the 'extent to which Labour's National Executive Committee has been drawn into what can only be described as the Marxist fold').[26]

The anti-communist campaign borders on the hysterical. Shortly after the row, at the end of 1977, when the Conservative MP Stephen Hastings suggested that some prominent British trade unionists had been the targets of communist agents, an article in *The Free Nation* claimed that communists controlled 10 per cent of the important posts in the major unions. It continued:

> If the Communists dominate the unions, they can also dominate the Labour Party as the block votes of the TGWU and the AUEW play a decisive role at the Labour Party Conference. The British Community Party has said for some years that all it has to do is 'float an idea early in the year and it can become official Labour policy by the autumn'.[27]

This simplistic 'analysis', presented in a wholly uncritical way, typifies NAFF's position. Socialism and trade unionism undermine freedom and blaze a trail for an even more sinister enemy:

> The message is simple: the major threat to our way of life comes from communist subversion throughout the world backed by the armed forces of the Soviet Union. It comes also from a naive tolerance of Marxism by Western intellectuals, politicians and industrialists who have lacked the determination to oppose it with the philosophy of freedom. It also comes because the results of Marxism in practice throughout the world are not well enough known by those who may become its victims.[28]

Such a view of world affairs has inevitably led NAFF to comment upon politics in other countries. In so doing further ammunition has been given to its critics, for whilst the denial of basic freedoms in Eastern Europe has been deplored an ambivalent attitude has been struck towards those countries seen to be in the front line of the fight against international communism. So, whilst not condoning the racist South African regime, a *Free Nation* editorial nevertheless stated: 'South Africa's government is neither a Communist nor a Fascist dictatorship. In this sense, it has some claim to belong to the small community of the free world. . . . Even with press freedom curtailed, South Africa is a relatively liberal society by comparison with the average U.N. member state.'[29] Similarly *The Free Nation* printed a full-page article 'exposing' communist and trade union influence in the Chilean Solidarity Campaign without commenting at all upon the mass killings or brutal repression of the regime which had given rise to the campaign.[30]

Strategies

In defending its vision of freedom NAFF moves on three main fronts: it seeks to alert the public to the nature of the challenge and to the consequences which will follow if it is not resisted; it attempts to influence and pressurise the political parties; and it directly confronts the perceived enemies of liberty in so far as resources and the law permit.

Taking the first of these, NAFF believes that the Left has made the running far too long. In Norris McWhirter's opinion,

The aim must be to try and concentrate people's minds on the consequences of going along with the serious legislative moves which reduce the importance of the individual and irreversibly create a corporate state in which everyone is beholden to the state. . . . We oppose the over-mighty of the moment and it is our role to show that the state and trade unions are abusing their powers.[31]

The Right, or as NAFF spokesmen would say, 'individualists and libertarians', must therefore now state their case and publicise their views. In this way the climate of opinion may be changed and the focus of intellectual argument shifted. Accordingly NAFF's main organ, *The Free Nation*, attempts a balance of, on the one hand, general discussion pieces on the nature of freedom, and on the other, examinations and 'exposés' of the many threats to liberty. In addition specific appeals are made, sometimes supplemented by separate leaflets addressed to sections of the population who it is thought might be particularly disposed towards NAFF's policies, e.g. the self-employed, those working in trades where there is a closed shop, and students (who are obliged to join their union).

Other measures to spread NAFF's message are many and have become increasingly varied as branches have established themselves and acquired a growing self-confidence. Much use is made of that now rather unfashionable and unsuccessful forum, the public meeting. Usually addressed by a leading NAFF spokesman – John Gouriet addressed 138 meetings in his two years as Director – and attended by upwards of 70 people, they serve a number of functions: publicity exercise, recruiting vehicle, and rallying point for supporters. Advertisements, outlining NAFF's principles and calling for support, are frequently placed in the national and local press. 'Freedom Proclamations', signed by local sympathisers – including whenever possible well-known names – are inserted in newspapers and magazines. Perhaps most interestingly of all, some of the more vigorous and well-supported branches, actively encouraged by Hartup who believes the left have 'ruled the streets for too long', have begun to use 'direct' methods of contacting the public, for example, by distributing literature in shopping centres and organising petitions on NAFF issues. As Hartup himself says, activism of this kind is as yet limited but it seems to be increasing: 'It's often very difficult for middle class people to get out onto the streets . . . they're very embarrassed . . . but they're beginning to get over it.'[32]

In pursuance of the second strategy – influencing the political parties – NAFF inevitably directs most attention towards the Conservatives. Indeed, such is the emphasis that at times it appears, in aims and strategy, almost as a right-wing Tory pressure group, not totally dissimilar in style to the Monday Club. To characterise it simply as such, however, would be to exaggerate for, though obvious parallels do exist, NAFF has gone out of its way to present itself as non-party-political. In so doing it has deliberately avoided some of the traditional right-wing Conservative bogies, such as immigration, capital punishment and 'the permissive society' which are guaranteed to stir the constituency rank and file. Further, whilst the great majority of NAFF supporters doubtless vote Conservative – and many are paid-up members of the Party – it is clear that most are deeply disillusioned with the performance of the leadership in recent years and are quite prepared to say so publicly. Meetings frequently develop into tirades, from the platform as well as the floor, against the neo-socialist inspiration of many in the upper echelons of the Conservative Party. To take just one example, one of the two platform speakers at the inaugural public meeting of the Lancashire Branch in April 1978, David Kelly, spent most of his thirty minutes explaining why his initial joy at the election of Mrs Thatcher to the Party leadership had been followed by an increasing disillusionment as it had become clear that she had been 'got at by the trendy liberals in the Party . . . the soft centre . . . the Heathmen with their line, "take my hand to a socialist paradise"'. He claimed that Conservative policies on a range of issues merely acknowledged the socialist advance, e.g. the refusal to outlaw the closed shop; the reluctance to de-nationalise; the unwillingness to reverse the movement towards comprehensive education; the avoidance of a commitment to reduce radically the level of taxation; and finally, the admission that the trade unions could not be defeated if they directly confronted a Conservative government.

NAFF spokesmen constantly stress the breadth of their appeal and claim to be as interested in influencing Labour and Liberal supporters as their more natural allies in Conservative ranks. Support for NAFF in these two parties is, however, minimal and in Labour's case virtually non-existent. Certainly Lady Morrison of Lambeth, Herbert Morrison's widow and a much prized member of NAFF's governing council, could hardly be said to represent a significant body of Labour support. Nor could Stephen Haseler and Douglas Eden, organisers of the fringe right-wing Labour pressure group, the Social Democratic Alliance, who have written for *The Free Nation*. Suggestions that NAFF has been associated with attempted right-wing infiltration into the Labour Party may be true, but there is no evidence of any influence having been exerted. Indeed, the uproar and indignation in the Party which followed upon the claim by Alex Lyon MP that NAFF may have assisted with the attempted 'moderate' takeover of Newham North East Labour Party (which had chosen not to re-adopt Reg Prentice as its candidate) illustrated the reception any attempted infiltration would receive.

But if NAFF cannot be reduced to a Conservative 'front' its relations with, and attitudes toward, sections of that Party are much closer than might be expected of a 'non-party' organisation. There are no formal organisational links – it is not part of the Conservative structure and it does not donate funds – but informal contacts and cooperation take place at all levels.

At the highest, Mrs Thatcher gave her general approval by attending, as guest of honour, NAFF's inaugural subscription dinner in January 1977. The 500 supporters who attended gave her a standing ovation. In addition, Robert Moss, who until the end of 1977 was NAFF's joint director and who continues as a member of its National Council, is known to be close to Mrs Thatcher and is indeed thought to have partly written her famous 'Iron Maiden' speech.

At parliamentary level, six Conservative MPs sit on NAFF's National Council: Jill Knight, Sir Frederic Bennett, Nicholas Ridley, Rhodes Boyson, Winston Churchill and Stephen Hastings. NAFF claims that they are but the tip of an iceberg: 'They have not acted as a concerted group but it could be possible for there to be some future loose form of association of sympathetic M.P.'s to act as a NAFF version of the Tribune Group. . . . We reckon some 100 or more Tory M.P.'s support our objectives. . . .'[33]

Such links are mirrored at local level where many NAFF supporters are actively involved in Conservative politics, as councillors, officials, or active members. NAFF organisers frequently make no bones about the fact that the Conservative Party is their main recruiting ground. Certainly there is little hesitation in urging members to vote Tory. John Gouriet himself, at the Lancashire meeting referred to above, stated: 'The Conservatives are causing us great concern as to whether they will deal with the matters on which they will be elected. . . . We have got to see that the Conservative Party, which we hope will be elected, does stand up for Conservative principles.'

Liaison has indeed been such that on one occasion Conservative Central Office was even able to use NAFF's mailing list for its own purposes. This was revealed by *Time Out* in the summer of 1977:

> 10,000 copies of a circular encouraging membership of the Small Business Bureau [see chapter 7] have been handed to NAFF for posting to its own supporters. The address on the pre-paid envelopes which accompanied the circulars was Conservative Central Office in Smith Square.[34]

The chairman of the Small Business Bureau, David Mitchell MP, was a founding member of NAFF.

Not surprisingly in the light of such 'overlap' NAFF takes a broadly pro-Conservative view in its public statements. *The Free Nation*, whose editor, Stephen Eyres, is a Party member and a prospective parliamentary candidate, gives generous space to articles by Conservative figures, and its editorial policy, whilst by no means uncritical – 'softies' such as Reginald Maudling and James Prior have been singled out for bitter criticism – makes clear its general support for the Party leadership. Indeed at times praise becomes positively fulsome:

> Mrs Thatcher's appeal to 'set the people free' (although she did not use Churchill's favourite phrase) was a memorable and refreshing speech – a model of how political leaders who are ready to describe things as they really are can set out to address a country where most people have grown sick and tired, through their personal experience, of the hypocrisy of the Socialist Establishment, and the excesses of the bureaucracy and of Left-wing trade unionists.
>
> We hope that more of Mrs Thatcher's colleagues on the Conservative front bench will be prepared to follow her example in other areas.[35]

That such a glowing appreciation should be accorded is not surprising. Mrs Thatcher represents much of what NAFF stands for and many of her speeches are similar to those to be heard from NAFF platforms. She is not committed to one key NAFF issue – a wholesale outlawing of the closed shop – but, that apart, her philosophy is very similar. This may be illustrated by referring to her address to the Bow Group of Tory MPs on 6 May 1978. Her central theme was the need to define the limits of state power, so as to preserve the superiority of the free system over communism. The state, she said, had three main roles:

First, to defend the population against the enemies within and without and to act as the force behind the law.

Second, to administer social services but in this it should not have a monopoly; there was a major role for private enterprise in housing, education and medicine.

Third, to oversee the economy; in doing this it should not only refrain from exercising monopolies but its every activity should be scrutinised to ensure that it could not be more effectively carried out by private enterprise.[36]

In the light of sentiments such as these, NAFF's openly expressed sympathies for Mrs Thatcher's view of the world are hardly surprising. They should not, however, be taken, as they frequently are in left-wing circles, as final and conclusive proof that the 'non-party-political' claim is bogus. The fact of the matter is that NAFF is a pressure group with objectives which are sympathetically considered by a section of the Conservative Party. That being the case, it quite naturally directs much of its attention towards that party. But that does not make it part of it.

John Gouriet claims that Britain has been at war intellectually since 1945. 'They are not all over there – they're over here as well.'[37] Accordingly he argued, whilst Director, that in addition to alerting the public and steeling the politicians NAFF's third strategy must also be vigorously pursued: direct action. In his view too many people had already concluded that the nation's fate was settled.

But Britain has shown its mettle in the past and can do so again if a conscious and active effort is undertaken by all those who believe in the democratic and competitive way of life, who wish to see freedom of choice exercised, who consider the weak should be protected, but who also believe that the strong should not be prevented from getting on with their endeavour or displaying leadership. . . . It is time to stand up and be counted or run the risk of losing our freedom for ever.[38]

In pursuance of this 'direct confrontation' strategy NAFF has relied principally, though not exclusively, on the courts. Its actions have included:

(1) Taking three cases of British Rail staff, sacked as a result of the closed shop, to the European Court at Strasbourg. (The results are not known at the time of writing.)

(2) Financially assisting, in the summer of 1976, the Tameside Parents Education Group in their legal struggle against the introduction of comprehensive education. The case was won in the House of Lords but NAFF incurred £8,000 in costs as a third party.

(3) Providing legal, physical and moral support to the management of Grunwick Film Processing Laboratories in North London in their protracted and much-publicised resistance, throughout 1976 and 1977, to the recognition

of union negotiating rights. (George Ward, managing director of Grunwick, claims in fact that he is not 'anti-union' but 'non-union' and that he is willing to accept union recognition if the majority of his workers so desire. He was, however, unwilling to allow the Government's Advisory Conciliation and Arbitration Service (ACAS) to hold a ballot of his employees' wishes, claiming that ACAS's intention to ballot workers who had been sacked or who had left since the outbreak of the dispute was unreasonable.)

Whatever the merits of the case, Grunwick quickly escalated into a major confrontation between the trade union movement and the management. Mass pickets, with Labour politicians and prominent trade union officials on the line, arrests, violence, the daily use of hundreds of policemen to allow the work-force to enter the factory, all combined in the summer of 1977 to put Grunwick in the headlines day after day. Inevitably NAFF was bitterly attacked by trade union officials. According to Jack Dromey, who, as secretary of Brent Trades Council and also of the South East Regional Council of the TUC, was closely involved in the dispute, 'The view within the trade union movement was and is that the NAFF is seeking to whittle away the hard won rights of trade unionists and to become a new "employers association" for companies like Grunwick.'[39]

In addition to providing Ward with moral support, NAFF made two drama-tic interventions in the case. When the Union of Post Office Workers (UPW) began 'blacking' Grunwick's mail on 1 November 1976, NAFF sponsored Grunwick's request in the High Court for an injunction against the Post Office and the UPW. The outcome was that within three days the UPW withdrew the boycott, believing that Grunwick had agreed to cooperate with ACAS. When it later became clear that they had no such intention the Post Officer workers at the local Cricklewood depot introduced their own ban on Grunwick mail. It was at this point that NAFF made its second intervention. With an enormous backlog of outgoing mail building up at Grunwick, NAFF's two directors, Gouriet and Moss, along with about twenty-five supporters, loaded 1,000 sacks of mail into vans during the night of 8–9 July. They then arranged for them to be mailed from post boxes 'as far North as Preston and Manchester and as far South as Plymouth and Truro'. Shortly after this exercise, now encased in NAFF mythology as 'Operation Pony Express', the blacking was ended.

(4) Obtaining, in January 1977, an injunction in the Court of Appeal against the boycott by postal workers of mail and telecommunications to South Africa. The application, which was made by John Gouriet on behalf of NAFF, was based on the argument that the threatened boycott broke the 1953 Post Office Act which makes it an offence to impede the delivery of mail. In announcing its verdict the Court, which was overturning a decision of the High Court, was highly critical of the Attorney General's decision not to allow the action to go forward in his name. The Court of Appeal's verdict was subsequently, in its turn, reversed by the House of Lords, a verdict which NAFF denounced as meaning 'that the Attorney General, a political appointee of a minority party in the pay of big unions, is basically not answerable to the courts'.[40]

These activities, and there have been others which have attracted less publicity, such as the establishment of a group, entitled Freedom in Advertising, to challenge the attempted imposition of a closed shop on commercial artists, have naturally required good organisation and substantial resources. NAFF has both.

Organisation and support

Formally overall policy is determined by the National Council. Chaired by Lord De l'Isle, it is composed of individuals from various walks of life. Business representatives include Sir Frank Taylor (director of Taylor Woodrow), Hugh Astor (with De l'Isle, a director of Phoenix Assurance), Lord Brookes (Life President of Guest, Keen & Nettlefolds), and Ernest Smith (President of the National Federation of Building Trade Employers). The principal representatives of 'similar minded' associations are Michael Ivens (director of AIMS), Ralph Harris (director of the IEA), Teresa Gorman (secretary of ASP), and Evelyn Hulbert Powell (director of the Income Tax Payers Society). There are three academics: Professor Flew of Reading University, Professor Denman of Cambridge, and Dr Watkins of Sheffield. Other prominent figures include the journalist Peregrine Worsthorne, the novelist John Braine, the chairman of the English cricket selectors Alec Bedser, and the director of the right-wing Institute for the Study of Conflict, Brian Crozier.

It is an impressive list, but with a total membership of over fifty the Council is too large and unwieldy to be an effective decision-making body. Quite apart from differences of opinion – and whilst it would be wrong to talk of a division in NAFF there clearly are differing emphases along a conservative/libertarian spectrum – it simply is difficult to arrange regular meetings when people with a wide range of commitments are all available. Thus, even during the most heated days of the Grunwick dispute meetings were rarely held. In consequence the Council, which meets on average once a quarter, is more of a sounding board of opinion than an initiator of policy. It may perform certain useful 'side functions' such as formally ratifying overall policy, assisting NAFF to display the support of leading figures publicly, and indeed gratifying the wishes of those 'notables' who wish to be formally associated with NAFF, but it is largely peripheral to decision making.

Policy on where and when to act is made by a small 'inner group', the Management Committee. In the early stages this appears to have been heavily influenced by the views of four people: the ex-army major, John Gouriet; the freelance journalist and editor of *The Economist*'s *Foreign Report*, Robert Moss; Lord De l'Isle and Norris McWhirter. Towards the end of 1977, however, this arrangement began to change. Moss, who as well as being editor of *The Free Nation* was, with Gouriet, co-Director of NAFF, resigned in order to concentrate on his journalism. This led to an internal reorganisation in which Gouriet became Campaign Director. At about the same time the Management Committee, which is drawn from the Council and which initially had operated in a very *ad hoc* way, moved to formalise and extend its role. It started to meet on a more regular fortnightly basis; it extended its membership to ten; most important of all, it sought to exercise greater control over NAFF's full-time staff, in particular Gouriet. This led to a protracted internal wrangle between Gouriet and the Management Committee which ended in June 1978 with Gouriet's resignation. The final straw for Gouriet was the refusal of the Committee to allow him to undertake a lecture tour of Australia on the grounds that it would be embarrassing to De l'Isle who, as the former Governor General, was forbidden by protocol from having any political contact with that country. With Gouriet's resignation the Management Committee, with McWhirter and De l'Isle as its most influential voices, had clearly established itself as the focus of power.

To implement decisions and generally conduct affairs the Management Committee and National Council are assisted by an organisational network that is impressive in terms of both administrative resources and popular support.

Head office works from a comfortable and well-equipped suite of rooms in central London. Employing around twelve full-time staff, who are aided by an array of part-time and voluntary helpers, it has been able to develop a division of labour and degree of specialisation not usually possible in non-occupational based pressure groups. The advantages of this are, of course, many. For example, Gerald Hartup, who as National Branch Organiser is most responsible for establishing an effective countrywide structure, can spend much of his time away from the office, talking to local officials and addressing public meetings; an efficient service can be provided to members; and individual queries – on, say, a closed shop dispute – can be quickly followed up.

Total support, claimed to number 50,000 in February 1978, is large for such an organisation, particularly one whose subscription is £5. In building up this base NAFF has drawn on a number of sources:

(1) The mood of anger and disillusionment, described in Chapter 1, has provided much of the momentum.

(2) The impact of the initial publicity greatly facilitated the always difficult task of getting a new venture off the ground. Widespread media coverage in the early stages, which doubtless owed much to Moss's knowledge of the newspaper world, enabled NAFF to make known to its potential audience both its existence and its purpose. Some sections of the press have continued to be sympathetic and have, in effect, provided free advertising space.[41]

(3) The decline of the Monday Club during the 1970s, following policy disagreements and personal differences, resulted in NAFF being seen, by many disgruntled right-wing Conservatives, as the only refuge.

(4) The collapse of the Voice of the Independent Centre (see Chapter 1) inevitably led to many of its members – claimed to number 5,000 – coming over to NAFF.

(5) The well-publicised interventions – at Tameside, Grunwick and in the High Court – have kept NAFF in the public eye and brought it to the attention of those sections of the population who want 'action' against 'the socialists and their union allies'.

But impressive though NAFF's support and network is, it must be kept in perspective, for three reasons:

Firstly, because levels of support in NAFF are graded, and not all of the claimed 50,000 have paid the full £5 subscription. There are five main types of supporter:

(*a*) ordinary members – £5 subscription
(*b*) pensioners   – £1 subscription
(*c*) contact members – five people join as a group and pay £10 between them
(*d*) those who have entered their names as 'supporters in principle', i.e. they have read and signed their names in support of the Charter. Their financial contributions vary though virtually all are significantly less than £5

(*e*) those who take *The Free Nation* but who do not fall into any of the first four categories.

Levels of commitment thus vary. According to Gerald Hartup, just over 20,000, in mid-1978, fell into one of the first three categories. (Which may be regarded as quite respectable since £5 is a very high subscription for a voluntary political organisation.)

Secondly, some of NAFF's seventy or so branches are only barely active. The occasional, stage-managed, public meeting can always be arranged, but vigorous and continual grassroots activity calls for real enthusiasm and this is not always available. Such was the case with the Greater Manchester branch before its leadership was changed early in 1978. Whereas national officials described Greater Manchester as a 'good area' in the North – and it did have around 200 members – investigations revealed the branch to be virtually dormant. Members received *The Free Nation* and that was virtually the sum total of their involvement. There were not even regular branch meetings. So, as with the ratepayers, the level of activity depends very much on the competence and enthusiasm of local organisers and committees. Whereas the main political parties and occupational based pressure groups can usually, in part at least, cover local apathy and inefficiency with their national and regional organisations, groups such as NAFF, which do not have a full-time regional network, cannot.

The leadership is aware of the problem and in attempting to overcome it most prominent NAFF figures – as well as sympathetic Conservative MPs – make themselves available to branches for meetings and rallies. In addition, at the end of 1977 the enthusiastic London area organiser, Gerald Hartup, was appointed National Branch Organiser. His role is quite specifically 'to set up branches, to encourage them to become active, to co-ordinate activities between them'.[42]

But at the same time as encouraging a strong branch structure head office has sought to keep a tight check on developments. Local organisers are, in effect, screened, and local initiatives are carefully monitored. Freedom may be the essence of NAFF's ideology, but control and centralisation are the hallmark of its organisation. In part this is because of a determination to ensure that it does not become associated with the racist right by being infiltrated by sympathisers of the National Front. This process took place in the Monday Club and contributed to its decline. Clearly this danger increases with decentralisation. In part, too, however, it is because NAFF was created not from the 'grassroots' but from the 'top'. A small number of people with a broadly similar outlook created an organisation which would assist the propagation of their views. In classic organisational terms the mass grew out of the centre.

But though the centralisation may be understandable it is probably counterproductive to the aim of creating a vigorous base. Frequently grumbles of 'too head office dominated' are to be heard from local activists, and with good reason, for there are few links between the two levels in terms of either participation or responsibility. Both the Management Committee and the National Council are virtually self-selecting bodies with membership being by 'agreement' and 'co-option'. Ordinary members have no means of putting themselves forward in the normal democratic way since there are no elections.

Nor can supporters discuss policy and make decisions in a democratic forum since there is nothing akin to an annual conference. The claim of NAFF's directorate that it is nevertheless closely in tune with members' views as a result of informal meetings, speaking engagements, and the introduction in 1977 of half-yearly branch chairmen's meetings, doubtless has some force, but it is no substitute for real participation and accountability.

The third reason for keeping NAFF's support in perspective is that, both geographically and socially, its base is limited.

Geographically, most supporters live in the South of England, in particular London and the Home Counties. So, whereas London itself has fourteen branches, most of which are active, many counties – the basis of branch structure outside London – have had difficulty in finding an organiser, let alone mounting a campaign. At the beginning of 1978 there were only two branches in the whole of Wales, and Scotland, with five, was only slightly better off. 'Branch News' – a regular feature of *The Free Nation* and a useful indication of activities – is dominated by reports from the South. A typical example, the edition of 28 April 1978, gives accounts of branch events in East Surrey, Weybridge, West Kent, West London, East Sussex, North West London, Wiltshire, Buckinghamshire and Worcestershire. Cheshire alone 'represents' the North, Wales and Scotland.[43]

As regards social composition it is impossible, without access to membership lists, to assess exactly what sections of the population support NAFF. Geographical distribution and observation at meetings, however, show it to be, as expected, overwhelmingly middle class, with a bias perhaps towards the self-employed. NAFF spokesmen, in fact, after making their ritual denial that social classes exist at all, usually concede the narrowness of the appeal. Chris Sneath, chairman of the North London branch, has stated, 'We tend to campaign in the, well, leafier parts of a borough.'[44] In the same vein, Roger Webster, former National Branch Organiser, spoke in 1977 of the difficulties in establishing a Scottish base, 'Our organisation is very weak in Scotland at the moment. We have only six branch organisers in the whole of the country. Our job in recruiting is very difficult because the main conurbations in Scotland are, what shall we say, less likely to provide members, and the rest of the country is so scattered.'[45]

Whether the social base can be broadened is doubtful. Quite apart from the fact that most 'issue related' pressure groups are predominantly middle class – who after all joins the National Council for Civil Liberties? – NAFF's ideology, not to mention subscription rate, is hardly designed to attract working class support. It is true that since the mid-1960s an increasing proportion of the population have become concerned about trade union power – NAFF's key issue – but there are few reasons for believing that this can be channelled, on a mass basis, in the direction of NAFF. Rather is it likely to stay primarily in the arena of the political parties. It thus seems unlikely that the campaign, launched in December 1977, to make NAFF more geographically and socially representative will make much headway.

Income

Given that support, whilst impressive, is not as great as it might at first appear, the question arises as to the sources of income. NAFF itself is evasive. The only set of published accounts are very general, as can be seen from Table 3. Spokesmen refuse to elaborate on these figures, confining themselves to denials that NAFF is heavily subsidised by industry. So, for example, Chris Tame, of NAFF's Research Department, when interviewed, would go no further than to say, 'about two thirds of our finance comes from membership fees, donations from individuals, fund raising events etc.; about a third comes from business groups'.[46]

TABLE 3

The National Association for Freedom financial statement 1977

Audited Accounts for NAFF for the year to 31st December 1977 have now been received. These may be summarised as follows:

	£	£
INCOME		
Subscriptions and donations including students and pensioners		
General Fund	121,889	
Legal Fund	42,530	
Interest (net)	664	
		165,083
EXPENDITURE		
Net loss on *The Free Nation*:		
Production costs	£59,838	
LESS: Revenue	32,155	27,683
Rumuneration of staff		41,219
Publicity and promotion		20,045
General office expenses		31,550
Legal and professional charges		149,232	269,729
Deficit for the year		104,646
Deficit brought forward		16,785
Deficit at 31st December 1977		£121,431
of which		
General Fund	15,036	
Legal Fund	106,395	
	£121,431	

Notes 1. A special Appeal to assist in the elimination of the deficit on the Legal Fund was made after 31st December 1977 and donations amounting to approximately £110,000 were received by 31st March 1978.
2. A proportion of the Staff and other costs has been charged against *The Free Nation*.

(Printed in *The Free Nation* 4–17 August 1978)

Inevitably the secrecy has given rise to speculation, for, however the calculations are made, it is clear that NAFF has commitments which far outstrip its income from subscriptions, garden parties, dinners and dances. The running of head office alone exceeds £70,000. On top of this there are very heavy legal expenses (£90,000 in the UPW High Court case), assistance to favoured organisations and causes, costly newspaper advertisements, and the printing and distribution of *The Free Nation*. (In the early stages, in particular, free copies were being 'thrown around like confetti'.)

Suggestions frequently heard in the left-wing press that business is the major contributor can be dismissed. Certainly some firms are providing assistance, but there is little to suggest that this is taking place on a major scale. It is indeed significant that the usually well-informed Labour Research Department in its analysis of NAFF funds came up with very little: £1,000 from the wire rope manufacturers, Bridon; £500 from Consolidated Goldfields; and £100 from the battery company, Ever Ready.[47] In addition to this it is reasonable to assume that some of the traditional donators to the *laissez-faire* cause are putting money into NAFF; certainly this would include those which have representatives on the National Council – such as Phoenix Assurance, Taylor Woodrow Group, and Guest, Keen & Nettlefolds – and those which advertise, at about £350 a time, in *The Free Nation*, such as Tate & Lyle.

According to Chris Tame, such donations as are forthcoming 'are in the hundreds rather than the thousands' (i.e. of pounds) 'and virtually all are from middle range and small businesses'.[48] This would certainly fit the pattern of contributions made to the organisations discussed earlier in the chapter. Big business, it was noted, tends to avoid assisting *laissez-faire* pressure groups, partly because it wishes to keep all its political options open, partly because big business is not an unreserved supporter of unfettered capitalism. It gains advantages from neo-corporatism in the form of incomes policies, state subsidies, tariff barriers, etc.

Apart from subscriptions, business donations, and social activities, funds come from a variety of sources, some known, some rather more shrouded. *The Free Nation*, at 15p a copy, whilst running at a loss, nevertheless covers much of its costs. Sympathetic and like-minded groups doubtless make contributions – AIMS, for example, admits to having assisted. The private fortunes of some of the wealthier members seem to have been tapped – the appeal, early in 1978, for £90,000 to meet Gouriet's legal costs was met in three weeks. Some of the funds supposedly available to anti-socialist groups from a variety of eccentrics may also have been realised. Gouriet, for example, submitted a claim in 1977 for the £1,000 legacy available to the group 'leading the fight against socialism' from a wealthy Cheltenham pig farmer.

In short, it can be said that although exact figures are not available, NAFF has substantial funds at its disposal and is able to raise – as the High Court action revealed – very large sums of money when circumstances demand.

Conclusions

Shortly after NAFF was founded, John Gouriet emphasised that its main activities 'will be in effecting communications between like minded groups, the exposure of the threats to our freedom, and in seeking legal remedies in cases of victimisation etc.'.[49] Clearly, a measure of success has been attained on all three counts. Having said that, however, there have also been failures, or at least disappointments, and these may be more significant than the successes in terms of NAFF's future development. Three are of particular importance:

(1) Whilst cordial relations have been established with a number of organisations – AIMS, IEA, ASP, etc. – NAFF has far from fulfilled its hopes of acting as a coordinator or centre of communication for like-minded groups. The ratepayers, for example, have kept their distance. NARAG – the ratepayers' main umbrella group during the 'revolt' – did attend a meeting, called by Gouriet, designed to bring the various protests together, but it did not follow up the initiative, mainly because of general unease over NAFF's motives and aims. Nor have relations with the self-employed been completely harmonious. ASP is represented on the National Council but the larger National Federation of the Self-Employed, after at first closely associating itself with NAFF, withdrew at the end of 1976, stating, in a letter dated 4 November: 'The national executive committee . . . has no alternative but to sever all connections, because of the extreme political views of your organisation.'[50]

Other possible linkages have been excluded by NAFF itself for fear of being labelled 'extremist'. (Not that this has noticeably deterred opponents.) Thus, protracted negotiations in 1976 with General Sir Walter Walker's Civil Assistance organisation (CA) broke down. According to Gouriet, in a letter to a member of the CA movement, the reason was as follows:

> We all have a high regard for Walter Walker. Unfortunately, the public impression of Civil Assistance is that it is a 'private army' although as we have made clear on many platforms nothing could be further from the truth. Nevertheless, the 'left' did a good smear job when it started, and we do not want to attract similar adverse publicity. Therefore, while we welcome individual members to join us and encourage local co-operation, we are not in a position to announce a merger.[51]

This explanation, that talks deadlocked over NAFF's reluctance to be associated with a movement that was widely regarded as a private army, was confirmed by Major-General Humphrey Bredin, a CA council member. CA itself subsequently split over the breakdown in negotiations and four council members, including Bredin, resigned and urged members to join NAFF. (At one time, in 1974, CA membership was claimed to be over 100,000.[52] According to some reports, this had declined to 15,000 by the time of the negotiations with NAFF,[53] though even this, in terms of potential activists, was probably an overestimate.) Significantly, after resigning, Bredin said: 'I felt it was ludicrous that there were a number of separate organisations which all had similar views. I have not yet joined the NAFF but I am considering it.'[54]

(2) Support, though impressive in purely numerical terms, has been confined, almost inevitably, to the 'natural' middle class pro-Conservative constituency. In consequence NAFF has been unable to make much headway in its proclaimed intention of making an impact on 'the public consciousness'. Working class people are no more inclined to buy *The Free Nation* or attend a NAFF meeting, let alone work for the cause, than, in the late 1960s and early 1970s, they were tempted to join the Monday Club.

Much effort has thus been restricted to reflecting and articulating the views of the already converted: those who were discontented and disillusioned with the Conservative Party after four years of 'soft' Heath government. Marshalling the sympathetic – as the Tribune Group has shown in the Labour Party – can, of course, be effective, but it narrows both options and possible avenues of influence. So, as NAFF has failed to broaden its base, it has increasingly addressed itself towards the Conservative Party, seeing a major part of its role as being to ensure that the next Conservative government does not follow its predecessor down the 'soggy road of intervention and capitulation'. In orientating itself in this way NAFF has assumed many of the characteristics of a Tory ginger group.

(3) Financial support from industry has been limited. Up to the time of writing alternative sources of income have been provided for the continuation of expensive campaigns, but it may be that these will not be so bountiful as initial enthusiasms fade. In that event NAFF would have to exercise major economies, and in so doing it would lose much of its distinctive appeal. For if it cannot afford to fight the occasional, well publicised, court battle, if it cannot afford to intervene in closed shop disputes, and if it cannot maintain a national popular campaign, it will lose much of the identity that at present distinguishes it from organisations such as AIMS and the IEA.

The problem for any popular based 'issue' group, whether it be the Campaign for Nuclear Disarmament, the Anti-Common Market Campaign or NAFF, is to maintain momentum. Activity can decline for a number of reasons, but usually it stems from either the fulfilment of objectives or from an increasing realisation that little can be achieved because the tide is too strong or the decision-making agencies are beyond its control. For how much longer NAFF can continue to generate increasing enthusiasm is difficult to judge, there being a number of imponderables involved.

On the one hand, a future Labour government continuing to give trade unions a central place in its social and economic strategy, or a Conservative government along the lines of the post-1972 Heath administration, might well 'favour' NAFF. On the other hand both major parties have sought to draw some of the teeth from the general mood of disquiet and protest which provided the background to NAFF's emergence (see Chapter 7). Rates increases have been dampened and special assistance has been introduced for small businesses and the self-employed. NAFF's interests, of course, go wider than such specific grievances, but accumulations of 'concessions' of this kind could in the long term, particularly if associated with a general improvement in the nation's economy, take much of the 'bite' out of NAFF's appeal. Certainly if the Conservative Government led by Mrs Thatcher attempts to honour its proclaimed ideals – of reducing state activity and more closely controlling trade unions – then the future of NAFF (or rather, since 1979, The Freedom Association) may become highly problematic.

NOTES

1 *The Free Nation*, pilot edition, February 1976.
2 An attempt to analyse donations is made in *Big Business and Politics*, Labour Research Department, 1974.
3 This information was provided by Michael Ivens, Director of AIMS, in a letter dated 6 April 1978.
4 *Must this happen?*, Aims of Industry, 1974.
5 *58th Annual Review*, Economic League, p. 2.
6 All these figures are from the *58th Annual Review*.
7 *The Observer*, 19 October 1969.
8 Letter from Colonel J. B. Hobbs, Director General of BUI, dated 1 March 1976.
9 *The Times*, 11 April 1973.
10 *The Daily Telegraph*, 4 July 1968.
11 *The Times*, 11 April 1973.
12 IEA *Occasional Paper* No. 14.
13 A review of the main themes of their publications is to be found in Hutchinson, T. W., *Half a Century of Hobarty*, IEA, 1970.
14 Watt, D., 'Mr. Martell and the Tories', *Spectator*, 26 June 1964; *The Freedom Group*, Information Pamphlet, Tileyard Press, 1963.
15 *The Times*, 20 September 1967.
16 *Guardian*, 28 November 1975.
17 *Time To Stand Up to The Unions*, Current Affairs Press, 1975. There is some doubt as to exactly when the Current Affairs Press was established. The idea appears to have first emerged in the early 1970s but there was no activity until 1975.
18 See *Majority*, 24 November–7 December 1975.
19 Ibid, 8 October 1975.
20 Ibid.
21 *The British Gazette: Journal of the Silent Majority and Self-Help*, 11–12 March 1976.
22 Ibid, April 1977.
23 *This is Murder Mr. Murray*, Anti-Strike Union leaflet, 1977.
24 For more detailed accounts of Self-Help see: Davis, G., 'Behind the Scenes', *New Statesman*, 16 December 1977; Davis, G., 'Inside Self-Help', *Isis*, 7 October 1977.
25 Interview, 17 February 1978.
26 *The Free Nation*, 25 June 1976, 9 July 1976, 1 October 1976, 18–31 March 1977, 30 September–13 October 1977.
27 Ibid, 21 December 1977–5 January 1978.
28 *The Communist Threat and the Lesson of Eastern Europe*, NAFF, December 1977.
29 *The Free Nation*, 28 October–10 November 1977.
30 Ibid, 22 December 1976.
31 Interview, 26 June 1978.
32 Interview, 17 February 1978.
33 *The Conservative Party and the National Association for Freedom*, NAFF, December 1977.
34 *Time Out*, 7 July 1977.
35 *The Free Nation*, 14 May 1976.
36 For a fuller report of the speech see *The Sunday Times*, 7 May 1978.
37 Speech at the NAFF Lancashire branch meeting, the Opera House, Blackpool, 24 April 1978.
38 Ibid.
39 Quoted in Rogaly, J., *Grunwick*, Penguin Books, 1977, p. 66.
40 *The Free Nation*, 5–18 August 1977.
41 See, for example, the article by Robert Moss in the *Daily Mail*, 16 February 1976, 'How long before the TUC storm-troopers take over?'.
42 Interview, 17 February 1978.
43 *The Free Nation*, 28 April–12 May 1978.

44 *7 Days*, 28 October 1977.
45 Ibid.
46 Interview, 6 January 1978.
47 *Labour Research*, Vol. 66, No. 8 (August 1977).
48 Interview, 17 February 1978.
49 Letter dated 26 February 1976.
50 *Guardian*, 23 December 1976.
51 Quoted by Peter Dunn, 'NAFF in Thurberland', *New Statesman*, 15 July 1977.
52 *The Times*, 5 September 1974.
53 *Guardian*, 2 March 1977.
54 Ibid.

Timothy May

5. Middle class unionism

In order to assess the significance of unionisation among the middle class for the overall theme of this book, the discussion that follows is centred around three main questions, to each of which a section of the chapter is devoted. The first section is concerned with the attempt to define the main terms that are being used – middle class and trade unionism – and to see how far we have reliable measures of the extent to which the middle class has become unionised. The second focuses on the nature or character of such unionisation, and in the third section there is some exploration of the implications of unionisation for the political parties and the TUC.

Definition and measurement of middle class unionism

An essential preliminary to any discussion of the significance of middle class unionism is an attempt to establish how extensively the middle class is organised in trade unions. As with most questions which seem straightforward in principle, in practice there is no single measurement acceptable to all those who have discussed the issues. The problems, as so often, lie partly in the definition of terms and partly in a lack of the necessary information.

Any measurement of middle class unionism obviously needs to aim at consistent definitions of both 'middle class' and 'trade unionism'. Most sociological discussion of class is organised around either objective or subjective criteria: typically the former divides the population into income or occupational categories, the latter asks respondents in a sample survey how they assess their own class position. So far as the objective approach is concerned, a dividing line has customarily been drawn between skilled, semi-skilled and unskilled manual workers who comprise the working class and the remainder who are regarded as the middle class. The justifications for this exercise are various, but one of the most common is that on a range of important determinants of life chances (income, education, home ownership, promotion prospects) such a division makes sense. Thus whatever the variation within what is admitted to be these somewhat heterogeneous categories of middle and working class the argument is that there *are* sufficient distinguishable characteristics that form some kind of a common core and serve to mark the two classes off from one another.

A further justification for the objective approach is that it produces results similar to those obtained using subjective methods: if one asks people in sample surveys to assess their own class position the results bear some similarity to a classification using objective criteria. However, the correspondence is certainly not exact, and this divergence between the objective and subjective methods is of some importance. For example, if one defines the behaviour of a particular group who objectively appear to be middle class as unusual or atypical, closer perhaps to what is seen as characteristically working class, such behaviour becomes much less puzzling if we recognise the possibility that the group may define their own position as working class rather than middle class. It would, of course, be perfectly reasonable to argue that there is still a significant problem to be looked at, namely why the results obtained by using the objective and subjective criteria diverge so markedly. But by recognising the possibility that individuals do sometimes define their situations differently from the observer we are prevented from following false trails.

When we turn to examine the other important term – trade unionism – we find, as with class, a whole range of possibilities on offer. The question of definition is often felt to be of particular importance when discussing the middle class and unionism because of the activity of professional associations which do not satisfy what some writers take to be the 'essence' of trade unionism. Hence it is argued that if we include the membership of such organisations in the total of those who are organised collectively, then a false picture is obtained of the extent to which 'true' or real trade unions have penetrated a particular section of the work-force. Conversely others have argued that though at some point in the past it may have been possible to make distinctions between trade unions and professional groups, it is possible no longer. This is not just another theological debate but an issue with important implications for the general theme of this book. For the notion that there is something unusual about the middle class joining trade unions does not make much sense if we are prepared to regard as trade unions various bodies that many members of the middle class have always accepted that it is right and proper for them to join. This clearly applies to many professional associations which set examinations and, for example, in the case of medicine and law, have been given the sole right to grant licences to individuals to practise the particular skills in question.

The important characteristic of a trade union for many of those who have concerned themselves with this question of definition is a concentration on the interests of the members as employees.[1] This is likely to mean that the regulation of wages and working conditions is a central concern of such organisations. It may be that this is important to many professional bodies and indeed that if it was formerly absent or of only marginal concern, it has become a great deal more important in recent years. While in principle we ought to be able to establish how far professional bodies are now concerned with the interests of their members as employees, in practice it would necessitate a lengthy and complex investigation to arrive at a satisfactory answer.

There is the further category of the staff association which also cannot be ignored in any examination of the middle class and unionism. The conventional view about the staff association phenomenon is that although it betokens some degree of commitment to collective activity it needs to be differentiated from the trade union proper. This differentiation is needed because the staff association usually has the blessing of the employer – indeed it may have been initiated and provided with continuing support by the employer precisely in order to ward off attempts by trade unions to recruit and organise the work-force.

Legislative definitions might offer a further possibility of distinguishing between a 'true' trade union and all other kinds of organisation. The Trade Union and Labour Relations Act 1974 and the Employment Protection Act 1975 embody a number of important provisions which relate to this matter. The Employment Protection Act established a Certification Officer who has to maintain a list of trade unions and further has to determine which of these shall be granted a certificate as an *independent* trade union on the basis of certain criteria. To be listed as a trade union is fairly simple:

> The essential requirement . . . is that the body concerned must be an organisation of workers . . . which has the regulation of relations between workers and employers as one of its principal purposes. The Act does not impose any test of size or effectiveness. . . .[2]

By the end of 1977, 485 organisations had been listed of which the Certification Officer estimated about 200 were directly or indirectly affiliated to the TUC. Since the TUC's affiliated membership was 11·5 million this means that the remaining 285 organisations shared the residual 600,000 members between them: many of the 285 are clearly staff associations organising quite small numbers of employees.

It is the second list which we might expect to provide us with a clear means of distinguishing trade unions from all other kinds of organisation. For acceptance as an *independent* trade union more stringent criteria have to be satisfied: the organisation must not be 'under the domination or control of an employer' and 'not liable to interference by an employer'.[3] While the intention of these provisions seems to be to mark off the 'genuine' trade union from the staff association, it has not worked out in this way, at least in the eyes of the TUC. By the end of 1977, certificates of independence had been granted to 273 unions, only 155 of which were affiliated to the TUC. Of the remainder, the claims of 83 were not opposed by the TUC, but this still left 35 to which the TUC did object. They did not agree that this last group were independent and it is clear that many of them were staff associations recruiting in areas which existing non-manual TUC affiliates wished to preserve for themselves.[4]

The net result of this discussion about definitions is that there does not exist any general and acceptable register of information about the membership of staff associations, professional groups and trade unions since there are no agreed and uniformly applied definitions. The Certification Officer is collecting a good deal of information, but there is no obligation for groups to register as 'trade unions' and, as we have seen, the definition of an independent trade union certainly covers associations that do not belong, and do not wish to belong, to the TUC.

We are therefore obliged to use what statistical material is available and to draw from it what inferences seem reasonable. By far the most important statistical examination of non-manual unionism in recent years has been by G. S. Bain, the Director of the Social Science Research Council (SSRC) Industrial Relations Unit, initially on his own account and subsequently with Robert Price.[5] What is interesting about their work over the last ten years is the way in which they have identified important changes in non-manual union growth. When Bain wrote his original paper in 1966, although he acknowledged that there had been a substantial numerical increase in non-manual unionism, he clearly demonstrated that this had failed (albeit only marginally) to keep up with the growth in non-manual employment. But the 1972 and 1976 papers (the latter taking the data up to 1974) showed that in the years since 1964 non-manual unions had succeeded in keeping pace with the increase in non-manual jobs. Thus the overall non-manual union density had increased by very nearly ten percentage points in the period 1964–74, from 29·6 per cent to 39·4 per cent.

Any attempt to break down these figures into particular groups confronts the limitations of the way in which the data have been collected. We would obviously like to be able to say how far clerical workers are unionised compared with managers – indeed, more specifically, how far managers in manufacturing industry are unionised compared to those working in the wholesale or retail sectors. The existing data allow only certain broad sectoral comparisons; for example, the highest rates of non-manual unionisation by far are to be found in the public sector, especially in central and local government. Bain's 1966 paper suggests a figure of over 80 per cent (and this is based upon data for 1960). At the other end of the scale the lowest density in 1960 was in manufacturing industry with 12 per cent, but substantial growth in the following fifteen years pushed the figure up to 32 per cent by 1974. One of the major unions attempting to organise white-collar workers in manufacturing industry, the Association of Scientific, Technical and Managerial Staffs (ASTMS), increased its membership by 700 per cent between 1964 and 1977.[6]

It would be particularly interesting if we were able to say something precise about unionisation among the general occupational group called 'managers'. There are a number of reasons for an interest in this group. In the first place, they are highly likely to emerge as 'middle class' on both the objective and subjective criteria previously distinguished. Secondly, of the six occupational categories into which Bain and Price divide the non-manual work-force they experienced the biggest growth between 1961 and 1971.[7] Thirdly, there has been a lot of debate about both the 'availability' and the 'suitability' of managers for trade unionism. Availability refers to the fact that managers remain one of the largest categories of poorly organised non-manual workers; suitability raises the issue of whether it is trade unionism they should be embracing or some alternative form of organisation that stands mid-way between capital and labour. This latter discussion merges with a broader political concern that has been much articulated in recent years about the real or imagined problems that managers have faced. We shall take up some of these issues in later parts of the chapter, but so far as the size of the group is concerned only the most general kinds of estimate can be given. John Elliott, on the basis of certain Government statistics, suggests that there are about two million managers in the country of whom some half a million are described by him as 'ripe for trade union recruitment'.[8] A more modest though still substantial figure of 100/300,000 professional employees and managers was given by David Churchill in an article discussing those unions most likely to bid for these potential members.[9]

Character of middle class unionism

Having discussed the available information on the extent of unionisation among the middle class we must move on to an examination of its 'nature' or 'character'. This is a very important question for the central theme of this book because it is critical in estimating how far the increasing membership of unions can be interpreted as an indication of rebelliousness or revolt.

In an attempt to encompass different analyses of middle class unionism which bear on the question of its character, our argument starts from the observation that the great majority of non-manual workers have not until very recently belonged to trade unions. If we assume that this reluctance to embrace trade unions derives partly from a set of values frequently encapsulated in the notion of individualism, and partly from their association with the working class and the Labour Party, then the growing propensity to join trade unions would seem to indicate changes of considerable significance. It would suggest that a sense of opposed, or at least differing, class interest is dissolving and a growing identity of interest developing between the two main social classes in Britain.

However, there are a number of objections that could be raised to this line of argument. In the first place, it is not clear that one can accurately characterise middle and working class values as individualist and collectivist respectively. Secondly, some of the studies of the growth of non-manual unions suggest that the crucial factors promoting their growth have been employment concentration and the increasing recognition of their role by employers and the government. Thirdly, we cannot assume that all non-manual workers will see themselves as middle class – we have already drawn attention to this possibility and to the implication that, for those who see themselves as working class, joining a trade union may be seen as perfectly normal. The final objection would, unlike the first, start from the assumption that the values and attitudes of the middle and working classes do differ. Precisely because of the difference in values it is argued that the unions in which the middle class predominate will differ in their strategy and tactics. So although this final objection has a different starting point from the previous three the direction in which they all point is the same: to cast serious doubt on the extent to which unionisation among the middle class can be seen as any sign of increasing social unity. None of the objections we have raised mean, of course, that increasing unionisation is without *any* significance: the pattern of industrial relations, the links with political parties and the role of the TUC may be considerably influenced by the growing strength of non-manual unions, and these possibilities will be examined in later sections of the chapter. What we need to do now is to examine more closely the four objections that have just been outlined.

The evidence about the existence of collectivist and individualist values, like most social science evidence, can be criticised in a number of ways. No survey has been carried out with the United Kingdom as its sampling frame; such evidence as we do have is derived from samples drawn from particular occupational or geographical contexts. Additionally, much of the material we can refer to is now rather dated: it was collected in the 1950s or early 1960s. Nevertheless this evidence does suggest that it is difficult to sustain any neat characterisation of the middle class as individualist and the working class as collectivist. This was the clear conclusion of Bain *et al*. writing in 1973 and reviewing much of the evidence of the 1950s and 1960s: '[we have] demonstrated that white-collar and manual workers cannot be polarised in terms of their images of society, industry or trade unions'.[10] In a report published in 1977, of fieldwork that did embrace the early 1970s, Roberts *et al*. endorse Bain's conclusion.[11]

A rather different argument, though pointing in the same general direction, has been put by Noel and Jose Parry.[12] They argue that the professional association, which has frequently been seen as the antithesis of a trade union, is formed to pursue collective social mobility. What therefore marks off the professional association – a characteristic organisation of the established middle class – from trade unionism is *not* a different value structure, at least in terms of individualism and collectivism. The main factor therefore, in their view, that marks off unionism from professionalism is the latter's commitment to changing the class and status position of its members and the unions' lack of interest in this.

So far as the second objection is concerned, one of the best known of all analyses of white collar unionism, George Bain's *The Growth of White Collar Unionism*,[13] is of central importance. Bain's book is notable both for what it dismisses and for what it emphasises. After examining many of the variables most commonly suggested as responsible for generating white collar unionism, it finds most of them not proven. At the same time its own explanation emphasises the importance of employer recognition of unionism and governmental action to promote such recognition, factors which, while not completely ignored, had received relatively little discussion in previous accounts of the growth of non-manual unionism.

Bain's theory is in fact built around three variables: he adds employment concentration to the two already mentioned of employer recognition and governmental action to encourage recognition. The underlying logic in each case is not difficult to see. Concentration implies that the group will be administered on the basis of standardised impersonal rules and regulations.[14] Hence the likelihood of contact with either the owner or senior management is reduced. It will be clear to many individuals that their wages and working conditions vary very little from one group to another and therefore a combined approach to their regulation makes sense. Bain's figures support an association between concentration and unionisation, and the predominant trend in the years since Bain's data were collected has been towards units of increasing size in both the public and the private sectors. David Lockwood, in the 1950s, noted how the growth of the National and Local Government Officers' Association (NALGO) had corresponded to the standardisation of working conditions for local authority employees.[15] Such tendencies will only have been reinforced in subsequent years, with substantial increases in the absolute numbers working in local government and its reorganisation into fewer and larger units.

The emphasis placed upon the second major variable – union recognition – does take us into the area of the attitudes and values of white collar workers. Bain's reasons for stressing the importance of recognition are, firstly, the propensity of white collar workers to identify with management; secondly, the risk to career prospects which is involved in joining unions *not* recognised by management; thirdly, the assertion that unions 'are usually accepted on instrumental rather than ideological grounds "as something to be used rather than as something in which to believe"'.[16] While these sentiments may be true for many members of the middle class, the research of Roberts *et al.* indicates that some of those who are engaged in routine white collar work do not identify with the management in the way Bain suggests; also that the degree of ideological commitment to unionism on the part of many working class trade unionists has been frequently exaggerated.[17]

The third variable is the one that has been particularly under-emphasised in previous discussions of white collar unionism – governmental action to promote the recognition of trade unionism. While important examples of this can be found before 1945, e.g. the *Whitley Report* of 1917, it is the years since the end of the Second World War that have been most notable for governmental encouragement of trade unionism. The increasing size of the public sector has been of great importance in creating a beneficent climate for union recognition. More specifically, the ten years from the *Donovan Report* of 1968 have been marked by a succession of positive statutory encouragements to unionism culminating in the Employment Protection Act 1975 and the establishment of the Advisory Conciliation and Arbitration Service (ACAS). Bain predicted in 1970 that the Commission on Industrial Relations (CIR), established as a result of recommendations in the *Donovan Report*, would contribute to a climate in which 'there will be a significant increase in white-collar unionism in Britain during the 1970s'.[18] Initially the CIR did have the support of the TUC, but even though this was subsequently withdrawn it has been argued that 'a preference for TUC style unionism over staff associations or staff committees was consistently shown by the CIR'.[19]

So far as the role of ACAS is concerned, the dispute which has given the service widespread publicity, at Grunwick Film Processing Laboratories where its recommendations were rejected, is far from typical. In introducing the third annual report of ACAS its chairman, after declaring that it was the job of the state 'to encourage, promote and uphold collective bargaining', noted that although the Grunwick dispute had had 'some effect on employers . . . 95 per cent were still willing to co-operate'.[20] It is important to note that the ACAS policy of supporting established unions among non-manual workers when making recommendations about recognition could have consequences for the degree to which those not at present in unions subsequently join them; this possibility is discussed in greater detail below.

One other aspect of governmental action which has received a great deal of public discussion since 1974 is the closed shop. While the extension of this principle may be a factor in promoting greater unionisation among manual workers, it is not widely established among non-manual workers. Roberts *et al.* demonstrate that while very nearly half the manual workers gave the existence of the closed shop as their reason for joining a union, among non-manual workers only just over one fifth gave this as the primary reason.[21] This survey predated the post-1974 legislation, but there have not, in fact, been any substantial extensions of the principle during the past four years so far as non-manual workers are concerned. Recently the civil service unions have been offered a form of the closed shop, but it is hedged around with so many escape clauses that the unions concerned consider that they have been offered very little.[22]

Thus the general implication of this second objection is that increasing unionisation has not got much to do with changes in the attitudes of middle class employees. Indeed, in its emphasis on the importance of employer recognition of unions because of the anxiety of employees not to antagonise the employer, it is accepting that white collar employees do have different attitudes to those of manual workers.

The third objection that we raised to the argument that increasing middle class unionisation denoted important changes in social attitudes and behaviour concerned the possibility that some members of the middle class saw themselves as working class: where this was the case, joining a trade union would be quite orthodox behaviour. It is clear from a number of surveys in recent years that many non-manual workers do indeed see themselves in these terms. Butler and Stokes reported that in 1963, among the four categories into which they divided non-manual workers, 22 per cent of Higher Managerial, 35 per cent of Lower Managerial, 40 per cent of Supervisory Non-Manual and 68 per cent of Lower Non-Manual saw themselves as working class.[23] While one must remember that the precise meanings attached to 'middle class' and 'working class' may be subject to considerable variation,[24] these figures certainly suggest that there are pit-falls in regarding the fourth category – Lower Non-Manual workers – as middle class.

Although proceeding along rather different lines, Roberts *et al*. identified a group of what they call 'white collar proletarians' among their non-manual workers. It accounted for 12 per cent of their total sample and they comment:

> In general as is common among manual workers, the white-collar proletarians regarded themselves as excluded from middle class privileges and were prepared to support both the political and industrial action necessary to remedy this situation. Their outlook was 'working class' in the full sense of the term.[25]

What we do not know, of course, is whether this group of 'middle class proletarians' has increased markedly in recent years. This is of some importance because discovering the existence of this group does challenge the idea of the middle class as individualist and suspicious of trade unionism, and if it could be shown that their outlook is shared by an increasing proportion of non-manual workers it would be powerful evidence of change within the middle class.

Roberts does not discuss this possibility directly. He sees the major reason for the 'proletarian' outlook as deriving from a reduction in the 'market advantages' enjoyed by some non-manual workers. There is little to distinguish the pay and fringe benefits which some of them have from those of manual workers and while they are not opposed to individual mobility they realise that they have reached their career ceilings quite early in their working lives. Hence their chance of improving their conditions necessitates collective action through trade unions. This argument of Roberts reflects a widespread view among sociologists who have discussed social stratification. They acknowledge that mobility chances for some have increased through the educational system but maintain that there is a corresponding reduction in the opportunities for career mobility on the part of those recruited to work at routine levels. Management and administration at the middle and upper levels are increasingly staffed by those directly recruited after university or degree level education rather than by those who arrive there after extensive internal promotion. Though the initial findings of the 1972 Nuffield survey on mobility challenge this interpretation,[26] such findings are not necessarily inconsistent with the fact that particular groups of routine non-manual workers do see their chances of promotion as having been curtailed. At any rate, though this analysis does suggest one source of middle class unionism it obviously does not apply to *all* middle class unionists.

We have already said that the fourth objection to our opening argument about increasing unionisation implying greater class unity is rather different because it takes more seriously the individualist/collectivist distinction. There are two possible versions of the argument, a 'strong' and a 'weak' version. The 'strong' version would argue that non-manual unions can be clearly differentiated from manual unions in both their aims and their day-to-day strategy and tactics. There will be a restrictive interpretation of the aims of non-manual unions with a concentration on economic protection and advancement and little interest in wide-scale social or political change. So far as strategy and tactics are concerned they will eschew the more militant forms of protest, especially the full-scale strike. The 'weak' version of the argument would agree that non-manual unions are less interested in wide-scale social change but would expect the unions to consider the full range of strategies and tactics open to all workers in order to prosecute the interests of their members. Indeed, it might expect to see a higher level of militancy in a number of cases precisely in order to maintain or re-assert differentials that the members see as having been unjustifiably eroded.

In considering the 'strong' argument we are confronted with a familiar problem in studying institutions: what evidence we are to accept in judging aims, strategy and tactics. Trade unions, like most formally structured organisations, have a written statement of their aims and objectives, and various parts of the organisation (e.g. the Executive Committee, President, General Secretary) elaborate upon these aims from time to time. But many social scientists insist that such statements are merely rhetoric and a poor guide to the actual behaviour of the organisation. Thus, it is argued, we should concentrate on what the organisation actually does (or indeed does not do) rather than what it says it believes in or would like to do. This view is strengthened if we accept another argument that is frequently put forward in this context, namely that statements made by the leadership of organisations with a mass membership may be a very imperfect guide to what the membership believes or would actually be prepared to do – again, the moral would be that we should concentrate on the behaviour of the organisation.

Certainly it is not difficult to demonstrate that so far as unions are concerned there are wide divergences between formally stated aims and actual industrial or political behaviour. A union such as the General and Municipal Workers (GMWU) is committed to a radical change in the social order, but it would be difficult to quarrel with the view that it has been 'a bastion of loyalty and moderation to the TUC since its foundation in 1924'.[27] This judgment is, of course, based upon an examination of the way in which the union has *behaved*: that is to say, the way it has cast votes at the TUC and the Labour Party Conference and the relative absence of industrial militancy during its past fifty years.

How far, then, does the behaviour of middle class unions support the 'strong' or 'weak' versions of the argument we have outlined? A summary verdict would be that the evidence does not support the strong version but does provide considerable support for the weak version. The difficulty about the strong version is that most middle class unions have resorted to the full range of sanctions, including national strikes, which are used by many working class unions; and there are examples of the latter which have hardly, if ever, resorted to the use of strike action. This obviously undermines any broad characterisation of non-manual and manual unions in terms of different strategies and tactics. It could be objected that the argument is not so much about whether white collar unions have *ever* resorted to industrial action but about whether their propensity to do so is markedly less than that of manual unions. To deal adequately with this argument we would need the data about different forms of industrial action to be collected on a quite different basis. Consequently any discussion of this argument has to rest on impressionistic evidence. Certainly it is true that much of the comment in the early 1960s and again in the early 1970s which highlighted the greater militancy of some non-manual unions assumed that such behaviour was *atypical*.[28]

If we examine the period between 1970 and 1974, which is generally regarded as one of increased militancy by the trade union movement, middle class unions do not emerge as prominent initiators or supporters of such activity and a number made their opposition plain. There were particular reasons why a number of unions like ASTMS and the National Union of Bank Employees (NUBE) found themselves strongly tempted to register under the Conservative Government's Industrial Relations Act and thus break ranks on the crucial TUC principle of non-registration.[29] But those unions whose self-interest was less directly threatened made it clear that the prospect of militant action against the Bill and the Act was not welcomed. Walter Anderson, the General Secretary of NALGO, criticised the industrial action that had already taken place when the TUC held its special Congress on the Bill in March 1971. It was 'highly irresponsible' and would 'convince hundreds of thousands of people that there is every need for such legislation'. Similarly Roy Grantham of the Association of Professional, Executive, Clerical and Computer Staff (APEX) declared that the Government would not be moved by industrial action 'but it would do damage to many of our unions, particularly the white-collar ones'.[30] The same two unions also stood aside from the various militant protests against the Conservative Government's statutory incomes policy during 1973. Though their emphasis was somewhat different – APEX, which is affiliated to the Labour Party, believed that working for a Labour Government was the only correct way to defeat the Conservative's incomes policy, whereas NALGO wanted the TUC to develop an incomes policy and be given the authority to implement it – their dislike and lack of support for any form of strike action was made clear.[31]

However, although the above evidence supports a view that white collar unions are more passive in their behaviour, it was not the case, especially with regard to incomes policy, that all white collar unions conformed to this stereotype. The Technical, Administrative and Supervisory Section (TASS) of the Amalgamated Union of Engineering Workers (AUEW) was a strong advocate of industrial action against the Industrial Relations Bill, and Bill Kendall, then General Secretary of the Civil and Public Services Association (CPSA), declared that the Conservative Government would not 'take a blind bit of notice' of the TUC's alternatives to statutory incomes control 'unless we punch home the message with some sort of industrial action'.[32] Similarly the National Association of Teachers in Further and Higher Education (NATFHE) and ASTMS jointly sponsored a motion the effect of which, had it been passed, would have been to involve the TUC collectively in any dispute over the statutory incomes policy that involved a particular union. One could raise the question of how far the speakers urging greater militancy were accurately representing the views of their members. Certainly, unlike those white collar unions opposing militancy who frequently made reference to the reluctance of their members to support such action and the damage it would do to their unions, those urging militancy did not choose to support their case by reference to the support such action would receive.

We have already suggested that the evidence does provide more support for the 'weak' version of the argument about the character of white collar unionism. The main thrust of this argument is concerned with the deterioration in the wages and working conditions of non-manual workers relative to manual workers in the post-war period. Resort to trade unionism is thus a defensive mechanism, at worst to prevent further deterioration, at best to re-assert differentials. As we have commented previously, the implication of this argument is that while the tactics they use may seem to indicate a growing identity with manual unions, the *purpose* of such activity is precisely to assert their differences.

The title of a detailed study of technicians by B. C. Roberts *et al. – Reluctant Militants*[33] – is a good illustration of the attitude of one important group who have strong feelings of relative deprivation. They do not consider that their pay levels establish anywhere near substantial enough differentials with those of manual workers. In the case of three of the four groups studied (draughtsmen, laboratory staff and quality controllers) more than eight out of ten thought the difference in pay was insufficient, and nearly three-quarters of the fourth group (planning and production engineers) thought similarly.[34] The authors conclude their study by emphasising that the bargaining strength of these different groups was aimed at 'improving or restoring their absolute and relative levels of earnings. In particular they wanted to see their own perceptions of their status compared with that of the shop floor workers rewarded equitably.'[35]

Engineers and managers are two further groups whose circumstances have been widely discussed in relation to trade unionism in recent years. The main reasons for their likely resort to trade unionism seem to be widely agreed: for both groups dissatisfaction about their incomes feature prominently. Linda Dickens argues that this is one of the main reasons for the growing abandonment by professional engineers of their former preference for individual bargaining.[36] Similarly, many managers would echo the view of the general secretary of a union for managers in shipbuilding (the Shipbuilding and Allied Industries Managers Association): 'Over a period of years as a result of government incomes policies and shop floor trade union pressures for single status, managers in shipbuilding, as elsewhere, have experienced a progressive erosion of differentials between themselves and their subordinates.'[37] The other major reasons suggested by Dickens for the movement of engineers towards unionism are rationalisation of firms through amalgamation and take-over which threatens security of employment, and the closely associated factor of organisations becoming more hierarchical and bureaucratic. Both these factors have been widely experienced by managers also. They serve to underline the diminishing status of both groups, for with reduced security and increased difficulty in negotiating working conditions on an individual basis, their positions seem closer to those of the bulk of manual workers.

But although the response of many is to turn to some form of collective action, the nature of this collective activity is a matter of considerable concern. So far as the engineers are concerned, when the Council of Engineering Institutions recommended their members to join trade unions in December 1975 they only nominated one TUC-affiliated union – the Engineers and Managers Association (EMA); the three non-affiliated unions suggested as suitable were the United Kingdom Association of Professional Engineers (UKAPE), the Association of Professional Scientists and Technologists (APST) and the Association of Supervisory and Executive Engineers (ASEE). TASS and ASTMS were not recommended as they were considered insufficiently professionally orientated and did not incorporate in their rules provision for a ballot before taking industrial action. Despite the fact that ACAS has favoured the large established unions like TASS, considerable resilience has been shown both by the EMA and by the three non-TUC affiliates in pressing for recognition, and a recent court verdict in favour of the UKAPE and reversing the recommendation of ACAS may oblige the latter to reconsider its policy.[38]

It is similarly clear that many managers, especially in private industry, do not wish to join existing TUC white collar unions. They are concerned about how far the management function is compatible with membership of a union which may include many of those over whom they exercise authority, as well as being sceptical about organisations which take political stances.[39] At the same time it is very apparent to many managers that staying outside any organisation is becoming increasingly difficult. Quite apart from the economic dissatisfactions already mentioned, the determination of economic policy appears increasingly to be the preserve of organisations – whether Government, CBI or TUC. There is clearly a feeling that the managerial voice is not articulated satisfactorily through the CBI and a disinclination on the part of many to align themselves with organised labour even when this can be done through a union like the EMA which is more approved than many.

The possibility of the British Institute of Management (BIM) emerging as a union or association of managers has been discussed, and its recently introduced practice of holding 'conventions' has suggested a move away from a study-based to a representative, 'pressure politics', type of body. The BIM has also relinquished its charitable status in order to campaign publicly to influence legislation and government policy. Though it may have some success in these objectives, there are a number of unresolved problems that it faces. One observer of its second convention has argued that its role is still ambiguous: partly an institute of management, partly a body representing managers. He suggested that the predominant sentiment at the convention was in favour of the latter,[40] but even if the BIM does evolve in this direction it would still face substantial difficulties as a representative body outside the tripartite structure of government, employers and the unions. This difficulty applies to all those groups or associations that are not linked to either the CBI or the TUC. Most of the white collar unions have had to face the fact that a 'middle way' between capital and labour has been rejected by successive Labour and Conservative governments. The affiliation of NALGO and the National Union of Teachers (NUT) to the TUC in 1964 and 1970 owed much to the realisation that influence could only be exercised within the TUC, with the rejection of the bids of the alternative organisation they had both supported for an equivalent status to that of the TUC.[41] The steady trickle of civil service unions into the TUC during the 1970s is further evidence of the belief that if influence is to be exercised on the vital matters of wages and working conditions, it will only be through membership of the TUC.[42]

It is true that some of the non-TUC affiliates argue that the particular interests of managers will be submerged in the TUC: 'even supposing half a million managers joined the TUC what influence would they have . . . we've already agreed our interests are different that's why we are reluctant to join traditional unions, for that very reason'.[43] Thus despite the discouraging precedent of the Conference of Professional and Public Service Organisations (COPPSO), two umbrella organisations have been formed outside the TUC with the aim of collecting together employee groups that do not wish to affiliate to the TUC. The first of these – the Confederation of Employee Organisations – has a membership of 70,000: this is made up of twenty-nine members and six associates. The membership is heavily concentrated in banking and insurance, in fact the three largest affiliates, Barclays Staff Association (30,392), Commercial Union Association (5,601) and Sun Alliance and London Staff Association (5,600), comprise nearly 60 per cent of the total membership.[44] These three chief affiliates all have slightly different status under the Employment Protection Act. Barclays Staff Association has been granted a certificate as an independent trade union, Commercial Union has applied for one but been refused and the Sun Alliance has not made an application. Given that unionism in banking and insurance is in a particularly volatile state at the moment with an unofficial but high-level enquiry into the whole area of banking representation, and feverish attempts by ASTMS and the NUBE to invade each other's 'territory', the prospects for the Confederation seem very uncertain. It has, in fact, become an associate of the second candidate to emerge as a positive rallying point for those unsympathetic to the TUC – the Managerial and Professional Staffs Liaison Group (MPSL).

The origins of this body are interesting and revealing. When the British Medical Association (BMA) attempted to make certain representations to government, the latter indicated that the BMA was not speaking on behalf of very many people. A similar response was experienced by some of the other groups who have joined with the BMA as founding members. These include the British Dental Association, the Confederation of Bank Staffs Association, the aforementioned Confederation of Employee Organisations, the APST and the UKAPE. The President is from the APST, the Secretary from the BMA and the Treasurer from the Confederation of Bank Staffs. The current (July

1978) membership is 250,000; although claims have been made that the organisation represents 500,000 employees, the additional quarter of a million are not yet full members – they are sending observers to MPSL meetings with a view to becoming full members. The President of the Group does claim that they are able to make representations to Ministers and achieve a degree of credibility that individually they did not possess.[45] How far they will be satisfied simply to make representations, particularly in connection with the Budget and incomes policies, it is too early to tell. The example of COPPSO does not provide much encouragement for any organisation that wants to break into the tripartite framework of Government, CBI and TUC, and this framework has become more, rather than less, firmly established during the 1970s.

Implications of middle class unionism

Having examined the growth and character of middle class unionism we will now look at its implications for the trade union movement as a whole and for the political parties, especially the Labour Party which has had such a close relationship with the trade unions. The major significance for the trade union movement of the development of middle class unionism is that the balance of power within the TUC – the major representative body of organised labour – has shifted, and continues to shift, in favour of non-manual workers and against manual workers. From being a clear minority with a need for the special protection of the Non-Manual Workers Advisory Committee and Conference, non-manual unions have moved to a position where they now comprise well over one third of the TUC's total affiliation, and a decision was taken in 1975 to abolish the special machinery of the Advisory Committee and Conference.

There are two main kinds of change that can be discerned from the increasing impact of non-manual workers within the TUC. Firstly, what will be described as internal changes such as pressure by these unions for increased representation within the TUC's formal structure, most obviously in the composition of the General Council; secondly, external changes, that is those that lead to the adoption of different policies and the use of different strategies by the TUC in its relationship with government, the political parties or the wider public.

The TUC does not make changes in its internal structure easily. Between 1921 and 1961 the General Council altered only very slightly: one new trade group was created and there were three changes in the membership of the remaining groups. The pace of change has accelerated considerably since then. Substantial occupational change, with its inevitable consequences for the expansion and contraction of particular unions, has made change impossible to resist, at any rate if the General Council was to continue to appear credible both internally and externally. Thus by the late 1960s two entirely new trade groups had been created, four of the existing groups had been amalgamated into two groups, and seven changes had been made in the membership of the remaining groups. A series of Industry Committees had been established in an attempt to overcome the problem of the haphazard growth of unionism which has led to trade union structures that are poorly related to the realities of contemporary collective bargaining.

Another lengthy re-examination of TUC structure was launched in 1975; it was not only initiated by a non-manual union but has turned out to be an enquiry in which the demands of non-manual unions for various kinds of change have featured prominently. John Lyons of the EMA had made clear in a number of comments prior to the 1975 Congress his dissatisfaction at the way in which the TUC had made representations on matters such as income distribution and the reconstitution of the Electricity Council without thorough consultation.[46] The only other speaker before the motion was remitted to the General Council was also from a non-manual union – Bill Kendall of the CPSA. His union had written earlier in the year to the General Council to highlight the unsatisfactory composition of the Council. In his speech to Congress he denied the General Council's contention that it was 'very representative of the Movement as a whole' and pointed particularly to the way in which the White Paper embracing the £6 pay policy 'had been written by the General Council without any mandate from this Congress'.[47]

The possibility of a fundamental change in the basis on which the General Council is elected was explored in some detail in a report to the 1977 Congress.[48] Most of the report is concerned with debating the merits of the 'automatic entitlement' principle: this means that unions would automatically receive seats on the General Council in proportion to their size. If it were to be adopted it would mark a complete break with the trade group principle. Perhaps in an attempt to ward this off and with the continuing pressure created by changes in trade union membership, the Council did recommend, and the Congress approved, an enlargement of the Council which increased its total membership from thirty-eight to forty-one. One of these additional seats was won by Ken Thomas who had succeeded Bill Kendall as General Secretary of the CPSA.

Whether the adoption of the principle of automatic entitlement would further improve the position of non-manual workers would depend critically upon the numerical threshold that was adopted, plus what resulted from the balloting among unions too small to qualify for an automatic seat. This is very clearly illustrated in the General Council's report. If, for example, all unions with a membership of 100,000 were to be given a seat, then their position would improve, for the Institution of Professional Civil Servants, the Society of Civil and Public Servants, the NUBE, and APEX would all gain automatic representation, and none of these unions have members on the General Council at the moment. Non-manual unions who are represented at the moment and would not qualify under automatic entitlement are the Inland Revenue Staff Federation (IRSF), the Association of Cinematograph, Television and Allied Technicians (ACTT) and the Musicians' Union, but it is quite possible that at least one of these would gain a seat in the balloting for unions with less than 100,000 members. Automatic entitlement at 100,000 would guarantee ten seats, but if it were fixed at 150,000 it would drop to six and at 200,000 to five. At the 1978 Congress the General Council once again shied away from any radical recommendation, but the General and Municipal Workers did propose a motion supporting the automatic entitlement principle with 150,000 as the qualifying figure. This motion was defeated, but only narrowly, and it seems highly likely that the issue will be raised again.

Parallel to this latest examination of its structure, the TUC has abolished the one part of its traditional arrangements that *did* appear to recognise the separate identity of non-manual workers: the Non-Manual Workers Advisory Committee and the associated annual conference. At first sight this may appear rather contradictory, but there are at least three considerations which help to explain the apparent inconsistency. Firstly, the origins of the special machinery lay in weakness – the small number of white collar workers who belonged to the organised union movement and the corresponding minority position of such unions within the TUC. As a result of growth, both in absolute numbers and in density, the impact of non-manual unions has been steadily increasing: in the short period between 1971 and 1975 nearly 600,000 additional white collar workers were affiliated to the TUC, and this raised their overall share of the TUC's membership from 27 per cent to 31·5 per cent.[49] This kind of advance has led to repeated questioning of the rationale of the special machinery. It was against the background of uncertainty that the 1970 Interim Report on the TUC declared that 'non-manual workers did have sufficient distinctive interests to provide valid grounds for maintaining the Non-Manual Workers Conference and Advisory Committee',[50] but in the comparatively short space of five years the balance of opinion had moved in favour of abolition.

A further reason that helps to explain abolition is the fact that neither the Conference nor the Advisory Committee had much real power. Decision making in the TUC lies with the Annual Congress, the General Council and some of its associated committees (especially the Finance and General Purposes and the Economic). So, at best, the Conference and Advisory Committee could only rehearse arguments that had to be finally settled elsewhere. This sense of being by-passed emerges from a slightly plaintive request made by the Advisory Committee in 1971 to the effect that 'it would be particularly helpful if other TUC committees could consult the Advisory Committee at an early stage when non-manual questions were under consideration rather than when policy was on the point of being decided'.[51]

The final reason for the abolition of this special machinery reflects the fact that many of the major problems that now confront non-manual unions are not seen as being essentially different from those of manual unions. Undoubtedly the growing degree of state intervention and regulation, especially in incomes policies, has acted to 'homogenise' unions and, given what has been said about the lack of authority of the special machinery, non-manual unions felt that the significant decisions were being taken by Annual Congress and the General Council and that that was where their voices were best deployed.

Nevertheless one should not exaggerate the degree of consensus among non-manual unions on their differences and how they can be articulated. When the General Council tested opinion in 1975 on the issue of abolition a clear majority of unions who responded supported abolition, but there were a number who did not express a view (representing 42 per cent of the white collar affiliations to the TUC) and a minority who were opposed. One has to assume that those who did not reply had no strong feelings either way, since when the General Council's recommendation to abolish the machinery was challenged at the 1975 Congress the challenge was defeated without any card vote being necessary. Those unions who did object argued their case on traditional grounds. They considered that there were still problems peculiar to non-manual workers, especially over recognition by private industry. They also believed their pay structures gave rise to different problems – and problems that were exacerbated by incomes policy, statutory or voluntary. Most manual workers were paid on the basis of 'the rate for the job', a phrase used by Mr Tony Christopher of the IRSF, one of the unions that objected to abolition. Consequently most incomes policies are based on this assumption and additionally have often included provisions for increases stemming from improved productivity. Both these features militate against the interests of most non-manual workers.[52]

Another important aspect of the TUC's procedures that has come under considerable strain as a result of the growth in non-manual unions has been the Bridlington Rules. These are a set of procedures worked out just before the Second World War and intended to regulate inter-union competition for members. Given all that has been said about the opportunities for the growth of unions among non-manual workers, it is only to be expected that conflicts have arisen between different unions competing for the same potential pool of new recruits. Two non-manual unions, APEX and EMA, have broken new ground in refusing to accept rulings given by TUC Disputes committees and utilising the judicial machinery to appeal against such judgments. In the case of APEX the issue centred around a merger between itself and the staff association at the General Accident Insurance Company. The proposed merger considerably annoyed ASTMS who had been attempting to gain recognition for a number of years against management hostility. The Disputes committee ruled in favour of ASTMS and the implication of this was that APEX should withdraw membership from all those who had previously belonged to the staff association. APEX resisted this and served an injunction on the TUC to prevent action being taken against it, for unions who refuse to comply with TUC rulings risk suspension and ultimately expulsion from the TUC. After some months of correspondence between the union and the General Council, APEX did eventually agree to comply with the Disputes committee ruling. However, the former chairman of the staff association was not willing to let the matter drop and instituted legal proceedings on his own account. The court ruled in his favour and the TUC, who were second defendant in the action, accepted legal advice against making an appeal. As a direct consequence of this case a number of alterations were made by the TUC to the rules and procedure governing the work of the Disputes committees.[53]

The dispute that the EMA has been involved in is another illustration of the unintended consequences of legislative action. The origins of the dispute are similar to the APEX case. A Disputes committee ruled against EMA recruitment at a GEC plant and in favour of TASS. As with APEX, the EMA was not prepared to accept this judgment and took out an injunction against the TUC to protect its position. The new twist in the situation, however, is that the EMA has sought to involve ACAS in the dispute by asking it to investigate its claim to recognition under the Employment Protection Act. John Lyons, the General Secretary of the EMA, has further threatened legal action against ACAS since he claims that it has been dilatory in investigating his recognition claim. If the claim has been deliberately delayed, that would not be altogether surprising, since ACAS was doubly embarrassed at finding itself embroiled in an inter-union dispute and even more in being used as a weapon to circumvent the TUC's internal disputes machinery. In an attempt to prevent this kind of situation arising, Ian Mikardo introduced a Private Member's Bill in January 1978, but it failed to pass all its necessary stages by the end of that session. Not surprisingly, it led to a strong complaint by Lyons, and Len Murray felt it necessary to intervene in the verbal battle.[54]

Unless some kind of *modus vivendi* can be worked out, the consequences of this kind of dispute could be quite serious. Since the EMA is involved in a number of similar disputes, it is not clear how long it will be content to remain within the TUC if judgments are constantly made against it. Equally the problems of the EMA are likely to reinforce the view among non-manual, non-TUC unions that the larger established unions will always be favoured and that they would be better off remaining outside the TUC.

So far as external changes are concerned, if we assume that non-manual unions do have different attitudes and that these can be clearly articulated within the TUC's structures, we might expect to see some changes in the TUC's strategies and tactics. As we have seen, there are some doubts as to how distinctive the policies of non-manual unions are, and even where they do have something different to say it is not clear that the present structures of the TUC will fully allow for this. We have also noted earlier that the belief among some managerial and professional groups that they cannot express their interests through the TUC is an important reason for the emergence of alternative 'peak' organisations like the MPSL. It is undeniable, though, that the TUC has achieved a broader base over the last fifteen years, and even if the articulation of non-manual unions' views is not perfect, sufficient notice has been taken of them for us to conclude that policy making in a number of areas is now more difficult. This conclusion certainly applies to incomes policies which, whatever the TUC's inclinations, have been one of its central preoccupations since the mid-1960s. A much broader band of incomes are now encompassed by the TUC's membership and therefore the formulation of an acceptable posture is more difficult. This greater difficulty is seen most clearly when the TUC moves from an 'oppositional' stance, where it is concerned with attacking a policy proposed by somebody else (e.g. Government or CBI), to an attempt to frame some positive proposals of its own.

When the TUC attempted to establish and administer its own 'vetting' machinery during the Labour Government of 1964–70, a number of white collar unions complained about the way in which this failed to take account of their particular problems.[55] When the £6 flat-rate policy was introduced in July 1975 non-manual unions were prominent in opposing it. TASS, ASTMS and the CPSA all indicated their dissatisfaction, though the grounds on which they chose to argue the case were general political ones rather than the deleterious effects it would have on their own members. The Society of Civil and Public Servants, the EMA and the National Association of Schoolmasters (NAS), though they did not all back the critical resolution, did complain about how the policy would reduce their members' standard of living. Terry Casey, the General Secretary of the NAS, echoed two familiar themes from the 1966–70 debates: firstly, that manual workers have opportunities for overtime and production bonuses denied to most non-manual workers, and secondly, that 'better paid trade unionists are every bit as worthy . . . every bit as necessary to our society', and that having welcomed non-manual workers to the TUC it could not now 'tell them they were some unworthy sector of employees'.[56] This slightly defensive tone and hesitancy in arguing the case of the higher paid non-manual workers is perhaps a sign of some insecurity and vestigial uncertainty about the acceptability of such groups to the TUC. A celebrated attack on non-manual work had been made some nine years previously by John Boyd of the AUEW when he told the General Secretary of NALGO that he represented people 'who produce nothing' but nevertheless enjoyed superior working conditions, salaries and holidays. This attack was disowned by Vic Feather and a number of other speakers. By 1975, with the increased weight of non-manual workers, Casey's defensiveness was probably unnecessary, and Jack Jones in his summing-up speech promised to give special consideration to the problems that had been raised by white collar unions.

To some extent this was done in the second stage of the voluntary policy which ran from August 1976 to July 1977. There was a more flexible formula which incorporated a percentage element; nevertheless, since it had a maximum cut-off point it was still discriminatory against higher paid workers. At the special Congress held in June 1976 to approve the policy both Clive Jenkins (ASTMS) and John Lyons (EMA) complained about the policy for this reason and similar criticisms were voiced by the Secretary of the Institute of Professional Civil Servants (IPCS) at the September Congress. However, the focus of much white collar discontent had shifted by this time to the reductions in public expenditure programmes. The successive cuts in planned public expenditure have certainly sparked greater unity among unions in the public sector, but there are, of course, many millions of manual workers involved as well as non-manual workers. One of the unions which has expanded most rapidly in the post-war period is the National Union of Public Employees which organises large numbers of public sector manual workers and which has played a leading part in the campaigns against reductions in public expenditure. An interpretation of the TUC's internal politics in terms of those with a vested interest in existing levels of public spending and those opposed, or at least indifferent, is more plausible than any attempt to range all non-manual unions on one side and all manual unions on the other. The evidence from the most recent period supports the conclusion that Jean Bocock arrived at in examining white collar politics between 1964 and 1970: 'Politically, then, white-collar unions demonstrate the same diversity of opinion as the manual unions.'[57]

One of the most important developments that has taken place in the period since 1970 is the establishment of the TUC/Labour Party Liaison Committee. This body, which was formally established in January 1972, had its antecedents in a liaison group formed to oppose the Conservative Government's Industrial Relations Bill of 1970–1. In its original form it brought together six representatives from the TUC General Council, six from the Parliamentary Labour Party (PLP) and six from the National Executive Committee (NEC) of the Labour Party.[58] Each of the groups has contributed its leading members, so that when it was first set up it included, for example, Harold Wilson, Denis Healey and James Callaghan from the PLP, Jack Jones, Hugh Scanlon and Vic Feather from the TUC, and Tony Benn, Barbara Castle and Ian Mikardo from the NEC.

One of the key factors in elevating the role of the Liaison Committee has been the growing divergence between unions affiliated to the TUC and unions affiliated to the Labour Party. This is a consequence of the steep reduction in the membership of many traditional unions who affiliated a substantial proportion of their members to the Labour Party and the growth of unions who do not affiliate in any form to the Party. The latter are, of course, non-manual unions. None of the civil service unions, the local government officers, or any of the teachers' unions affiliates to the Labour Party. The growing gap this produces can be illustrated by figures in Table 4.[59] Even where white collar unions do affiliate to the Party the contracting out rate – that is, those who decline to pay the political levy – is frequently high. Two of the four unions whose returns were singled out by the Certification Officer in his 1977 Report as examples of those where less than half the membership paid the political levy were TASS with 48 per cent and ASTMS with 37 per cent.[60]

TABLE 4

Affiliation to the Labour Party and to the TUC, 1956–76

Year	Union members affiliated to the Labour Party	Union members affiliated to the TUC	Labour Party affiliates as percentage of TUC affiliates
1956	5,658,249	8,263,731	70
1965	5,601,982	8,771,012	64
1976	5,800,069	11,036,326	52·5

It was essentially from the Liaison Committee that the social contract emerged. The TUC took the initiative on industrial relations matters, mapping out a programme of legislation which would be introduced by a future Labour government. Two of these proposals – the repeal of the 1971 Industrial Relations Act and an extension of trade union rights and recognition – were promptly acted upon by the Labour Government that took office in March 1974.[61] The third proposal, on industrial democracy, has been the subject of an official enquiry which reported in terms favourable to the TUC, but the legislative outcome is uncertain.[62] It was hoped that in exchange for this legislation and other appropriate action the trade unions would observe some limitation on wage claims. Initially the response of the TUC to this hope of pay moderation was somewhat equivocal and many individual unions negotiated high settlements.[63] However, with a rapidly increasing rate of inflation the £6 pay policy was formulated by the TUC and marked a return to a firm incomes policy. The Liaison Committee continued to be of importance during the Labour Government's period of office and in so doing it confirmed, at any rate so far as the trade unions were concerned, a diminution in the status of the NEC of the Labour Party.

In view of the increasing divergence between trade unions affiliated to the TUC and trade unions affiliated to the Labour Party, one might have expected the Conservative Party to have made rather more of this. However, though the circumstances surrounding the fall from office in February 1974 have certainly provoked a lengthy re-appraisal of its relationship with the trade unions, an appreciation of the opportunities that changes in the movement offer the Party seems to be lacking. In one way the increase in non-manual unionism complicates matters for the Conservatives, because trade unions increasingly embrace voters with Conservative Party preferences. Hence the Party has to be wary of adopting any straight 'anti-union' stance, since many of those from whom it needs votes are union members. Such an awareness may underlie one strategy which has been adopted, namely to encourage Conservatives to join trade unions and play an active part within them.

It is not clear how systematically this strategy is being implemented, but there are a number of other organisational indications – for example, the appointment of a special officer at Conservative Central Office and a number of conferences of Conservative trade unionists – that suggest this is an area where the Party could make some advances. One or two well-publicised instances such as the decision by ASTMS to close its Central London branch, to which a number of Conservative Central Office officials had belonged, have demonstrated that an exploitable strategy is being implemented here and there, but it is too early to see whether this will have more than an irritant effect.

Conclusions

This examination of middle class unionism has been concerned with three main questions – how far are the middle class unionised, what is the nature of that unionism, and what are the wider consequences for the political parties and the TUC?

The answer to the first question is bedevilled by difficulties of definition and the absence of important information. The discussion has equated middle class with non-manual workers while being well aware that this may lead to some individuals being seen as middle class who certainly do not regard themselves in that way. Again, so far as unionism is concerned we have chosen to define the term fairly widely and to regard any association which has 'the regulation of relations between workers and employers'[64] as a manifestation of unionism. This definition obviously entails a concern with staff associations and some of the activities of professional groups as well as bodies that call themselves unions and affiliate to the TUC. While it is not possible with this kind of approach to measure precisely the impact of unionism upon non-manual workers there is little doubt, in the light of the work of Bain, that it has increased. But the increase – or, to be more precise, the increase in density, which is the important measure – dates from the middle 1960s and has not been a phenomenon of the mid-1970s as have some of the other examples of 'revolt' discussed in this book. Neither is there much indication of an appreciable quickening of pace during the post-1974 period. The consideration of the reasons for the increase of unionism takes us directly to the second of the major questions – the nature or character of such unionism.

The tactic we adopted here was to assume that an individualist ethic characterised the middle class and had kept them away from the economic collectivism of associations and unions. If they were now joining such groups this would seem to imply that an important social change was taking place. We discussed this hypothesis by examining four different objections to it. This discussion suggested three main conclusions. Firstly, that a small element of middle class unionism can be described as 'proletarianisation'. It is clear that some non-manual workers identify with the working class and, like them, join trade unions in order to make advances collectively since the chances of individual mobility appear slight or non-existent. What we do not know is whether this category is growing. Even if we assume that there is a fairly close connection between subjective consciousness and objective circumstances, it does not take us much further, for we would need to know what the prospects are for the continued expansion of non-manual employment and in what areas and at what levels future growth will take place. The 1972 Nuffield Mobility Survey indicated that substantial expansion in non-manual employment since 1945 was an important reason for the continuing possibility of upward career mobility.

The second conclusion emphasises the important role that increasing government and employer recognition has had in promoting non-manual unionism and the fertile soil that has been created for such recognition through changes in employment conditions. So far as government is concerned, the expansion in the public sector work-force and successive laws have been the most important factors. Though it has not yet passed into law, the very prospect of the introduction of industrial democracy in which employee representation would be through trade unions has led many managers to consider joining a trade union in order not to be left out. Changes in the size of companies and in the size of work units has encouraged recognition procedures to be used. The doubts, hesitations and reservations that are displayed by many, especially about embracing unions affiliated to the TUC, are illustrated by the continued existence of many staff groups and the attempts at building an alternative peak organisation to the TUC.

The final conclusion to emerge from the discussion of the character of middle class unionism was that while many of the middle class belonged to organisations which were quite prepared to use the tactics of 'traditional' unions, including the full-scale strike, such tactics were not being used as a gesture of solidarity but for precisely the opposite reason – in order to re-assert differentials with manual workers. It is here that one finds the closest correspondence to the kinds of 'revolt' described in other chapters in this book. The impact of very high levels of inflation, increases in taxation and highly restrictive pay policies have fuelled a sense of resentment on the part of many salaried workers. The differences that marked them off from the bulk of manual workers are less clear, and in turning to unionism they are adopting the apparently successful techniques of manual workers to reclaim advantages that they see as being unjustifiably reduced.

The third section of the chapter examined some of the consequences of increased unionism. It was argued that, despite the conservatism of the TUC, some changes have been made and others appear likely in order to satisfy the demands of the increasingly strong non-manual element within it. With the affiliation of all the major public-sector non-manual unions the TUC's claim to representativeness has been enhanced, but, as with any body spanning a range of diverse interests, the problems of designing viable policies are considerable. Nevertheless in 1975–6 and 1976–7 the TUC committed itself to two stages of incomes policy which, in contrast to previous attempts, were successful in that all affiliates kept to them in their pay settlements. Beyond the desire for improvements in representation and consultation and some concern about the effects of flat-rate pay policies on differentials, it was not possible to see white collar unions displaying much unity. Such unity as has been evident is further limited by the fact that there are a small but significant number of unions and associations representing non-manual unionists who do not wish to affiliate to the TUC and have combined in the MPSL to promote an alternative peak association.

There are also divided views on the relationship with the political parties. Most non-manual unions have chosen not to affiliate to the Labour Party and among the minority who do (such as ASTMS) nearly two-thirds of the members do not pay the political levy. With the decline in the membership of a number of traditional unions, barely half the TUC's membership is now affiliated to the Labour Party. This development enhanced the importance of the TUC/Labour Party Liaison Committee as the major formal channel through which the Labour Party during 1972–4 and the Labour Government after 1974 conducted relations with the trade unions. In principle the growing gap between the trade union movement in the Labour Party and the trade union movement in the TUC should make the Conservative Party's relationship with the TUC easier, since the latter has always emphasised its role as a negotiator with whatever party currently forms the Government. However, there were few signs, as the Conservatives took office in May 1979, that this would necessarily be the case.

NOTES

1 Blackburn, R. M., *Union Character and Social Class*, Batsford, 1967; Lumley, R., *White Collar Unionism in Britain*, Methuen, 1973.
2 *First Annual Report of the Certification Officer 1976*, HMSO, 1977, p. 3.
3 Ibid, p. 7. All statistics are drawn from this *Report* and *Annual Report of the Certification Officer 1977*, HMSO, 1978.
4 See, for example, the debate at the 1976 TUC Congress: *TUC Report 1976*, pp. 451–5.
5 The principal discussions are Bain, G. S., 'The Growth of White Collar Unionism in Great Britain', *British Journal of Industrial Relations*, Vol. 4, November 1966; Bain, G. S., and Price, R., 'Union Growth and Employment Trends in the United Kingdom', *British Journal of Industrial Relations*, Vol. 9, November 1971; Price, R., and Bain, G. S., 'Union Growth Revisited: 1948–1974 in Perspective', *British Journal of Industrial Relations*, Vol. 14, November 1976; Bain, G. S., *The Growth of White Collar Unionism*, Clarendon Press, 1970.
6 The 1964 figure is based upon figures in Bain, 1966, for the Association of Scientific Workers and the Association of Supervisory Staffs, Executives and Technicians which merged in 1968 to form ASTMS. The 1977 figure is from *TUC Report 1977*.
7 Price and Bain, 1976. The category is, in fact, 'managers and administrators' and therefore will include personnel in both public and private sectors.
8 His figure of 500,000 is obtained by subtracting already unionised civil servants, certain supervisors and company directors from the total figure, *Financial Times*, 2 February 1976.
9 'Unions Start Recruitment Campaign', *Financial Times*, 8 June 1976.
10 Bain, G. S., *et al.*, *Social Stratification and Trade Unionism*, Heinemann, 1973, p. 148.
11 Roberts, K., *et al.*, *The Fragmentary Class Structure*, Heinemann, 1977 – see especially Chapters 4 and 7.
12 Parry, Noel, and Parry, Jose, *The Rise of the Medical Profession*, Croom Helm, 1976.
13 Bain, 1970.
14 In a recent note on Bain's theory Roy Adams argues that Bain is really talking about bureaucratisation, not concentration; the two may be associated but not necessarily. Adams, Roy, J., 'Bain's Theory of White Collar Union Growth: A Conceptual Critique', *British Journal of Industrial Relations*, Vol. 15, November 1977.
15 Lockwood, D., *The Blackcoated Worker*, Allen & Unwin, 1958.
16 Bain, 1970, p. 123.
17 Ibid, especially Chapter 7.
18 Bain, 1970, p. 180.
19 Thakur, M., and Naylor, M., *White Collar Unions*, Institute of Personnel Management, 1976, p. 16.
20 *Financial Times*, 14 April 1978.
21 An investigation into a major city branch of NALGO produced a similar figure – see Nicholson, N., and Ursell, G., 'The NALGO Activists', *New Society*, 15 December 1977.
22 See the report in the *Financial Times*, 5 June 1978, which indicates the nature of the offer and the objections to it of the unions concerned.
23 Butler, D. E., and Stokes, D., *Political Change in Britain*, Macmillan, 1969.
24 Runciman, W. G., *Relative Deprivation and Social Justice*, Routledge, 1966, especially Chapters 8 and 9; Roberts *et al.*, op. cit.
25 Roberts *et al.*, op. cit.
26 Goldthorpe, J. H., and Llewellyn, C., 'Class Mobility in Modern Britain: Three Theses Examined', *Sociology*, Vol. 11, No. 2 (May 1977).
27 Taylor, R., *The Fifth Estate*, Routledge, 1978, p. 229.
28 See, for example, Burke, V., *Teachers in Turmoil*, Penguin, 1971.

29 See particularly Chapter 8 of Moran, M., *The Politics of Industrial Relations*, Macmillan, 1977.
30 *The Industrial Relations Bill – Report of the Special Trades Union Congress*, TUC, 1971, pp. 72–3 and 85.
31 See the speeches of G. J. Phillips (NALGO) and Roy Grantham (APEX) in *Economic Policy and Collective Bargaining – Report of a Special TUC, March 1973*, TUC, 1973, pp. 69 and 82–3.
32 Ibid, p. 71.
33 Roberts, B. C., *et al.*, *Reluctant Militants*, Heinemann, 1972.
34 Ibid, p. 146.
35 Ibid, p. 323.
36 Dickens, L., 'UKAPE: A Study of A Professional Union', *Industrial Relations Journal*, Vol. 3, No. 3 (Autumn 1972).
37 Quoted in Crisp, J., 'How Managers are struggling to make themselves heard', *Financial Times*, 19 June 1978.
38 See *Financial Times*, 1 July 1978, for a report of the case.
39 See Crisp, J., op. cit.; Dickens, L., op. cit.; and Wigham E., 'What of the Managers who want to participate in the trade union movement?', *The Times*, 28 June 1977.
40 Crisp, J., 'Is the BIM managing to make itself heard?', *Financial Times*, 10 March 1978.
41 The organisation was the Conference of Professional and Public Service Organisations (COPPSO). For a discussion of it, see Coates, R. D., *Teachers' Unions and Interest Group Politics*, Cambridge University Press, 1972, Chapter 8.
42 The Society of Civil and Public Servants, the Institute of Professional Civil Servants and the First Division Association all affiliated between 1972 and 1977.
43 Quoted in Crisp, 'How Managers are struggling to make themselves heard', *Financial Times*, 19 June 1978.
44 Thakur and Naylor, op. cit., pp. 87–8.
45 I am grateful to Dr M. Gillibrand, the Executive Secretary of APST who is President of the MPSL, for information about the Group.
46 See, for example, his letter in *The Sunday Times*, 20 July 1975, in which he alleged that in its evidence to the Royal Commission on the Distribution of Income and Wealth, 'not only were we not consulted in any shape or form by the General Council . . . but so far as I am aware neither were any of the unions representing technical, managerial and professional staffs'.
47 For the full response to the CPSA and the speeches of Lyons and Kendall, see *TUC Report 1975*, pp. 37–9 and 378–80.
48 *TUC Report 1977*, pp. 321–6.
49 Figures from *TUC Report 1971*, p. 80, and *TUC Report 1975*, p. 81.
50 *TUC Report 1971*, p. 81.
51 Ibid.
52 *TUC Report 1975*, pp. 81–2, for details of the General Council's survey, and pp. 408–9 for the debate.
53 The details can be found in the *TUC Report 1975*, pp. 39–43, and *TUC Report 1976*, pp. 95–9.
54 See Lyons, John, 'Trade Union Recognition: Why is Mr Mikardo taking this line?', *The Times*, 26 January 1978, and a letter from Len Murray, *The Times*, 31 January 1978.
55 See, for example, *TUC Report 1968*, pp. 356–7, and some of the speeches at the 1967 Conference of Trade Union Executives: *Incomes Policy – Report of a Conference of Executive Committees of Affiliated Organisations, March 1967*, TUC, 1967.
56 *TUC Report 1975*, p. 475.
57 Bocock, Jean, 'The Politics of White-Collar Unionisation', *Political Quarterly*, Vol. 43, 1973.
58 It was subsequently modified by increasing the PLP and NEC membership to ten each.

59 Labour Party figures from *Labour Party Annual Conference Report*, 1977; TUC figures from *TUC Report 1977*.
60 *Annual Report of the Certification Officer 1977*, p. 24.
61 In the form of the *Trade Union and Labour Relations Act*, 1974 and the *Employment Protection Act*, 1975.
62 *Report of the Committee of Inquiry on Industrial Democracy* (under the chairmanship of Lord Bullock), January 1977.
63 See May, Timothy C., *Trade Unions and Pressure Group Politics*, Saxon House, 1975, pp. 40–3, for initial uncertainty about the social contract.
64 The definition employed by the *Trade Union and Labour Relations Act*, 1974.

Dallas Cliff

6. Religion, morality and the middle class

Introduction

Many sociologists would now agree that the effect of the so-called 'counter culture' of the 'swinging sixties' was over-stressed at the time, both as a movement unifying all youth in a homogeneous youth culture and as an assault on the dominant values of society.[1] Yet the ideas a society has about itself may themselves be potent facts. In the words of W. I. Thomas's famous dictum, 'If enough men define a thing as real, it is real in its consequences.'[2] The 'permissiveness' of the sixties had, in any case, a tangible basis in reality as far as many were concerned. Explicit sexual magazines have become a familiar sight at the corner newsagent. Every provincial town now has its specialist cinemas for 'skin-flics'.

The period also saw a number of much-publicised legislative innovations, all of which could be regarded as shifting legal definitions of morality in a permissive direction. The law relating to homosexuality was amended in 1967 to legalise sexual relations between consenting male adults; the 1969 Divorce Law discarded the notion of 'matrimonial offence' and established 'irretrievable breakdown of marriage' as the sole criterion for divorce; and the 1967 Abortion Law enabled women to take this option to end unwanted pregnancy legally and with comparative ease. The same period was marked by a steady upward trend in the statistical figures relating to social problems of all kinds which led many to believe that the social fabric was coming apart at the seams. The figures for divorce, delinquency, violent crime, truancy from school and other indicators of social malaise were, and still are, rising. Attendances in churches, the proportion of time devoted to Christian religion in schools, and commitment to established values generally were falling. For many these trends were causally related. British institutions were felt to be under attack from within, in the shape of the misguided disciples of 'permissiveness'.

We may characterise the reaction to permissiveness in terms of a commitment to a set of values linked historically to the traditional middle classes. The German sociologist Max Weber saw these values as being derived from the 'Protestant ethic'.[3] They can best be seen as manifesting themselves in certain core beliefs in the value of hard work, individual initiative, self-restraint, responsibility, honesty and delayed gratification. If the middle classes are 'in revolt', then we find them fighting not only on the economic front, but also on the moral front, in such groups as the National Festival of Light and the National Viewers and Listeners Association. These are just two of the better-known groups who are involved in combating what they see as a definite decline in contemporary standards of morality. There is, as will be shown in a later section of this chapter, substantial evidence to suggest that support for such organisations is drawn disproportionately from the middle classes.

Organisations like these which aim at changing the definitions of morality prevalent in society have been described by Howard Becker as 'moral entrepreneurs'.[4] They involve themselves in attempts to explicate moral principles and to define certain activities as deviant. This automatically brings them into conflict with the major 'definers' in modern society, those in the communications industry, media, advertising and publishing on the one hand and the education system on the other.

The senior group of those to be considered here is the National Viewers and Listeners Association (NVALA) which was formed in 1964. The others were all founded or assumed their form in the late sixties or early seventies. The Association was formed specifically to question and combat the subversive values and images of society which were felt to be disseminated by the broadcasting media. The NVALA has links with many other groups involved in moral protest and its leader, Mrs Mary Whitehouse, is an important co-ordinator. The Association aims at being the 'nations's watchdog' on television and radio broadcasting standards, in order that 'the Broadcasting Authorities should fulfil their obligations to ensure that programmes do not offend against good taste and decency, incite to crime and disorder, take sides on matters of public interest, or give offence to public feelings'.[5] With a membership of over 2,000 in 1978, the NVALA is the largest organisation we shall examine and its example has been an important factor in the foundation of similar groups.

The National Festival of Light (NFOL) came to public notice in a most spectacular manner in 1971 and 1972 when it held mass rallies in Trafalgar Square. The Festival owes its conception to Mr Peter Hall who, on returning from India where he had been working for the Christian 'Operation Mobilization', was appalled to find that a 'moral landslide' had taken place in England.[6] Acting as a coordinator for many groups, largely drawn from the evangelical wing of British Christianity, he staged the 1971 and 1972 rallies which attracted an estimated 35,000 and 20,000 people respectively. Since that time the NFOL has undergone a process of change. By 1979 the organisation no longer held mass rallies but aimed at the more limited task of collecting, collating, and disseminating information across the whole range of moral concerns. A small team distributes 15,000 copies of a quarterly broadsheet through various Christian and other sympathetic organisations. The Festival proclaims itself to be 'For Love, Purity and Family Life' and claims 'to speak out for Christian community standards' to 'warn against destructive influences in contemporary culture', and to ensure that 'Christian concern is expressed where it really matters'.[7]

The Order of Christian Unity (OCU) was founded in 1956 by Ernest Tapp as an organisation to foster ecumenicalism. In 1971, however, it was taken over by Lady Lothian and after three years of preparatory work it was launched as a crusading, anti-permissive, moral protest organisation with a similar platform to the NFOL. An inaugural rally was held in 1974 where the Order called for 'moral moderates to unite against the forces of cruelty'.[8] The Order produced a six-point charter calling for the defence of Christian education, opposition to euthanasia, unrestricted divorce, and abortion, the advancement of Christian sex education, and the furthering of Christian values in broadcasting. Whilst the NFOL contents itself with a small central organisation and attempts to work through established groups, the OCU recruits members and has small regional branches. In 1978 membership stood at 1,200 with an estimated further 800 associate members.

The Responsible Society (RS) differs from the other groups in that it has a wholly secular orientation and takes a scientific approach to problems of moral pollution. The Society models itself on various learned societies and aims to combat irresponsibility in society at large through the sponsorship of research and the spread of scientific information. Thus the RS claims 'our primary aim is the encouragement of responsible behaviour in sexual relationships by educating and informing the public about the real consequences of irresponsibility'.[9] Formed in 1971 by a number of people in the medical profession, it had a membership of 719 by 1978.

In addition to these national organisations two groups will be examined who are organised at, and seek to achieve an impact on, a purely local level. The Community Standards Association (CSA) was formed in 1974 in the Bodmin area of Cornwall to 'awaken the conscience and mobilise the concern of the community over the encroachment of mental and moral pollution with its disastrous consequences for the physical and psychological health of the individual and its damage to society as a whole'.[10] The Association had about 300 members in 1978.

The Bristol Family Life Association (BFLA) dates from 1976. It lacks a definite membership, working as it does through local church groups, and is coordinated by an executive of about twenty people. Its primary aim is 'to promulgate and uphold the Christian standards of family life and public morality in the area'.[11]

No claim can be made that this represents an exhaustive list of groups engaged in the sort of puritanical moral protest which attempts to re-establish traditional values. No attempt has been made, for instance, to deal with those groups who concern themselves with relatively narrow issues, like the anti-abortionist lobby. It may be fairly claimed, however, that the above groups are perhaps representative of those who seek to make an impact across the broad spectrum of moral concerns. This chapter will be concerned with examining the beliefs and activities of these groups in the context of recent social and cultural change with a view to establishing how far these organisations, who all see themselves as responding to threats to moral standards, beliefs and behaviour, can be properly understood as part of an alleged 'middle class revolt'.

Unifying ideologies

Roy Wallis[12] has called the underlying ideology of the NVALA 'cultural fundamentalism'. Certainly if there is a general coherence between the standpoints of all these groups it is the call for moral certainty, a return to the essential values of British culture. Such a call, however, must be viewed in the context of the specific issues and concerns around which it is mobilised if we are to understand it fully.

One important concern is the preservation of religious values. Indeed, the most recent research conducted into the NVALA sees the impetus behind the organisation as largely a response to secularising trends in British society.[13] Only one group, the Responsible Society, has no overt commitment to the Christian religion. The others have all made this a specific part of their platforms to a greater or lesser extent. The CSA aims to 'encourage the understanding of the relevance of religious and moral values and personal character (honesty, self-discipline, love, purity and family concern), to the health of the community'.[14] The NFOL 'speaks out for Christian community standards'.[15] The Order of Christian Unity 'are Christians from all denominations united in trying to uphold the Christian standards which have been constantly eroded'.[16] The BFLA takes the view that 'the marriages, children, and single people of Bristol all need Christ'.[17]

Such militant and forthright Christianity, often presented in a rather dogmatic and inflexible manner, has not always been welcomed by the established churches. Indeed, the churches themselves have often been prime targets for attack on the grounds that they have been opting out of their responsibilities. The position of the Church of England is particularly interesting in this respect. The publication of *Honest to God* in 1963 and the follow-up work on 'situational ethics' by radical theologians such as those in the Southwark group are seen by Mrs Whitehouse as a crucial event in the retreat of many individual clergymen, and of the Church of England in general, from their moral responsibilities.

> The significance of the support for the Southwark theologians which flooded in from left wing humanists, will not be lost on anyone who has learned the hard way, that these people, who reject all concept of man as the child of God both for themselves and everyone else, make common ground with soft permissives wherever they can find them – in or out of Church.[18]

The Church of England itself was clearly divided. On the one hand there were those who, like the Southwark group, wanted to increase the church's relevance to the modern age and were sensitive to those who caricatured the Church of England as 'the Tory Party at prayer'. They saw radical change as the only way to make the church meaningful to a society which was becoming increasingly secular and in which matters of faith were seen as largely irrelevant. On the other hand there were those who felt that the church should stand by its established position.

This division led the church to consider the whole question of its relationship to the establishment. The debate culminated in the publication of *Church and State*[19] in 1970. Edward Norman pointed out at the time that a curious reversal was involved whereby conservatives in the church were arguing for nationalisation and the radicals for private enterprise.[20] In the event the church chose to continue to see itself as 'a national church professing a mission to the nation',[21] effectively continuing its establishment position. This naturally disappointed the radicals. Mervyn Stockwood wrote angrily in an article entitled 'Church and State: Empty Pews – Empty Debate': 'The Church of England might be better employed in finding ways and means of making the church a reality in the life of the state rather than in concerning itself with constitutional priorities.'[22]

Others, however, saw even a partial retreat from firm authoritative claims on behalf of the church as a disaster. When the church did speak it often did so anyway in a liberal voice, as when it supported the 1969 Divorce Act. Nor was the church's willingness to air its own internal divisions welcomed by everyone. After a television debate between clergymen of different social and political persuasions Mrs Whitehouse wrote: 'Many people felt that the cause of Christianity was not forwarded by the spectacle of so wide a disparity of views, and apparent lack of sympathy between a group of people all calling themselves Christian.'[23] The Director of the NFOL summed up his organisation's attitude to the churches in the following way:

> it was the silence that worried us so much. The church leaders right down to parish level seemed ignorant of or unwilling to face the facts of moral decay. Although they were the people who had the tools for identifying and combating it. That makes for a very serious responsibility.[24]

Certainly, the influence of the church has waned dramatically in the modern age. The time has passed when clerical teaching dominated administration and government. As J. R. Seagrave has recently noted,

> in making observations on moral issues the church has to rely for its scientific knowledge on working parties of lay experts in each field. The separation of the church from the political parties, the depolitization of religion and the acceptance of Christian heterogeneity by western government, the divergence in education, the rise in civil marriages, the growth of divorces and the increasing areas of moral neutrality have contributed to the church's difficulties.[25]

In a *Times* survey in 1971[26] a sample drawn from *Who's Who* were asked to rate the influence of certain groups and organisations on public life. Only 2 per cent thought that the Church of England was 'very influential', as opposed to 33 per cent who thought that this was true of the TUC and 52 per cent who thought it was true of the BBC. To a large extent the groups dealt with in this chapter share a desire to see Christian values influence public life far more than they actually do. This commits them to a more forthright, muscular Christianity which seeks to lay down and impose strict 'standards'.

A clear religious impetus, however, would obviously not, on its own, be enough to substantiate the claim that these groups share a common standpoint. After all there are Marxist Christians and there is a 'Gay Christian Movement' both of whom are anathema in the eyes of the moral protest groups considered here. We must, therefore, look closely at the directions in which their energies are harnessed in order to come to a full understanding of their significance. The concern with pornography, the effects of television, sexual permissiveness, divorce, abortion, the age of consent, and all the other myriad issues which have led moral protest groups to take up the cudgels can only be understood in terms of a more fundamental issue which shapes this concern. This is the problem of the family and its relationship with the bringing up of children which is seen as the central and most important 'victim' of permissiveness.

The protection of the family is obviously a central concern of the BFLA, which argues that 'all adults must be encouraged to put their family obligations first'.[27] The CSA also seeks to 'resist those influences which are undermining the family. The basic unit of our society.'[28] The OCU Charter states that 'any nation's stability depends on the quality of its family life'. It is this concern that allies the secular Responsible Society with those groups with an overtly religious viewpoint. The RS believes that 'the basic unit of society is the family which is founded on marriage. A lasting, happy marriage forms the best environment in which children can develop the uniquely human capacities for affection, generosity and creative imagination.'[29] The statement of intent drawn up by the NFOL in 1971 gave a similar prominence to the family, suggesting that 'there is clear evidence that a determined assault is being made on family life, moral standards and decency in public entertainment and the mass media'. The NVALA also sees the family as a major victim of media effects. 'Sexual innuendo and explicit sex trivialise and cheapen human relationships and undermine marriage and family life', states its introductory pamphlet on beliefs and aims.

This central concern with the family gives each of the concrete issues taken up by these groups its specific form. If the family is seen to be under assault and actually crumbling, then it is the child who suffers most, for children are especially vulnerable to exposure to permissiveness. Mrs Whitehouse's biographer recounts that, as a teacher,

> She saw a generation of youngsters exposed to a new form of insecurity – no longer the economic one that had been the plague of previous centuries but that of lack of moral guidance; through a failure within the Established English Church and within English Society itself, they were left without any yardstick of behaviour by which they could judge the world around them.[30]

The Responsible Society echoes these fears. 'We believe it is necessary to uphold standards of responsible sexual behaviour lest anarchy in this field should not only endanger the health and happiness of the present generation but in the end destroy the ideals of parental care and affection.'[31] The CSA proposes to 'protect children from exploitation and unwarranted intrusions into their privacy, specially in the field of sex, whether in the context of education or entertainment'.[32]

The vulnerability of school children to the effects of radical influences within education is a further major preoccupation which unites all the groups. Two issues predominate: the lack of effective Christian teaching and the failure to provide a moral context for the teaching of sex education. On the former issue, the OCU is particularly energetic in its call for the 'fourth R' to be given equal weighting in the curriculum of schools.

> In British state schools, Christian Education is in imminent danger of being replaced by so-called Religious and Moral Studies, which includes political philosophies. This means that children may soon be denied the right to discuss and study what Christ himself taught.[33]

One of the events which confirmed these fears and led to vigorous campaigning by both Mrs Whitehouse and the NFOL was the dismissal of Mr David Watson from a comprehensive school in Rickmansworth for refusing to treat the story of creation in Genesis as myth and not as literal truth. Mr Watson refused to implement a Department of Education and Science directive not to contradict the theory of evolution when dealing with Genesis. The NFOL commented:

> The Festival of Light is not setting itself up as a judge on how biblical interpretation relates to modern science. It is probable that even amongst Bible-believing Christians Mr Watson's personal views are not those of the majority. But they can command

considerable intelligent support, and it is quite wrong that such opinions should be suppressed and never mentioned to children. Mr Watson was, at all times, willing to put the views of liberal thinkers on Genesis before his students and there is every evidence that he did so regularly. The implications of the case for the teachers of religious education are very serious indeed.[34]

The nature of the call with respect to sex education is simple and straightforward. The BFLA exhorts its members 'to encourage the schools each one of us has contact with to teach sex education in the context of a committed life-long married relationship', and asserts that 'if sex education is taught only in Biology, an experimental science, then it is hardly surprising if children treat it as such'.[35] The NFOL warns parents that they 'must not take it for granted that sex education will be responsibly presented and NFOL has often stressed enquiries should be made as to what their children are being taught and the kind of moral values underlying the course'.[36] All the groups would agree with the sentiments of the OCU Charter, which states that 'the psychological and physical welfare of school children depends on guidance that inspires stable relationships, based on the ideal of chastity outside marriage and fidelity within it'.

Another target in this connection is the Family Planning Association which, again, is accused of dealing only with technical information, devoid of moral precepts. In a pamphlet aimed at 13–16-year-olds the FPA asserted: 'it is an act of irresponsibility to make love if you do not intend to have a child and have not taken adequate precautions'. The Responsible Society retorted:

> apart from the harm that this kind of advice can cause to young people's emotional lives by making it more difficult for them subsequently to enjoy a natural loving relationship, there is reason to think that the denigration of self control may be linked to the growing problem of drug addiction and violence among children.[37]

Similar fears are held about the publishers and editors of teenage magazines, who again are seen to be undermining the moral standards of young people by the dissemination of false standards, this time with a view to their commercial exploitation. BFLA members conducted a survey of such magazines and criticised them for their neglect of moral and religious concerns and their tendency, particularly in letter columns, to condone extra-marital sex. They concluded: 'we cannot wholeheartedly recommend any of these magazines for regular consumption. Apart from their serious religious shortcomings we feel they give an imbalanced view of life and create expectations that are unhelpful to teenage development.'[38] The Chairman of the Responsible Society also feels that such magazines are a subversive influence on the family: 'Within the field of the teenage magazine cult there is a very real attempt to separate teenagers from their parents and make the teenagers feel that their parents are old fashioned and don't know what's best for them.'[39]

Pornographic trends in the media and entertainment industries are clearly another major source of anxiety to these groups. This applies particularly to that combination of pornographic photographic material with 'permissive' and 'promiscuous' sexual attitudes and behaviour. The Responsible Society feels that 'one of the most serious threats to the future of the family and hence to the coming generation is sexual irresponsibility masquerading as freedom'.[40] The CSA newsletter bemoans the fact that 'there has been a sudden increase in the material in "girlie" magazines, which is frequently now of an utterly perverted and perverting nature, likely to disturb the normal sexual maturation of young people'.[41] Again the young are seen as particularly vulnerable. This point is echoed by the BFLA, which urges its members that 'newsagents need to be told when we find their displays indecent and offensive to us and our children. The least they can do is put offensive material out of sight.' 'Silence,' they remind their members, 'is taken by the media as acceptance, so let us be heard.'[42]

The battle-front with the communications industry is not, however, confined simply to pornography, but includes the much wider accusation that the media are responsible for falling standards generally, by propagating 'permissive', 'irresponsible' and 'decadent' values. The television and broadcasting industries are the main focus of these attacks. The NVALA claims that increasing television depiction of violence, immorality and blasphemy is itself a major cause of these activities in real life. 'Violence on television,' states its pamphlet *Aims and Objectives*, 'is a key factor in social violence and must be significantly reduced.' The OCU urges its members to 'use their customer power to require from the media Christian content and accurate information'.[43] Such complaints about the values underlying media products are always likely, despite claims to the contrary, to spill over from the moral to the political. Mrs Whitehouse, for instance, has objected to bias within the BBC's programmes because a schools programme on ethology 'constantly reiterated that man is merely a superior ape, likely to be guided by his feelings';[44] to *Cathy Come Home* because it gave a 'slanted' picture of homelessness;[45] and to Colin Welland's play *Leeds United* because it was a piece of propaganda for the left.[46]

The decline in standards is seen as a problem across the whole of society. Great concern is felt over recent legislative changes which, it is claimed, encourage promiscuity and undermine the family. The laws concerning abortion and divorce create particular concern in this context. The OCU claims:

> In the first ten years since the 1967 Abortion Act more than 1,000,000 unborn babies have been killed in Britain. In 1975 there were 147,000 abortions and 30,000 babies were killed at a stage when medical evidence proves that they can feel pain and many can breathe and cry. We believe this to be the greatest cruelty.[47]

The implications of the Abortion Act are equally worrying to the Responsible Society which fears that 'the widely publicised use of the word "unwanted" in relation to pregnancy and babies by the Health Education Council is creating a climate which encourages young people to trivialise the consequences of sexual relationships and insinuates that an unplanned pregnancy is disposable, simply because it is inconvenient'.[48]

It is the Divorce Act, however, which raises most hackles amongst the members of these groups. Rising divorce rates are cited again and again as the crucial evidence of the dangerous state of the modern family. When asked what had prompted the formation of the BFLA, the Chairman replied: 'we were really prompted by the divorce figures. These seemed to be not only increasing but accelerating. We were particularly concerned by the number of people involved in broken homes through divorce.'[49] The OCU similarly opposes unrestricted divorce because 'problems of violence, juvenile delinquency and mental illness increase daily as a direct result of broken homes'.[50] The Responsible Society also lays the blame for many social ills on the relaxation of divorce laws and claims that these are responsible for 'the steady increase in the number of disturbed children deprived of security and affection and incapable of forming stable loving relationships'.[51]

A further legislative concern is the much-publicised issue as to whether the age of consent should be lowered. As we have seen, the vulnerability of children is a central theme for these groups and, not surprisingly, they are adamantly opposed to what they see as the law turning its back on its duty to protect children. The NFOL makes clear its support for the present law:

> One of the great protections for girls has been what the law knows as the 'age of consent'. It is unlawful for a man to have intercourse with a girl under the age of sixteen because she is not regarded as being able to give realistic, responsible consent to such a serious act below age. This legal device must have saved thousands of girls from exploitation by unscrupulous men. It was introduced in the last century after many years of campaigning by dedicated Christians, horrified by the extent of child prostitution.[52]

In this context we may look further at the reaction to those deviant minorities who 'come out', in the sociologists' phrase,[53] and proclaim their sexual deviance and seek to convince the majority either of its essential normality or of its right to tolerance. Laurie Taylor has noted that sex offenders typically resort to some evasion of personal responsibility when accounting for their actions. 'I don't know what came over me' and 'I don't know what happened' are typical responses. Taylor further argues that sex offenders are covertly encouraged to take this view of themselves.

> It may be disturbing to some when abnormal ideologies are increasingly articulated but at least we can argue with their advocates. Perhaps the most disturbing alternative is to go on accepting that a large section of our society is subject to blackouts, over which they have no control.[54]

One group which has tried to articulate an 'abnormal ideology' is Paedophile Action Liberation (PAL). Mrs Whitehouse is clearly disturbed by its activities. Paedophilia (sexual desire in an adult for a child) is the latest abnormality on the list for 'normalisation'.[55] The NFOL is equally disturbed by the close association between certain 'subversive' groups, the National Council for Civil Liberties, the Campaign for Homosexual Equality and the paedophiles.[56] Whilst paedophiles are the recipients of more or less unqualified condemnation, hitting as they allegedly do at the very foundations of family life and childhood innocence, a much more circumspect view is taken of homosexuals. The Responsible Society's view is typical: 'In regard to the complex problem of homosexuality, for instance, social responsibility dictates that while the minority who feel attracted to their own sex should certainly not be persecuted or despised, they should refrain from proselytising a tendency which is increasing.'[57] Mrs Whitehouse also sees this as the main danger. 'Society, to its shame, once hurled this word at the homosexual. In our crazy "value free" society the "shame" is now attached to those who dare to say that homosexuality is less than "gay".'[58]

The stand that these groups take on each issue reflects their underlying concern with moral values, particularly as they affect the family and the upbringing of children. These views, of course, contain within them implicit assumptions about the causes of the 'decline' they are fighting against. To some extent the issues raised are political and have political implications. All the groups in fact claim to be non-political and are quick to point out that even though they may be looked on with approval by certain political figures they do not have any straightforward political connections. Despite these claims, however, certain groups and sections of society are singled out as 'the enemy' and are held to be responsible, either directly or indirectly, for the ills which they seek to combat. Views vary here from those who want to identify particular groups and conspiracies to those who talk vaguely of 'undesirable influences' and seem to imply that the 'enemy' is those well-intentioned but misguided liberal humanists and intellectuals who, to quote the Responsible Society, mistake 'the pollution of men's minds' for 'artistic freedom'. The influence of these people is seen as pernicious, precisely because they constitute an 'enemy within' powerful traditional institutions. 'Highly vocal minorities have so far secured something like a monopoly of influence, through entertainment, the media and indeed in many public bodies operating in the field of welfare and health and social problems.'[59]

At times, however, they are willing to be more specific and to accuse their opponents of being not merely misguided but actually engaged in the undermining of British society. All the groups, within varying degrees of intensity, name 'communism' as a major opponent and attribute some part of the recent moral decline to communist influence. The political implications of this can be overstressed. More sophisticated thinkers amongst these groups, such as the present director of the NFOL, are more circumspect about the 'communist menace':

> I don't think we can discount them, but I do think there are some people who overstress this particular thing. I think the number of people consciously trying to overthrow our society are very few. Now, there are some, I think, doing it unconsciously.[60]

Morrison and Tracey in their study of the NVALA take the view that the concern with communism in fact merely summarises a whole complex of attitudes. 'Frequent use of the term communist, as the embodiment of secularity, rests on its functionality as a summary statement, enclosing a variety of disparate groups and individuals, whilst at the same time metaphysically embodying the philosophical assumptions which NVALA opposes.'[61] Other groups which are considered to come under the communist umbrella include the National Council for Civil Liberties, the Albany Trust, the Campaign for Homosexual Equality and the Humanist Society.

The decline in society's moral order is not solely attributed to 'left-wing' enemies. The rampant commercialism of capitalism, unrestrained by moral values, is seen as almost as great a danger. As we have seen, not only are commercial enterprises engaged in pornography the objects of attack, but so too are the publishers of teenage magazines, the broadcasting companies and the entertainment industries generally. These implicit political concerns, opposing communism on the one hand and naked capitalist exploitation of the profit motive on the other, present us with an interesting parallel to the economic concerns of middle class groups, who feel squeezed between the more powerful interests of organised labour on the one hand and large corporations on the other.

Tactics and support

One of the most significant trends in the political life of modern societies has been the move to 'direct action' by groups of all kinds, particularly those not normally noted for irregular political activity. Bridget Pym made the following prognosis in 1974.

> Campaigning groups would still appear to have a function left, and in the 1970's we see them being joined by groups standing for new causes, such as conservation, pupil power etc. All completely unthinkable ten years ago. Another clear development is the resurgence of groups like Mrs Whitehouse's NVALA or the Festival of Light, formed to defend the traditional values of religion and purity. In the past the orthodox could depend on their values being defended by institutionalised groups such as the church, the Conservative Party, social workers, teachers etc. without having to think about the matter, but in the current world none of these agencies is totally reliable.[62]

This accurately summarises recent developments. The groups considered here all exhibit a similar structure and most campaign with an emphasis on their members' direct action. There is a core of central committee members who collect and collate information which is then distributed to the wider membership in the form of news-sheets, broad-sheets and the like. In these, members are urged to act on the various issues which are outlined by writing letters to their MPs, supporting petitions, contacting local councillors and other officials, making their presence felt in local schools, and generally creating an impact on the community. They are most successful when tackling relatively concrete specific issues. Thus, all the groups supported the very effective ABUSE (Action to Ban the Sexual Exploitation of Children) campaign through letters to the local and national press, the circulation of petitions, and contacting MPs. Their action culminated in the first reading of a private member's bill. Efforts to mobilise support for moral and religious issues in a broader front are more difficult to sustain. The history of the NFOL is salutary in this respect.

The general impetus behind the early rallies was by the mid-1970s being channelled into much narrower and more specific activities. As Roy Wallis noted in 1972,[63] there was an initial tension within the movement between the legislative orientation of those like Mrs Whitehouse who were interested in tangible changes to laws relating to obscenity and pornography, and those with an evangelical orientation. This, as another commentator noted,[64] was characterised by 'a lack of intellectual weight, a sharp division of the world in the "damned" and the "saved", salvation by faith, a lack of interest in political and social activity, and a reliance on the "conversion experience" as the test of genuine Christianity'. In 1971 and 1972 the evangelical wing predominated. Speakers on the platform denouncing contemporary social values, the corruption of the media, and the prevalence of pornography were drowned by young evangelists chanting 'Jesus, Jesus'. Booklets such as *Living Jesus Style* by Billy Graham were produced and distributed by the organisation.

The fervour of the first mass rallies did not persist. The organisation found that it could not go on having festivals for ever. As Roy Wallis has pointed out, the NFOL underwent a process of goal displacement when 'it became incongruous that such charismatic enthusiasm should be programmed annually, scheduled and organised, indeed that it should be routinized'.[65] With the appointment of Raymond Johnston as director in 1974 a new policy emerged. It has since operated as a moral pressure group researching problems, bringing these to the attention of its supporters and recommending various kinds of direct action to them. It also lobbies influential people such as broadcasting officials, MPs and ministers, puts out press releases on key issues and contributes to official bodies like the Williams Committee on Obscenity and Film Censorship to which it submitted a special report recommending that 'a reform of the law is long overdue if our society is to remain civilised and sensitive'.[66]

The influence of key personalities cannot be overemphasised. Mrs Whitehouse's newsworthiness and her ability to get her statements widely reported have made her an important focus for coordinating the activities of moral groups, as she did so successfully in the ABUSE campaign. Petition forms were distributed from the NVALA through other groups and returned there for collation. Letters from Mrs Whitehouse appeared in both the national and provincial press explaining the reasons for the campaign and urging support for it. Lesser known figures stand at the centre of each of the groups, but again their commitment and energy are crucial.

The example of the NVALA was an important influence on the foundation of both the BFLA and the CSA in that enthusiastic members felt they should take steps to set up local organisations to take a stand on moral issues in their regions. In fact there is both overlapping membership and extensive leadership contact between all the groups dealt with here, including the secular Responsible Society. Newsletters, details of meetings and publications of all sorts are sent to other groups as a matter of course.

The most important antecedents for each group seem to have been local church organisations, although, as we have seen, the NFOL and the OCU developed into their present forms from earlier and slightly different types of organisation. Whilst most of the groups are happy to see themselves as 'moral pressure groups', the Responsible Society differs in its secular standpoint and scientific orientation. Many of its founder members, including its present chairman, come from the medical profession and it sees itself more as a learned society than as a moral pressure group. Its major aim is 'to stimulate and promote appropriate scientific research into the social, medical, economic and psychological consequences of irresponsible sexual behaviour and to publish the results of such research'.[67] Therefore, whilst it does put out press releases, it does not engage in the lobbying of local and national figures engaged in by the other groups. This kind of work is not completely confined to the Responsible Society, however. The NFOL shares this more intellectual and academic approach in some respects. Both groups publicise the work of academics like William Belsen, David Holbrook and Dr John Court, who challenge 'liberal permissiveness' on the grounds of psychological and sociological evidence.

Elsewhere, attitudes to the social sciences are often ambiguous, if not downright hostile. Social scientists themselves are often seen as amongst the main propagators of permissiveness. Mrs Whitehouse accuses Herbert Marcuse of encouraging 'the suspension of guilt in the face of the perversion and inhumanity of pornography'.[68] In fact, Marcuse's analysis of the consequences of exploitative pseudo-sexuality in modern societies has much more in common with her own views than she realises.[69] As is often the case, radical and conservative social critics share a similar view of a problem, but differ widely over solutions.

When social scientists produce results that fall in the 'right' direction, however, they are eagerly seized upon and used as 'evidence' for the advancement of the cause. Research into the effects of television, for instance, has been particularly disappointing until recently. Psychological and sociological studies of communication have all tended to stress the importance of mediating variables between the content of programmes and their effects on recipients. Thus, a person's present attitudes and values, his location in the social structure, the social situation in which he received the communication, and the credibility the media had for him have all been shown by Tudor to be important intervening variables.[70] This work was highly critical of the 'hypodermic syringe' model which hypothesises uniform media effects and is implicit in the denunciations of the NVALA. However, William Belsen's recent research,[71] which is merely one project among many, was heralded as having at last furnished convincing proof of a measurable pernicious influence. The NFOL, for instance, claimed that the link between television violence and 'real' violence was now 'crystal clear'. Belsen himself is much more circumspect about his results although he does claim to have established some connection between television viewing and certain types of violence.

The other groups seem much more at home on the practical matters of getting involved with live issues such as sex education in schools, pornography in the local area, and putting out press releases on those moral matters which are creating the news of the day. Thus, many of the groups have had an upsurge of interest following incidents like the blasphemy trial of *Gay News* and the public interest in Jens Jørgen Thorsen's attempt to make a pornographic film about the life of Christ in this country. By and large the organisations feel that their press releases are not taken up by the media as often as they would wish, but this seems to be as dependent on the general news situation as on any systematic bias. Not surprisingly, the *Daily Mail* and *The Daily Telegraph* were mentioned in interview by more than one group as more likely to take up a press release than other newspapers.

Whilst most of the groups see the lobbying of MPs as a major activity, and many claim special 'friends' in both houses, as we have seen none are willing to claim party allegiance. By and large the Liberal Party seems to be the one that is felt to give least support and it is certainly the party with the least contact with any of the groups. At least one influential organiser feels that, whilst the Conservative Party is the most overtly favourable to their endeavours, in reality important progress is halted on certain issues because commercial interests become involved. The Labour Party, with the strong nonconformist religious backgrounds of many MPs, is felt to be at least as sympathetic on many questions.

It is probably at local level that we find some of the most interesting and active projects of these groups. These are also often the most successful. Thus, Mrs Whitehouse and the NFOL were certainly influential in the decision of the Greater London Council to retain its prerogative of censorship, a decision taken as the NVALA and the NFOL prayed in the rain outside County Hall.[72]

The CSA, as we have seen, was formed in order to ensure that local councils in Cornwall took their powers of film censorship seriously and was successful in persuading them to vet each film shown in the area. Since then the Association has become involved in monitoring sex education in schools and in persuading local newsagents not to stock pornography, and generally tries to keep moral issues live in the area.

The BFLA has also had a campaign aimed at newsagents for which it claims some success. It fought an unsuccessful battle with the Bristol Council to try to prevent a homosexual festival being held at the Corn Exchange in the city in 1978. In spite of losing that particular fight, the BFLA declared its intention of monitoring proceedings so as to make sure that they kept within the law, particularly with regard to minors. A further project which the BFLA hopes to get off the ground involves a Christian marriage counselling service. Likewise, both the OCU and the NFOL have been active in the inception of Pilot, a counselling service for Christian homosexuals.

The concern with moral issues is an international phenomenon, and all the groups have attempted to establish some international contacts. Many of these were fairly tenuous, and most of the groups express a desire to do more in this field. The OCU has sent a delegate to COFACE (Committee of Family Organisations in the Community of Europe) and the director of the NFOL has attended a Council of Europe conference on pornography in Strasbourg. Contact has been established with similar groups in North America, Australia and New Zealand and the British groups seem to reciprocate in the exchange of newsletters, pamphlets and information sheets. Certain groups like the Network of National Councils for Righteousness seem to have been active in establishing these contacts.

The success of such groups is impossible to ascertain. In general, tangible success has been more likely at the local level and over very specific issues like the ABUSE campaign and local government censorship. The groups have had, as yet, little impact on such large legislative issues as the Divorce and Abortion Acts. However, for both major political parties the defence of the family has been put on the agenda for inclusion in policy manifestos. Furthermore, the appointment of a minister for the family, a specific aim of the OCU, cannot be ruled out as a future possibility.

The support for such groups comes largely from the middle aged and middle class. Their spokesmen are even more defensive on this point than on their political affiliations, and it is very much against their basic beliefs to acknowledge 'class' as an important category. But in their analysis of support for the NVALA Morrison and Tracey conclude that it is mainly middle class, female and elderly. It is also over-represented by those in rural areas, the clergy, the older professions, small businessmen, traders and shopkeepers.[73]

Most of the organisations do not have full details of membership. Some, in fact, do not have members in the recognised sense at all. We have two sources of direct evidence apart from the NVALA study, however. In 1976 Roy Wallis was able to conduct a postal survey on people attending the NFOL rally in Trafalgar Square.[74] As one might expect at such a rally, the age distribution favoured the young, the majority being between 15 and 30 years old. The social class composition is clearly biased towards the middle class, as Table 5 shows.

TABLE 5

Respondents' distribution by Registrar General's
Social Classes (from R. Wallis and R. Bland,
Five Years On, SSRC, 1978 p. 32)

Class	Percentage
RGI	21·5
RGII	40·7
RGIII non-manual	16·6
RGIII manual	10·5
RGIV	5·3
RGV	1·1
Services	1·0
Unemployed	3·3
	100·0

N – 1056 (60 uncodable)

The membership of the Responsible Society (Tables 6 and 7) is, like that of the NVALA, biased towards the elderly, and interestingly, men slightly outnumber women.[75] Given its objective of modelling itself on the learned societies and not conceiving of itself as a popular organisation, such an overwhelmingly upper middle class composition is not surprising. It casts doubt on its claim to articulate a general view on behalf of the common man or the silent majority. This again need not surprise us. It fits in with much of the sociological research evidence which has universally found support for voluntary organisations in general, and religious participation in particular, to be a largely middle class phenomenon.[76] Morrison and Tracey relate, rather amusingly, that in reply to a clergyman who suggested that the NVALA had a poor public image because it drew most of its support from elderly middle class women, Mrs Whitehouse retorted that this was also the typical supporter of the

TABLE 6

Membership of the Responsible Society by age

	Percentage	Number
Under 30	7	47
30–39	12	93
40–49	23	166
50+	58	398
	100	704
	(unclassified)	15

TABLE 7

Membership of Responsible Society by Registrar
General's social classes

	Percentage	Number
RGI	33	248
RGII	29	207
RGIII non-manual	7	42
RGIII manual	–	–
RGIV	–	2
RGV	–	–
Unclassified (retired, housewives)	31	220
	100	719

Church of England and by the same logic did he want to question their teaching?[77]

In the next section we will explore the relationship between the middle class and moral protest more fully.

The roots of moral protest

The values that are being defended by the sort of puritanical moral protest groups examined here are those of the traditional middle classes. This is not to argue that their support is confined to such groups but simply that it is disproportionately located in them. Indeed, Roy Wallis quotes a letter in the NVALA periodical *Viewer and Listener*: '. . . it is an insult to the working class that anyone should suggest that the desire for standards of decency is a feature of middle class morality. The middle classes do not have and never did have a monopoly on virtue . . . for quite large sections of the working class moral codes have been very strict indeed.'[78]

To associate a particular set of values with the rise of a particular group is not, however, to argue that adherence to those values does not become more general. As Raynor argues,

The rise of the middle class accompanied the growth of an industrial society. In a sense they acted as a yeast to economic activity, serving to break down the old traditional loyalties and gaining for themselves the privileges of groups of higher social standing, through a thrusting and aggressive spirit of economic enterprise. To a large degree, then, we should expect that the ethics of this most dynamic part of the class system would be manifest in the ethics of the whole industrial community.[79]

Wallis makes a similar point in his assessment of the support for the NVALA with regard to the connection between support for that organisation and traditional middle class values by arguing that, once established 'as the dominant norms of a society and therefore as the basis for the attribution of respectability, they tend to become "lodged" in certain areas of the social structure where they are resistant to change'. He sees the middle classes as being differentiated between the traditional middle class and a new 'bureaucratic, salaried, and often effectively tenured middle class [that] has emerged with the technologization of production'.[80]

An influential attempt to explain the association between moral protest and the traditional middle classes has been made by 'status defence' theorists. This was first elaborated by Joseph Gusfield, an American sociologist in connection with the temperance movement in the United States.[81] Gusfield argued that status groups in decline in a society typically engage in a different style of moral reform to those status groups that are in a secure ascendant position. When secure, the style is assimilative and self-confident, seeking to win over the deviant and convert him. When in decline, however, such groups tend to favour a repressive and coercive style that seeks to defend their own threatened position. A repressive style of moral protest is seen as a form of 'status defence'.

Wallis originally took this view of the activities of the NVALA but has since repudiated the position,[82] suggesting that such concepts are only used to 'explain' beliefs which sociologists do not themselves hold and that the result is to explain away and invalidate those beliefs. He proposes the alternative concept of 'cultural defence' which seems to suggest that such groups should be seen as acting in response to cultural changes rather than to a decline in economic status. Morrison and Tracey are also critical of 'status defence' as an adequate explanation of moral protest with reference to the NVALA. They point out the lack of opposition to other groups inherent in the NVALA's policy statements and conclude that 'in general, questions of social status did not enter their universe of discourse and their concerns rested elsewhere at both the symbolic and concrete level'.[83] They prefer to analyse the NVALA in terms of responses to secularising trends in modern British society and to emphasise the religious values which underlie its members' views.

Roland Robertson argues,[84] however, that secularisation can be seen as evoking many different responses, all of them religious. The clergyman who espouses radical causes in order to bring the church nearer his parishioners is also responding to secular trends. But we still need to ask why the response takes the form that it does. The relationship between recent economic, social and cultural changes in British society and their effects on traditional middle class values, and family life, are worth exploring in order to understand the impetus behind moral protest.

The notion that the middle classes are a coherent group is clearly suspect. As Roy Lewis and Angus Maude noted in 1969, the debate about values divides the middle classes themselves. Black paper educationalists confront 'liberal' educationalists, theatre critics revile radical directors, while

the middle classes have seen their own middle class representatives (in all political parties) lessen the fabric of the traditional middle class moral code almost to the point of dissolution. Legislation on capital punishment, homosexual practices, gambling, divorce, abortion, censorship and race relations have been carried through by middle class MP's despite the doubts of many middle class people. . . . The middle class is at odds with itself.[85]

It is possible that the source of this cleavage can be understood in terms of differentiation between a traditional middle class that sees its values as being regarded as increasingly redundant and irrelevant to more and more areas of social life and a salaried, organisationally based middle class, whose values are essentially personal, expressive and consumerist. Bridget Pym elaborates the implications of this theory:

> According to this thesis the basis of morals had to change because it had become an obstacle to the economic interests on which we all depend. If this is true, it leads to the interesting conclusion that Mrs Whitehouse, with her stand for traditional values, is doing more to destroy capitalism than left wing MP's like Abse and Jackson.[86]

In looking at the composition of those pressure groups instrumental in the 'permissive' reform of the laws relating to divorce, abortion and homosexuality, Pym finds no evidence for the involvement of business interests and concludes that there is only a 'grain of truth' in this position. This may be to look for too obvious a link between structural change and overt political activity, however. Business interests are always wary of their reputation and would be unlikely to put themselves in the public eye by supporting 'permissive' causes. Yet the significance of advertising and marketing techniques for consumer values can hardly be doubted. The Midland Bank, for instance, is unlikely to see itself as an institution engaged in undermining the British way of life. Yet nothing could be further from the Protestant ethic than the exhortation to its customers to avail themselves of an Access card in order to 'take the waiting out of wanting'.

Many sociologists have in their various ways tried to characterise the trend away from the Protestant ethic in modern societies. David Reisman's influential work in the 1950s[87] suggested that nineteenth-century societies were characterised by the development of 'self directed' personalities, typical of the entrepreneur; people with firm inner convictions which enabled them to see through arduous life-projects. Man in modern society is, by contrast, 'other directed'. In an age of media and advertising we take as our main source of reference, not an inner ideal, but the approval of others. Our success is evaluated in terms of popularity, having the right image, being the right kind of person.

More recently Daniel Bell has put forward a similar thesis. He sees the old conventional bourgeois world view, based on traditional religious values, as being replaced by new cultural values:

> Modern culture is defined by this extraordinary freedom to ransack the store house of the world and to engage any and every style it comes upon. Such freedom comes from the fact that the axial principle of modern culture is the expression and remaking of the 'self' in order to achieve self-realization and self-fulfilment. And in this search there is a denial of any limits or boundaries to experience. It is a reaching out for all experience, nothing is forbidden, all is to be explored.[88]

However, these cultural values stand, for Bell, in sharp contradiction to the routinised, rational, bureaucratic, hierarchical nature of the techno-economic system of modern societies. This contradiction he sees as a continuing source of tension and conflict within modern societies.

In order to move between structural and cultural change and individual action, however, we need to see how such changes are experienced in everyday life. It has been argued earlier that the key issue for these moral protesters is the defence of the family and a concern with the vulnerability of children. In order to understand these more fully we must turn to two related problems.

The first is the consequences of the increasing cultural pluralism that these changes have prompted and the ways in which this has led to the normalisation of attitudes that others still see as deviant. The second is to look more closely at that area of living, the family, where these changes are experienced as being most threatening.

Albert Cohen has argued that an important element in the changing definitions of acceptable behaviour which accompany social change is the relationship between a person's identity, his conceptions of social reality and his definition of deviance:

> The counter culture, for example, is not only an attack on the existing institutions of property, authority, social stratification and so on. It is also an attempt to render worthless the currency in terms of which the identities of those who dwell comfortably within these institutions are currently valued. Were the counter culture to succeed, moral as well as material fortunes would be wiped out.[89]

One of the correlates of 'permissiveness' within British culture has been a willingness to tolerate diversity in the moral sphere. Thus many groups whose deviance would once have remained hidden in the dark corners of our society have felt able to come forward and justify themselves and their chosen activity. Paul Rock has called these people 'expressive deviants',[90] people for whom the ability to proclaim their difference from the rest of society represents the greatest personal liberation. The badges of the Gay Liberationists are not simply to identify themselves to each other but to proclaim publicly both their differentness and their lack of concern at that difference. This involves not accepting one's deviance apologetically but positively affirming it. Yet, Rock points out, 'expressive deviance prompts organized response'.[91] It represents a threat to the reality definitions of the world that it opposes. This is particularly true where these new definitions are taken up by the young. Whilst the young are, contrary to popular imagery, remarkably conformist (the young Conservatives are by far the largest political youth group), they are none the less more likely to become involved in expressive deviance, be it through seemingly bizarre pop cults like punk rock, delinquent groups like Hell's Angels or groups like Gay Lib.[92]

The media and communications industry, especially television, are likely to create moral indignation because they bring the expressive deviant with his subversive view of reality right into the home. These messages arrive in the centre of the family, the pre-eminently private sphere where men and women strive to maintain their view of the world as sacrosanct.[93] Small wonder that some people feel outraged and indignant when this inner sanctum is invaded by alien ideas.

If the family is, as we have seen, the key concern for these groups, then how far is there a crisis of the modern family? If such a crisis does indeed exist, are the middle classes particularly affected by it? Sociologists used to take a fairly optimistic view of the modern family. The main changes that had taken place were thought to be a move away from the family as a unit of production, based on extended kinship, towards the small nuclear family as a unit of consumption. Such a small unit was seen by Talcott Parsons to 'fit' the needs of industrial society for a geographically and socially mobile population,[94] whilst W. J. Goode[95] stressed the liberation of the individual from traditional family authority.

More recently, however, sociologists have reviewed the history of the family and a new emphasis has emerged. The modern family, it is now argued, is not unprecedented in terms of its size but unique in its child-centredness, and this feature is seen as being inextricably linked to the rise of the middle classes. A major influence here has been the work of Philippe Aries. Indeed, for Aries childhood itself is seen as a product of the modern family:

> In medieval society the movement of collective life carried along in a single current all ages and classes, leaving nobody any time for solitude and privacy. In these crowded collective existences there was no room for a private sector. The family fulfilled a function: it ensured the transmission of life, property and names; but it did not penetrate into human sensibility.[96]

The key transition was the development of the family as the pre-eminently private sphere which began in the emerging middle classes and which spread to the rest of society. This meant that children assumed a new significance and 'the family ceased to be simply an institution for the transmission of name and estate – it assumed a moral and spiritual function; it moulded bodies and souls. The modern family satisfied a desire for privacy and also a craving for identity: the members of the family were united by feeling, habit and their way of life.'[97]

Edward Shorter shares a similar view of the structural changes which distinguish the modern family. Its main characteristics are threefold. Firstly, there is a romantic rather than a pragmatic view of the relationship between husband and wife. 'Property and lineage would give way to personal happiness and self-development and criteria for choosing a marriage partner.' Secondly, children assume a prime importance. 'Whereas in traditional society the mother was prepared to place many considerations – most often related to the desperate struggle for existence – above the infant's welfare, in modern society the infant came to be the most important; maternal love would see to it that his well-being was second to none.' Thirdly, the family has become more isolated from the wider society.

> The traditional family was more a productive and reproductive unit than an emotional unit. It was a mechanism for transmitting property and position from generation to generation. While lineage was important, being together round the dinner table was not.[98]

Peter Willmott and Michael Young, writing specifically of the English family, argue that the traditional family was severely disrupted by industrialisation and that the modern 'symmetrical' family with its equal relationship between marriage partners and its private concerns took shape within the Victorian middle classes and only slowly spread to the rest of society through a process of 'social diffusion'. In an increasingly bureaucratic and impersonal society, they suggest, the family is increasingly seen as a haven of personal satisfaction. 'As the disadvantages of the new industrial and impersonal society have become more pronounced, so has the family become more prized for its power to counteract them.'[99]

The stress on individual satisfaction within the family may, however, have a 'centrifugal effect' especially as material restraints are lifted. 'The wife will be off to pottery or (as ever) her mother's, the husband to sailing or golf, the children to pop sessions and dances and all to their own friends.'[100]

Christopher Harris has taken these kinds of argument a stage further. He sees the modern privatised family as above all the arena where individuals 'seek to reproduce not their society/line/family but themselves through their children'.[101] This creates certain strains and tensions. Harris notes the consequences of these 'contradictions', which riddle the family. Parents may attempt to live vicariously through their children, swamping them with their own emotional needs and demanding too much of them. Laing's analysis of the relationship between schizophrenia and family life is considered by Harris to be concerned with this problem. Alternatively parents may opt out of their parental responsibilities because they fail to provide the satisfaction they require, such 'disintegrated' families leading to 'latch key' children and those whose life is lived mainly on the streets.

Another major contradiction, according to Harris, is the conflict between public and private responsibilities regarding the socialisation of children. Hence, attempts to contradict the 'reality' definitions within the family by educationalists over such matters as sex education may be strongly resisted, as will attempts to influence children through the dissemination of 'pop culture' through the media and entertainment industries. This contradiction is also well illustrated by reference to ambiguous attitudes to social welfare interference in the family. Public opinion pilloried the social workers who 'allowed' Maria Colwell's parents to beat her to death and waxed equally indignant over the 'police state methods' that Morecambe social workers were engaged in when they compiled a confidential list of homes where children may have been at risk of being 'battered'. In a similar vein to Harris, Shorter contends that the modern family has two main problems to face, 'an inherent instability in the couple itself and loss of control over adolescent children'.[102]

The 1978 Reith Lecturer summed up the plight of the modern family very ably indeed:

> It is not enough, as it once was, to look after bodily and physical security. Parents must, more than ever, answer for the mental and moral character of their sons and daughters, despite influences from the street, the so-called peer group, the mass media and youth culture, which they may fear they cannot escape. They are increasingly made to feel amateur in a difficult professional world. The old 'us and them' is now a generalised division between the inner life of families of all classes and the external forces.[103]

If any discernible themes emerge from a consideration of recent work on the family, they would, then, be the increasingly privatised nature of family life, with a concomitant increase in the strains on the marriage partnership and the tension between public and private responsibilities in the socialisation of children. As we have seen, the modern family has its roots historically in the middle class and it seems that these groups are still the most resistant to threats to it.

Of course, it would be surprising indeed if the members of these moral protest groups were articulating a full-blown sociology of the decline of the family. Whilst a sociologist would tend to see both the cultural changes associated with permissiveness and changes in the nature of family life as related outcomes of long-term structural changes in post-war British society, moral protesters tend to see a simple cause and effect phenomenon where the growth of permissive values is seen as straightforwardly leading to the undermining of the family.

When asked to give their own views on the state of the modern family and to say exactly why it is in need of 'protection', members of all the organisations discussed in this chapter were clear that the crisis of the family was essentially a crisis of 'values'. The Chairman of the BFLA summed up those which he saw as undermining the family: 'More leisure, more money, more independence of women, more sexual awareness, so-called liberation, but not really liberation, and a sort of if you don't like this then get something different approach – hedonism, I suppose, lack of effort.'[104]

The evils of affluence and a spurious commitment to individual liberation and freedom form common themes for members of these groups. Such values are seen as promoting a more egotistical attitude to life and to lead directly to the individual opting out of his family commitments and responsibilities.

A second major theme is that the dissemination of such values has led even the well-intentioned modern parent to lack the appropriate moral certainty for effective child rearing. Parental uncertainty was one of the main keys to the problem of the modern family emphasised by the Director of the NFOL:

> There is a lack of parental authority. I am not saying that they should use more stick. What I am saying is that there is a lack of certainty in their minds about moral values in general and they are not able to take a clear line almost from birth.[105]

This lack of certainty in the exercise of parental authority is thought to be exacerbated by the growth of professional groups claiming child-rearing as an area of expertise. Their influence is felt to undermine further the confidence parents have in their own moral standards with respect to their children. The Chairman of the Responsible Society summed up this view admirably:

> The impression one gets is that parents are no longer considered by some to be capable of making the right sort of decisions about their children. They don't feel capable of doing this and for some reason they are led to believe that they are not expert enough to know what is best for their children and ought to call in the experts, the paediatrician, the educationalist.[106]

As we have seen, the major victims in the retreat from parental responsibility are felt to be children. Moral laxity, uncertainty and the prevalance of false hedonistic values are all seen as major factors underlying contemporary problems such as truancy, violence and delinquency. These are the outward manifestations of the dissolution of the family. The Responsible Society feels that 'there is sufficient evidence from past studies of what the human child needs to establish some sort of parameters of what are best in family life'. It argues that 'a number of these secure building blocks are being torn apart'.[107]

Whilst the explanations given are different, the sorts of question asked and the kinds of problem raised do seem to reflect the contradictions and tensions in family life that are highlighted by social scientists. Indeed, their views do themselves seem to be subject to similar kinds of contradiction. Thus the problem of the family is seen to involve too much external interference with the way in which parents bring up children, on the one hand, whilst, on the other, parents are seen as failing in their duties either through having inappropriate values or by simply being uncertain about what values to apply. Clearly, if the second view is true then some sort of intervention is justified, and this is exactly what is advocated.

The criticism of 'professionals' for being both 'interventionist' and subverting parental authority is misplaced. The groups themselves are highly interventionist in terms of the legislative changes which they are seeking to institute. They would like to see the restoration of traditional notions of parenting and child rearing and are willing to see coercively imposed measures taken towards this end.

Conclusions

In conclusion it can be argued that anti-permissive moral protest amongst sections of the middle classes can be best understood in the context of two related social changes. The first relates to social and cultural changes in post-war British society in the direction of an increased emphasis on expressive and consumerist values and a correlative decreased emphasis on traditional values, particularly those connected with established religion. Loss of confidence in 'the Establishment', Church of England, civil service, education and government has been a major source of disillusionment and has provided the basis of much of the protest activity. The second concerns recent changes in the nature of the modern family. These have gone far in shaping the stand taken by the protest groups on issues such as divorce, education and the effects of the media.

As a final assessment it must be said that the collective and individual efforts of the groups have produced short-term local successes, and indeed some national victories too, albeit on relatively narrow issues. The long-term prospects, however, for their efforts to reverse major structural changes must be doubtful.

NOTES

1 See, for example, Mungham, G., and Pearson, G. (eds), *Working Class Youth Cultures*, Routledge, 1976.
2 Thomas, W. I., *Social Behaviour and Personality* (ed. Volkart, E. H.), Social Science Research, 1951, p. 81.
3 Weber, M., *The Protestant Ethic and the Spirit of Capitalism*, Allen & Unwin, 1930.
4 See Becker, H., *Outsiders*, Free Press, 1963, especially Chapter 8.
5 National Viewers and Listeners Association, introductory leaflet *What NVALA Believes*, 1966.
6 See Capon, J., . . . *And There Was Light*, Butterworth, 1972, p. 5.
7 Nationwide Festival of Light, introductory leaflet *Love, Purity and Family Life*, 1976.
8 Order of Christian Unity, *Crusade Against Cruelty*, 1974.
9 The Responsible Society, *An Invitation to Join*, 1975.
10 Community Standards Association, *Schedule of Purposes*, 1974.
11 Bristol Family Life Association, *Immediate Targets*, 1976.
12 Wallis, R., 'Moral Indignation and the Media: an analysis of the NVALA', *Sociology*, Vol. 10 (1976A), pp. 271–95.
13 Morrison, D., and Tracey, M., *Opposition to the Age – A Study of the NVALA*, Report to the SSRC, 1978.
14 Community Standards Association, *Schedule of Purposes*, 1974.
15 Nationwide Festival of Light, *Broadsheet*, Spring 1977.
16 Order of Christian Unity, *Our Christian Charter*, 1974.
17 Bristol Family Life Association, *Immediate Targets*, 1976.
18 Whitehouse, M., *Whatever Happened to Sex?*, Wayland Publishers, 1977, p. 15.
19 Church Information Office, *Church and State*, 1970.
20 Norman, E. 'Church and State: Establishment versus Radicals', *Spectator*, 12 December 1970, pp. 762–3.
21 Church Information Office, op. cit., p. 30.
22 Stockwood, M., 'Church and State: Empty Pews – Empty Debate', *The Times*, 10 December 1970, p. 8.
23 Whitehouse, M., *Who Does She Think She Is?* New English Library, 1970, p. 172.
24 Interview with Mr O. R. Johnstone, 21 March 1978.
25 Seagrave, J. R., 'A Model of Organized Group Behaviour for the Church in British Politics', *Parliamentary Affairs*, Vol. 27 (Autumn 1974), p. 399.
26 *The Times*, 1 October 1971, p. 10.
27 Bristol Family Life Association, *Immediate Targets*, 1976.
28 Community Standards Association, *Schedule of Purposes*, 1974.
29 The Responsible Society, *An Invitation to Join*, 1975.
30 Caulfield, M., *Mary Whitehouse*, Mowbrays, 1974, p. 17.
31 The Responsible Society, *An Invitation to Join*, 1975.
32 Community Standards Association, *Schedule of Purposes*, 1974.
33 Order of Christian Unity, *Christian Curriculum – The Crisis*, 1976.
34 Nationwide Festival of Light, *Broadsheet*, Autumn 1977.
35 Bristol Family Life Association, *Immediate Targets*, 1976.
36 Nationwide Festival of Light, *Broadsheet*, Autumn 1977.
37 The Responsible Society, *The Case for Responsibility*, 1975.
38 Bristol Family Life Association, *Teenage Magazine Survey October 1977 – February 1978*, 1978.
39 Interview with Dr S. E. Ellison, 23 March 1978.
40 The Responsible Society, *The Case for Responsibility*, 1975.
41 Community Standards Association, *Newsletter* No. 5 (Winter 1977), p. 1.
42 Bristol Family Life Association, *Immediate Targets*, 1976.
43 Order of Christian Unity, *Love and Life*, Summer 1977, p. 2.

44 Whitehouse, M., *Who Does She Think She Is?*, 1970, p. 147.
45 Ibid.
46 Caulfield, M., op. cit., p. 146.
47 Order of Christian Unity, *Our Christian Charter*, 1974.
48 The Responsible Society, *The Case for Responsibility*, 1975.
49 Interview with Mr A. Bush, 22 March 1978.
50 Order of Christian Unity, *Our Christian Charter*, 1974.
51 The Responsible Society, *The Case For Responsibility*, 1975.
52 Nationwide Festival of Light, *Broadsheet*, Autumn 1977.
53 See, for example, Musgrave, F., *Margins of the Mind*, Tavistock, 1977.
54 Taylor, L., 'The Significance and Interpretation of Replies to Motivational Questions: The Case of Sex Offenders', in Wiles, P. (ed.), *The Sociology of Crime and Delinquency in Britain*, Vol. 2, Martin Robertson, 1976, p. 52.
55 Whitehouse, M., *Whatever Happened to Sex?*, 1977, p. 59.
56 Nationwide Festival of Light, *Broadsheet*, Autumn 1977.
57 The Responsible Society, *The Case For Responsibility*, 1975.
58 Whitehouse, M., op. cit. (1977), p. 186.
59 The Responsible Society, *The Case For Responsibility*, 1975.
60 Interview with Mr O. R. Johnstone, 21 March 1978.
61 Morrison, D., and Tracey, M., op. cit., p. 31.
62 Pym, B., *Pressure Groups and the Permissive Society*, David & Charles, 1974, p. 148.
63 Wallis, R., 'Dilemma of a Moral Crusade', *New Society*, 13 July 1972, pp. 69–72.
64 Longley, C., 'Casting Some Much Needed Light, on the Festival of the Same Name', *The Times*, 9 July 1973, p. 14.
65 Wallis, R., 'Processes in the Development of Social Movements: "Goal Displacement" and "Routinisation of Charisma" in the Nationwide Festival of Light', *Scottish Journal of Sociology*, Vol. 1, No. 1 (1976B), p. 85.
66 Nationwide Festival of Light, *Obscenity, Indecency and Violence in Publications and Film Censorship*, submission to the Home Office Committee under Professor Bernard Williams, 1978, p. 30.
67 The Responsible Society, *The Case For Responsibility*, 1975.
68 Whitehouse, M., op. cit. (1977), p. 177.
69 Marcuse, H., *One Dimensional Man*, Routledge, 1974.
70 See Tudor, A., *Image and Influence*, St Martins Press, 1975.
71 Belsen, W., *Television Violence and the Adolescent Boy*, Saxon House, 1978.
72 See Caulfield, M., op. cit., pp. 157–8.
73 Morrison, D., and Tracey, M., op. cit., p. 103. For the full analysis of NVALA membership see their forthcoming book which is to be published by Macmillan.
74 Wallis, R., and Bland, R., *Five Years On*. Report of a survey of participants in the Nationwide Festival of Light in Trafalgar Square, London, on 25 September 1976, SSRC, 1978.
75 I am very grateful to the Responsible Society for allowing me access to their comprehensive records.
76 See both Reid, I., *Social Class Differences in Britain – A Source Book*, Open Books 1977, especially Chapter 7, and Brothers, J., *Religious Institutions*, Longmans, 1971.
77 Morrison, D., and Tracey, M., op. cit., p. 29.
78 Wallis, R., 1976A, op. cit., p. 283.
79 Raynor, J., *The Middle Class*, Longmans, 1969, p. 86.
80 Wallis, R., op. cit. (1976A), p. 283.
81 Gusfield, J., *Symbolic Crusade and Status Politics; The American Temperance Movement*, University of Illinois Press, 1976.
82 Wallis, R., 'A Critique of the Theory of Moral Crusades as Status Defence', *Scottish Journal of Sociology*, Vol. 1, part 2 (1977), pp. 195–203.
83 Morrison, D., and Tracey, M., op. cit., p. 18.

84 Robertson, R., *The Sociological Interpretation of Religion*, Blackwell, 1970, Chapter 8.
85 Maude, A., and Lewis, R., 'The Modern Middle Class – Values that are Worth Preserving', *The Times*, 20 October 1969, p. 10.
86 Pym, B., op. cit., p. 125–6.
87 Reisman, D., *The Lonely Crowd*, Yale University Press, 1970.
88 Bell, D., *The Cultural Contradictions of Capitalism*, Heinemann, 1976, pp. 13–14.
89 Cohen, A., 'The Elasticity of Evil: Changes in the Social Definition of Deviance', in Hammersley, M., and Woods, P. (eds), *The Process of Schooling*, Routledge, 1976, pp. 51–2.
90 Rock, P., *Deviant Behaviour*, Hutchinson, 1973, Chapter 2.
91 Ibid., p. 99.
92 See Milson, F., *Youth in a Changing Society*, Routledge, 1972.
93 See Berger, P., and Kellner, H., 'Marriage and the Social Construction of Reality', in Open University Reader, *School and Society*, Routledge, 1971.
94 Parsons, T., and Bales, R. G., *Family Socialization and Interaction Process*, Free Press, 1955.
95 Goode, W. J., *World Revolution and Family Patterns*, Free Press, 1963.
96 Aries, P., *Centuries of Childhood*, Penguin, 1962, p. 395.
97 Ibid, p. 396.
98 Shorter, E., *The Making of the Modern Family*, Fontana, 1977, pp. 25–6.
99 Willmott, P., and Young, M., *The Symmetrical Family*, Penguin, 1975.
100 Ibid, p. 273.
101 Harris, C., 'Family and Societal Form', in Scase, R. S. (ed.), *Industrial Society: Class, Cleavage, Control*, Allen & Unwin, 1977, p. 86.
102 Shorter, E., op. cit., p. 263.
103 Halsey, A. H., 'Reith Lecture No. 5', reprinted in *The Listener*, 9 February 1978, p. 178.
104 Interview with Mr A. Bush, 22 March 1978.
105 Interview with Mr O. A. Johnstone, 21 March 1978.
106 Interview with Dr S. E. Ellison, 23 March 1978.
107 Ibid.

Roger King

7.   The middle class revolt and the established parties

Introduction

In examining the response of the established parties to the middle class revolt it is important to note that the three major political parties are not monolithic machines but rather are capable of varying and sometimes contradictory reactions to events. Political parties are collective organisations, but they are also the actions and statements of individuals, groups, factions and committees. Some of these are more authoritative, influential or representative of party opinion than others. Consequently, in discussing the 'responses' of the political parties to ratepayers' protests, for example, or the demands of the self-employed, the actions of individuals, the pronouncements of semi-official groups, and authoritative party policy must be carefully distinguished.

It is possible to identify at least four ways in which the political parties could be said to have responded to the 'middle class revolt' of the mid-1970s. Firstly, they reacted through authoritative policy statements in party manifestos, official party publications, and commitments publicly given by party spokesmen. Two examples are the Conservative promise, in the manifesto for the general election in October 1974, to abolish the rating system, although they have subsequently become noncommittal on this; and undertakings by leading Liberals at National Federation of Self-Employed (NFSE) rallies in 1974 and 1975 to press for the abolition of the Class 4 National Insurance payments imposed on the self-employed by the Social Security (Amendment) Act 1975. In government even more authoritative expressions of party policy are contained in Bills, White Papers and circulars. An example here is the relief afforded small businessmen from capital transfer and corporation taxes by the Labour Government in the 1976 and 1978 Finance Acts.

Secondly, a party may react to events through the statements of groups within it, such as the Monday Club or the Selsdon Group in the Conservative Party, or the Tribune or Manifesto Groups in the Labour Party. This may involve conflict with other parts of the party. The Selsdon Group, for example, which advocates a movement back towards a free market society, has criticised proposals by the Party leadership for positive state intervention to help home owners and small farmers. In addition to such 'unofficial' pressure, and of greater importance in formulating the parties' responses to the 'middle class revolt', have been the activities of official working parties. Conservative and Liberal parliamentary committees on small businesses have produced major documents that form the basis of respective Conservative and Liberal policy towards the self-employed and small businessman.

Thirdly, influential individuals in the parties have responded to the middle class revolt with well-publicised and much-discussed speeches. Roy Jenkins and Peter Walker, members of opposing political parties, interpreted the middle class revolt as symptomatic of a general political malaise – the alignment of party loyalties around outmoded and disruptive class-conflict. Both called for a coalition of the centre, an alliance of moderates in all the major parties, which would reduce class tension through responsible government.

Finally, parties respond to political events locally as well as nationally and these responses may indicate different priorities. The Conservative reaction to the Ratepayers' movement in 1974–5 is a good example. Whilst the Parliamentary Party was mainly concerned with formulating general housing and rating policy, local constituency organisations were left to take electoral decisions about alliances and tactics when confronted with the prospect of Ratepayers' candidates in local elections.

It should also be emphasised that decisions by governments are not always fully consonant with the wishes or priorities of the rest of their party. For example, the Labour Government's efforts to help the small businessman after 1976 were as much a reaction to the persisting problems of unemployment and inner-city blight as the expression of general Party concern for the problems of the small employer.

Let us turn now to a fuller consideration of each of the parties' reactions to the 'middle class revolt'.

The Conservative Party

The Conservative Party is a natural habitat for the middle class. At elections the Party attracts most of the middle class vote whilst the themes of much middle class protest – claims for reduced public expenditure, lower taxation and greater economic freedom for the individual – are also strongly emphasised in Conservative rhetoric. Conservatives frequently refer to the indispensability of 'middle class values': allegedly those of independence, enterprise, order and family centredness. These are all seen as being central to the economic and moral wellbeing of the nation.

As has been shown, most members of groups comprising the 'middle class revolt' have Conservative sympathies. There are close individual links between the Conservative Party and organisations such as the National Association for Freedom, the Middle Class Association and many local Ratepayers' associations. Indeed such groups are part of the attempt by some Conservatives to 'ginger up' the Party, so as to return it to non-consensual and more bitingly partisan policies. Middle class militancy also coincided with the return of a Labour government in 1974 and legislation which appeared to threaten middle class interests. This included the repeal of the Industrial Relations Act, the increased power given to trade unions in the Trade Union and Labour Relations Act 1974 and the Employment Protection Act 1975, the introduction of Capital Transfer Tax, and the increase in National Insurance contributions for the self-employed in the Social Security (Amendment) Act 1975.

Yet it would be wrong to regard middle class protest as simply a Tory reaction under non-party labels to a new Labour government. Although the

Conservative opposition from 1974 used middle class protests as a stick to beat the Labour government, a Conservative government would probably have been faced with similar militancy. Heath's final two years in office were marked by measures which were opposed by many Party supporters: the turn towards tripartism and accommodation with the unions following the lack of success by 1972 of more aggressive economic and industrial strategies; salary and price freezes; the three-day week, which seriously affected small businesses; apparently expensive local government reorganisation; and persistent inflation and increasingly higher interest and mortgage rates.

Conservative budgets had added to middle income distress by redistributing income and benefits to the poor and rich,[1] and although the Government exempted small businesses from the worst of the price freeze restrictions, their competitive position with the larger firms was affected by the price constraints on their larger market leaders. Popular indignation that some were benefiting from inflation particularly afflicted Conservative supporters. Private opinion polls taken during the election campaign of February 1974 showed them to be even more angry than Labour supporters at lucrative property speculation and large bank profits.[2] A reservoir of disaffection amongst some of the Conservative Party's traditional middle class supporters had been created that would almost certainly have been directed at a re-elected Conservative administration continuing with similar policies and having to cope with the inflationary consequences of higher oil prices.

But a Conservative Party in opposition was better placed than a Conservative Government would have been to take advantage of the middle class protests that swelled throughout 1974 and 1975. At least five reasons may be advanced to account for the increased receptivity of the Conservative leadership to this disaffection.

Firstly, in opposition from February 1974, the Conservatives had most to gain from 'anti-government protest', particularly when it came from quarters normally sympathetic to the Party.

Secondly, opposition parties have to demonstrate policy distance from the party in office if they are to reassure supporters and emerge as a credible alternative government. This has become increasingly difficult in recent years as both major parties have employed similar approaches to managing the economy. But the 'middle class revolt' enabled the Conservatives to make the running on issues such as mortgage relief, rating reform and the plight of the small businessman.

Thirdly, Conservatives traditionally turn to their Party roots in opposition. A number of writers have noted the pre-eminence of the Party's 'free market' wing in these circumstances: an emphasis on market forces, with restrictions on state interventionism in the economy, lower public expenditure, and a stress on individual freedom in the face of large, collective organisations, notably the trade unions. Entrepreneurial activity, particularly that of the small businessman who is regarded as providing the 'seed corn' of future capitalist development, is particularly commended. This replaces the typical Conservative stance in government when the Party's 'collectivist' wing, that associated over the years with Butler and Macmillan, is in the ascendant. Policies then are 'progressive', socially aware, and involve state intervention and harmony between society's principal 'estates', employers and trade unions. Emphasis is placed on the directive role of a rational state, avoiding class or partisan goals and operating with the consent of fair-minded people in the interests of 'one nation'.[3]

Two explanations for this oscillation are usually offered. One, which Moran labels 'the theory of petit-bourgeois Conservatism', suggests that the re-emergence of 'liberalism', when the Party is returned to opposition, stems from the weakening influence on the Party leadership of civil servants and powerful interest groups such as the CBI and the TUC, all of which incline towards collectivism. The Party becomes more directly influenced by its petit-bourgeois activists who, like Sir Keith Joseph, 'express an anti-collectivist ideology hostile to big government, big unions and big business', which becomes reflected in party policy.[4]

An alternative explanation suggests that the oppositional ethic of British party government forces the parties to formulate policies that please their supporters but are unrealistic for the modern economy. The complexity of modern industrial society imposes objectively necessary policies on all British governments, Conservative or Labour, such as state interventionism and income controls. Once in office the 'irresponsibilities' of opposition are gradually shed.[5]

Although evidence for both viewpoints is sketchy, the Conservatives returned, rhetorically at least, to free market themes from 1974. Economic individualism, competition and the importance of small business activity were much more markedly commended by leading Conservatives than they were during office. To some extent this was because of the election of Margaret Thatcher as leader and the apparent dominance of 'liberal' economic thinking amongst her closest advisers, such as Joseph and Biffen.

The fourth reason explaining the increasing receptivity of leading Conservatives to the middle class revolt throughout 1974 is closely linked to the previous point: the middle class protest coincided with the leadership crisis in the Party that followed expulsion from office. Events leading to Mrs Thatcher's election as leader in 1975 highlighted the strengthening influence of the 'liberal' school within the Conservative Party. Tripartite and interventionist policies and those associated with them, particularly Heath and colleagues such as Walker, Carr and Gilmore, were openly criticised. Joseph, Boyson and Biffen were amongst those who strongly advocated a freer market economy, lower public expenditure and stricter control of the money supply. The decline of electoral support in February, and again in October, was interpreted as the consequences of fallaciously seeking the 'middle ground', a policy of appeasement which, it was claimed, alienated Conservatism's traditional middle class support.[6]

The swelling demands of ratepayers and small business groups reinforced the ascendancy of those demanding a break from consensual policies. Thatcher's leadership campaign was able to use these signs of general middle class disaffection to challenge Heath on a 'mistakes in government' platform. Both Thatcher and Joseph argued that Conservatism's traditional supporters were alienated by Heath's 'corporatism', and would only return to the Party once the values of freedom, enterprise, incentive and defence of the family were more sharply proclaimed by Conservative leaders.[7]

Thatcher was also helped in her challenge to the incumbent leadership by her direct association with Tory policies designed to rally disaffected supporters. As Opposition Spokesman on the Environment she was closely identified with Conservative proposals in the October 1974 election campaign to reduce mortgage interest charges, abolish rates, and provide help for the first-time house buyer. These are popular themes for Conservative supporters, particularly when rates and mortgage bills are high. Additionally, her skilful opposition to the Capital Transfer Tax proposals in the House of Commons debates in January 1975, especially her defence of small business interests, provided parliamentary support for her challenge at a crucial period in the leadership campaign.

Finally, there were straightforward electoral reasons for the Conservatives to take note of the middle class protesters. Having lost office the Party needed to attract potential votes from every possible source. A Department of Community Affairs was therefore created at Central Office aimed at establishing better organisational contacts with several important sections of the population. In particular, a Small Business Bureau was formed to combat small business disaffection with Conservatism's increasingly close association with big business. Its *raison d'être* was to form part of the concerted drive of the new leadership to boost flagging support; it was not simply a consequence of internal Party pressure by petit-bourgeois activists on the leadership. Small business passivity, not activism, was the problem that faced Conservative leaders as many traditional supporters preferred to make themselves heard in ratepayers' and small business associations rather than through Party channels.

We turn now to a more detailed examination of the Conservative reaction to specific aspects of the 'middle class revolt' described in the preceding chapters.

Ratepayers

The 'Ratepayers' revolt' surfaced shortly after the February 1974 general election. Disquiet had been expressed earlier, with criticism of the rating system voiced at the Labour Party local government conference in January and, in the same month, with the Association of Metropolitan Authorities warning of big rate increases to come. Only the Liberal election manifesto, however, addressed itself directly to the rates question. The Party committed itself to reforming the whole system by levying rates on sites only rather than the established practice of relying on the value of site plus buildings.

Protests remained muted until ratepayers were presented with their bills in March and April. Only then, when the full impact of the increases was felt – an overall average of 30 per cent, but much higher in some areas – did opposition become vociferous and organised. The explosion of discontent clearly surprised many politicians, including Anthony Crosland, Minister for the Environment and directly responsible for local government finance. Suggesting that it was 'a new social phenomenon', he remarked that 'certainly in my lifetime I have never known such universal anger and resentment at the level of rates'.[8]

Both Crosland and the Opposition Spokesman on the Environment, Margaret Thatcher, were lobbied in June by the two national Ratepayers' associations: the long-established National Union of Ratepayers' Associations and the newly-formed National Association of Ratepayers' Action Groups. NARAG sought immediate interim relief for ratepayers and the restructuring of local government finance. Among NURA's demands were: a government inquiry into local authorities' capital expenditure; an immediate increase in the rate support grant; the transfer to the Exchequer of education costs borne by the rates; and a local income tax to replace the rating system.[9]

The Conservative response to these aims, not surprisingly, was sympathetic. Conservatives share with Ratepayers' associations a commitment to low public expenditure, and Party leaders were impressed by the size and anger of the revolt. It appeared as a golden opportunity to berate the Government and also to appeal to disaffected Conservatives living in suburban and dormitory areas where Liberals took large slices of the Conservative vote in the February election. These areas had been particularly hit by Labour's decision to switch the emphasis of rate support relief away from the rural to the urban authorities.

Conservative determination to demonstrate its concern for the hard-pressed householder took a number of forms in the run-up to the inevitable general election later that year. At the end of June the Government was defeated by nine votes on a Conservative proposal which stressed the need for a fundamental reform of the rating system, urged the Government to introduce immediate interim relief, and asked that water and sewerage charges be included for rate rebate.

In the meantime the backbench housing policy group chaired by Margaret Thatcher was particularly influenced by the rates revolt. Convinced that rating reform could be a major electoral asset, the group rushed through a number of proposals for inclusion in the Conservative manifesto, which was published in August, and which was clearly designed 'to assist the middle classes'.[10] The manifesto proclaimed that housing was 'second only to the fight against inflation', and the various proposals were a major advance on those outlined in the February election. The Party promised to abolish the rating system 'within the normal lifetime of a Parliament'; pledged itself to reduce mortgage rates to $9\frac{1}{2}$ per cent; offered special help for first-time house purchasers in paying deposits; and guaranteed a statutory right to council tenants of three years' standing to purchase their homes at a price one-third below their market value.[11] Butler and Kavanagh remark:

> The housing policy was designed to remedy one of the most widely admitted weaknesses of the 1970–4 government: its failure to look after its own, the little man, the suburbanite, the would-be home buyer. Reports from candidates and agents emphasised this even more than private polls. If a specific policy could win back the new Liberals and at the same time hearten the party workers, it was the offer to help the owner-occupier.[12]

The Party's housing policies were well received by activists and were developed further during the election campaign. Mrs Thatcher was encouraged to announce that the cost of teachers' salaries up to a specified number of teachers for each local authority would be transferred to central government; expenditure on police and fire services would also qualify for increased Exchequer grants; first-time house buyers would receive £1 for every £2 they themselves saved towards a deposit; a 'broadly-based local tax' would replace the rating system; and the $9\frac{1}{2}$ per cent mortgage rate would be introduced 'by Christmas'.[13]

These policies clearly pleased the Ratepayers' groups. A number of their key aims were met by the proposals, including the plan to abolish the rating system, the transfer of education costs to central government, and the hint of a local income tax. NARAG was especially jubilant. It felt that 'the Conservatives have met our demands'.[14] Conservatives also claimed, with some justification, that the interim subsidy of £150 million to domestic ratepayers in the Government's July budget and the establishment of the *Layfield Committee* in June to investigate the whole basis of local government finance were a consequence of their pressure in the Commons.

Conservative housing policies surprised the Labour Party. Crosland described the proposals as 'midsummer madness' and vowed not to compete. But not all Conservatives were entirely happy with the schemes either, even if they were designed to win back the aggrieved middle class. Although home ownership is a moral virtue for nearly all Conservatives and to be encouraged because it strengthens initiative, independence and family-centredness, its positive pursuit by the state runs the risk of transgressing other Tory beliefs. For 'free market' exponents these interventionist policies in the housing market 'smacked of socialism' and appeared inconsistent with opposition to other subsidies (which mainly aided the working class).[15] They conflicted also with the competitive market ideology with which Margaret Thatcher later became identified in her leadership campaign.

The housing proposals of 1974 thus highlight the tensions in the Conservative Party between ideological consistency and class interest, and particularly between economic individualism and demands from supporters for state assistance. Although most 'liberal' Conservatives, including Mrs Thatcher, take care to emphasise that their commitment is not to a completely unregulated *laissez-faire* economy, but to a 'social market economy' where intervention is accepted so as to preserve competition by preventing restrictive practices, the emphasis remains on the competitive discipline of market forces. Ratepayers and small businessmen, however, prefer the immediate comfort of financial assistance to exposure to the cold draughts of a 'stand-on-your-own-feet' policy, and Thatcher's proposals recognised this.

The decision to transfer the cost of teachers' salaries to central government and at some future point abolish the rating system entirely also produced divisions between local Conservative councillors and Party leaders. The loss of power to raise revenue was an unacceptable blow to the belief in local autonomy which is deeply felt by many Conservatives, and they have continued to lobby the leadership for a reversal in policy. A Bow Group pamphlet written by Roland Freeman, a member of the Greater London Council and a former chairman of the Finance Committee of the GLC and Inner London Education Authority, argues that the pledge to abolish rates 'leaves the party with no definitive standpoint on local government finance'.[16] It suggests that education should be financed by a 100 per cent Exchequer grant, and social services by a 60 per cent grant. Housing would be financed as at present and the balance of expenditure by the districts would be met by rates, charges for local services and income from tourist taxes, stamp duty on house purchase, development land tax and relaxed limits for local lotteries.

Three major propositions on reforming the rating system are advanced in the pamphlet. Firstly, valuation should be abolished for the assessment of dwell-ings and a new method of assessment should be based on square metres. Secondly, non-domestic rating should be collected on a national rate pound-age. Finally, a tax relief scheme for domestic rates would give relief at the standard rate of income tax to all the ratepayers, and rating authorities would claim the amount of rates lost from the Exchequer. Whether they are adopted or not, these proposals indicate the difficulties the Conservatives are experienc-ing, following their pledge to abolish domestic rating and replace the revenue by 'taxes more broadly based and related to peoples' ability to pay'. The search for the alternative has proved fruitless and criticism within the Party over the commitment will undoubtedly continue.

The extent of the influence exerted by the Ratepayers' groups is difficult to gauge. They conveyed the 'gut' intensity of the issue to leading Conservatives, and Party policy in the October election included a number of Ratepayers' objectives. But middle class housing interests are part of the Conservative universe and the Party was seeking a *rapprochement* with its traditional, but disillusioned, followers after its defeat at the polls in February. NARAG and NURA were pushing at an opening door.

Furthermore, relations between the Conservative Party and the Ratepayers' organisations were not free from mutual distrust. Many Ratepayer activists, particularly in NARAG, laid at least part of the blame for the huge increase in rate bills on local government reorganisation which was passed in 1972 by the Conservative Government, and came into operation in April 1974. The growth of public expenditure under Labour and Conservative administrations, and the genuine belief of many ratepayers in non-partisan local politics, ensured a degree of coolness between Ratepayers' organisations and both major parties.

Conservative attitudes towards the Ratepayer activists were also ambival-ent. Although local Conservatives played a prominent role in a number of Ratepayers' associations, and some encouraged the withholding of rates pay-ments in the summer fo 1974,[17] Conservatives tended to view Ratepayers' methods with disquiet. Many in the Parliamentary Party in particular felt the Ratepayers' groups lacked proper political courtesy, had no idea how to lobby effectively (preferring mass, noisy demonstrations to quiet, informed brief-ings), and verged towards lawlessness, especially with the threat to withhold rates payments. To some leading Conservatives, the Ratepayers had little constructive to offer. Demands to cut the rate bill, coupled with calls to improve services, simply revealed that they wanted the earth the day before yesterday. Other Conservative members, recognising the strength of feeling behind the discontent and its electoral possibilities, tried to harness it to Conservative-led protests, such as the organisation of a national petition.

Relations between the Conservative Party and Ratepayers' associations at local level have depended on electoral circumstances. Where Ratepayers' groups are composed mainly of local Conservatives, they have tended not to intervene in local elections so as not to split the 'anti-Socialist' vote. In some cases, post-election alliances in the council chamber have been formed.

But local Conservatives have been increasingly irritated by the willingness of many of this new breed of Ratepayers' associations to keep their distance from the Conservative Party and run their own candidates in local elections. Many attracted support both from non-manual and manual workers in 1974 and 1975 and were not confined to the areas in which Ratepayer movements had previously tended to flourish. Some captured seats that would otherwise have gone to Conservative candidates. The newly elected councillors have thus frequently been regarded as untutored in the ways of political bargaining, partly because they lack the organisational back-up of the more established political parties.[18]

The announcement of Conservative rating policies in 1974 reduced much of the lobbying by Ratepayers' groups on the Party. Decreases in public expenditure, lower inflation and reduced rates increases took much of the force from the ratepayers' revolt. As a consequence, the influence exerted by Ratepayers' organisations on the Conservative Party, which mainly consisted of conveying the sense of injustice and depth of feeling of many ratepayers, has ebbed. None the less, where Ratepayers stand for council, they are frequently courted by the Conservatives and may enter into coalitions with them.[19]

Small businessmen and the self-employed

Most small businessmen normally vote Conservative and many are active in Conservative constituency associations. Workers in small enterprises, less unionised and reluctant to strike, are also likely to be more sympathetic to Conservatives than those in larger concerns. Even the self-employed skilled craftsman, who has stronger links with the Labour Party, symbolises, alongside the small employer, many of the virtues which Tories admire – thrift, order, innovation and independence.

Although Conservatives regard the small entrepreneur as a source of economic vigour and enterprise – 'the seedbed from which a wealth of innovative technology and new products spring' – he has social and moral importance too. David Mitchell MP, chairman of the Party's Small Business Bureau, has described the small businessmen's social contribution as 'providing key local services to the consumer around the clock', offering a more personal environment to the employee and enriching neighbourhood life at every turn. Politically, they provide a 'counterbalance to the concentration of economic and political power in the hands of the state'.[20] At the 1975 Conference, Edward du Cann characterised small independent businesses as 'the seed-corn of our future prosperity, lively, ingenious, self-reliant, the anti-Marxist barrier, Conservatism in practice, and the true picture of free enterprise, honourable, patriotic and acceptable'.[21]

Yet the feelings are not always reciprocated by the small sector, and the Conservative Party's hold on its political loyalties is often less than secure. Amongst shopkeepers, Bechhofer *et al.* have indicated that whilst 'support for the Conservative Party is strong' it is none the less 'tinged with scepticism'. They suggest that the Conservatives' ambivalence in office, the neglect of the small traders in favour of big business, reduced the shopkeeper's commitment to a sceptical acceptance of the Conservative Party 'as the lesser of two evils'.[22] Recent economic and political events have reinforced this anti-politician cynicism. The small business sector has declined in most advanced industrial societies in post-war years, but nowhere more so than in Britain. The Report of the *Bolton Committee* on Small Firms (1971) remarks that 'the declining share of small enterprises in economic activity is a universal process but . . . has gone further here than elsewhere'.[23] Inflation and large rate rises have added to the financial difficulties of many small enterprises, eroding liquidity and increasing bankruptcies. The inability of both parties to deal effectively with the economic situation has augmented small business distrust of government. More specifically, the Heath Government's neglect of the claims of the smaller employer and actions which were less acceptable to them than their larger competitors, such as price and rent controls, credit restrictions, and the introduction of VAT, led to disaffection with the Conservative Party and loss of support, often to the Liberals, in the 1974 general elections.[24]

The Conservatives have tried strenuously to reforge these damaged links with the small business sector since the 1974 defeats. Loss of office and the need to recover electoral and activist enthusiasm; Labour legislation; a new, more sympathetic, leadership under Mrs Thatcher; and the challenge of the small business and self-employed associations have helped their efforts. Specific actions have included: parliamentary harrying of the Labour Government; the creation of the Small Business Bureau to provide better institutional connections to the small businessman; the publication of a new policy document on small businesses; and regular individual contacts with the small business sector.

The initial policies of the newly returned Labour Government in 1974 were especially helpful in enabling Conservatives quickly to portray themselves as defenders of small business interests against the depredations of a Socialist administration. Healey's first budget in March, which increased income and corporation tax and raised employers' flat rate National Insurance contributions, was condemned by Sir Keith Joseph as 'a declaration of war on the middle classes'.[25]

Members associated with the newly constituted Conservative backbench small businesses committee were thus handed a number of opportunities to defend the small businessman by an administration seeking to pass or publish as many of its legislative proposals as it could, as quickly as possible before the expected early election. Some of the proposals appeared especially threatening to the small entrepreneur: the repeal of the Industrial Relations Act and the strengthening of the closed shop provisions; a Capital Transfer Tax to replace the much-evaded estate duty; a Social Security (Amendment) Bill implementing a special Class 4 National Insurance contribution from the self-employed; and the Employment Protection Bill which was to make it more difficult for employers to sack their workers and which extended the rights of trade unions to information about company affairs.

None of this legislation was aimed specifically at small businessmen. But they were most vulnerable to it. Larger companies have specialised legal and personnel departments and are able to handle administrative burdens imposed by government better than small firms. Most even viewed many of the provisions in the Employment Bill as good industrial practice. Smaller firms, however, faced with encroaching trade unionism in their sector, were worried by the closed shop legislation and the restrictions on dismissing employees. Capital Transfer Tax, too, also threatened smaller, family-owned businesses passed on from generation to generation.

Labour's price restrictions also harmed small companies, though, in the main, they were simply a continuation of policy initiated by the Heath Government. The first Prices Bill introduced by Labour abolished the Pay Board and imposed a 10 per cent cut in gross profit ceilings. Price-fixing and other restrictive practices in almost all commercial services, from travel agents to undertakers, were also outlawed, thus disturbing small businesses' preference for maintained price levels.

Conservative MPs used government decisions to demonstrate their own commitment to the small business sector. They initiated debates on the price restrictions, opposed the new tax proposals, sought easier rates payment facilities for small businesses, and were particularly active during the passage of the Finance Bill. A series of amendments pressed for the exclusion of small traders from certain sections of the price code; for relief from the corporation tax increases; and (successfully) for raising the level of profits before corporation tax was imposed.

The October 1974 manifesto reflected this redoubling of effort on behalf of the small trader. A much more substantial section on small businesses than had been contained in the February manifesto included plans to 'shield' small businesses from 'crippling' taxation; promises of an enquiry into the availability of long-term finance for small firms; proposals to ask planning authorities to consider the 'social' contribution of smaller firms in city centre redevelopments; and ways of extending tax relief for small employers. All, however, were vague and short on detail.[26]

The Social Security (Amendment) proposals, which stimulated the formation of the National Federation of the Self-Employed, provided the Conservative Party with its major opportunity for re-establishing better relations with the small trader. The NFSE's campaign to fight the 8 per cent Class 4 levy was warmly welcomed by Conservatives, and Geoffrey Howe, speaking at an NFSE rally, went so far as to promise that the Party would be prepared to use its majority in the House of Lords to remove the self-employed provisions.[27]

The new Conservative leadership was sympathetic to the NFSE, and its emergence was warmly welcomed by such leading figures as Heseltine, Du Cann and Thatcher at the first Conservative Conference under the new leadership in October 1975. During her first public speech at the Conference, at a reception given by the NFSE, Mrs Thatcher criticised the Heath Government 'for allowing the cause of small businesses to go by default', welcomed the formation of 'an effective working group', and, remarking that she had been 'born into trade', went on to hope 'that next time you will know which party to support'.[28]

Yet Conservative attitudes to the NFSE, and their aim to abolish the 8 per cent Class 4 contribution in particular, were to some extent hypocritical, for the principle that the self-employed should have graduated National Insurance contributions had been introduced by the previous Conservative Government in the 1973 Social Security Act. This mirrored the commitment by both major parties to the idea of graduated pension benefits and graduated contributions required to pay for them. The Act had introduced the Class 4 contribution on the self-employed, albeit at 5 per cent, and the Labour Government was proposing to extend this to 8 per cent.

Conservative leaders were thus in a potentially embarrassing position when faced with the NFSE's demand that the Class 4 contribution should be abolished entirely. Their solution was to wage a vigorous campaign against the increase, although it could be argued that this largely reflected the erosion by inflation of the value of the original proposal, which dated from 1972. Furthermore, the self-employed were to benefit from higher pensions and also earn the same pension rights as employees, although they were to pay only 65 per cent of the combined employer–employee contributions. Compared with the principle of the Class 4 contribution, to which the NFSE was and is implacably opposed, it is difficult to see that the rise in the levy which the Conservatives were opposing represented the 'grave and growing danger to personal independence and freedom' claimed by Geoffrey Howe. Since the Conservative failure to press for the complete abolition of the Class 4 principle, the NFSE has remained distrustful of Conservative intentions.

Perhaps a clearer recognition of Conservative concern for the small business sector has been the creation of the Small Business Bureau. This was formed as a section within the Department of Community Affairs at Central Office in 1976. It is chaired by David Mitchell MP, who is also chairman of the Conservative backbench committee on small businesses, and is a subscription-based organisation with over 2,000 individual and 300 corporate members. There are branches in nearly 80 constituencies. Group membership includes the NFSE, the Union of Independent Companies, the Association of Independent Businesses, and the Association of Self-Employed People, and contacts have been established with similar European organisations such as the European Medium and Small Business Union (EMSU) and the Mittelstand in Germany. The Bureau organises national and regional conferences, publishes a monthly newspaper with a 50,000 circulation and provides Conservative speakers for small business organisations.

Under the aegis of the Party's backbench committee on small businesses, and serviced by the Conservative Research Department, the SBB collates small business grievances, often collected from questionnaire campaigns, such as 'Operation Letterbox' on the Employment Protection Act. It thus provides a valuable source of information for the backbench committee, whose members used its services to pursue the Labour Government over plans to regulate small business contractors, the effects of the Employment Protection Act, and the extension of municipal trading sought by some Labour councils. The Bureau also supplied much of the research back-up for the Conservative policy document on the small business sector, *Small Business, Big Future*.[29]

Three major reasons behind the development of the SBB may be identified.

Firstly, towards the end of the Heath Government and well before Mrs Thatcher's successful challenge for the leadership, a number of Conservative backbenchers had become seriously alarmed at the increasing distance between the Party and the small business community. The result was the backbench committee on small businesses, many of whose officers are small businessmen themselves. In turn, the SBB was conceived as a means of institutionalising better contact with small businessmen and the self-employed through the Central Office machinery. The SBB could also provide well-researched briefs, invaluable to any backbencher, that would enable the parliamentary campaign on behalf of the small business sector to become more effective.

Secondly, it became part of a wider organisational effort, following Thatcher's election to the leadership, to establish links with sections of the electorate previously ignored or alienated by the Party. Although the new leadership is sympathetic to small business interests, they are not the only group with whom better relations are desired. The Department of Community Affairs coordinates a reinvigorated Conservative Trade Unionist section, the revived Federation of Conservative Students and new Anglo-West Indian and Anglo-Asian divisions, in addition to the Small Business Bureau.

Thirdly, the growing number of associations representing the self-employed and small businessmen posed a challenge to the Conservative Party's claim to speak for the small sector which was difficult to ignore. The Party could only be weakened if large numbers of 'natural Tories' campaigned in associations outside it, many of which were determined to stress their non-party affiliations. The SBB is thus a forum for establishing relations with these organisations and a way of influencing small business politics. It also claims the overriding advantage of political influence lacked by the small business associations – a 'direct line to the Shadow Cabinet'.

Yet a sense of mutual suspicion still pervades relationships between the Conservative Party and the associations. Initial approval of the NFSE, for example, waned with the internal divisions and financial problems which beset that organisation. The general reluctance of small business protesters, espe-cially the NFSE and ASP, to moderate their stridency and to insist on the repeal of legislation such as the Employment Protection Act, the Social Security provisions, and Capital Transfer Tax, which the Conservatives simply wish to modify, also irritates many Conservatives, particularly in the Parliamentary Party. It reinforces their view that small businessmen are political unsophisti-cates and they prefer the quieter methods of other, well-established organisa-tions, such as the CBI Small Firms Division and the National Chamber of Trade.

In return small business organisations remain sceptical of Conservative intentions. Previous Conservative administrations have favoured larger inter-ests and the NFSE remains critical of the introduction of the Class 4 National Insurance contributions by the last Conservative government. Present Conser-vative policy on the small business sector abounds with vague promises. Both *The Right Approach to the Economy*[30] and *Small Business, Big Future* make few detailed proposals for helping the small businessman. An earlier promise to repeal Capital Transfer Tax is missing from both documents and there is a refusal 'to go for another widespread upheaval in the tax system'.[31] The emphasis is on reducing rates of taxation and 'drawing the teeth' of the much-hated Employment Protection Act. Even the favourably disposed 'social market economy' wing of the Party is prevented, by its adherence to a more competitive climate, from advocating positive subsidisation of small busi-nessmen.

Strong criticism of these 'piddling amendments' have come from ASP and AIB/SBA who fear amended Labour legislation would simply be restored by the next Labour government.[32] It is also doubtful whether small entrepreneurs would benefit as much as the bigger employers from a central plank in Conservative economic policy – the reduction in higher rates of taxation. Tories regard this as encouraging initiative, rewarding success and generating savings for investment in smaller enterprises. But few small traders are liable for income tax at the higher levels.

Notions of what constitutes a 'small business' vary. The *Bolton Report* settled for employers with no more than 200 workers as their basis, although the figure varies in official definitions used by governments of the industrialised nations, from as low as 100 in Belgium to 500 in the United States. For some the term 'small businessman' may conjure up a picture of a small shopkeeper or trader whilst for others it may be a reasonably large manufacturing employer. What Conservative leaders think of as 'small business' is very much bigger than what many 'small businessmen' think of themselves as engaging in. George Ward may have become a symbol of the small employer battling against big collectivist battalions, but to the small shopkeeper he must look – with his employees, his factory, his money and his racehorses – very much like a large businessman. Tory leaders and small businessmen may be using the same label to refer to different animals. Hence the suspicions and disappointments over tax cuts. To a self-employed painter and decorator or a struggling shopkeeper the highest rates of tax have little relevance; but the Tory leadership's 'small businessman' is really a small-scale employer of labour earning big money but facing severe tax problems.

Small business organisations are aware of the tensions between small and big interests in the Conservative Party. Their suspicions are fed by Conservative acceptance of most of Labour's closed shop legislation. The actions of some big business contributors to the Conservative Party – Allied Breweries, for example – in insisting to its small suppliers that goods must be delivered only by union labour is cause for considerable anxiety.[33] Closed shops are anathema to many small employers, although regarded much more favourably by bigger firms who see them as guaranteeing order and discipline in industrial relations.

Small businessmen are as likely to fall foul of local government decisions as they are of central government action. Thus a complaint voiced with feelings at the 1978 Small Business Bureau annual conference was the lack of control Conservative councillors exercise over their officials. Planning departments are especially resented, and some Tory local authorities are accused of allowing, or even encouraging, planning officers to increase the number of enforcement orders against small business premises or delay small business planning proposals.[34]

Finally, a further problem for Conservative relations with the small business organisations is the all-party consensus that has developed on the need to develop the small sector. As the next section indicates, the Labour Government became more receptive to small business interests and a number of measures were introduced to help them. This has made it that much more difficult for Conservatives to re-establish their 'special relationship' with the small entrepreneur. Until the present Conservative government translates its promises to help the small entrepreneur into more positive aid than that supplied by the last Conservative administration, mutual suspicion between the small business organisations and the Conservative Party will persist.

White collar trade unionism
Tensions between small and big business in the Conservative Party are also reflected in attitudes to trade unionism. Small employers, generally anti-union, lead calls to outlaw the closed shop. But the big corporations prefer strong and effective trade unions, and many believe that post-entry closed shops, where a worker has to join a union, are positively desirable.

The Conservatives have clearly accepted the arguments of the big employers on this issue. Although proposing to give better compensation to those sacked as a result of closed shop legislation, and widening the 'conscience' exemption clauses, Thatcher and Prior have resolutely set themselves against the introduction of new legislation outlawing the closed shop. The Tory leader has also continued to appeal to Conservatives to join unions wherever possible in an effort to build up a political alternative to Labour in the trade union movement.

An organisational consequence of these moves has been the strengthening of Conservative Trade Unionists (CTU) who now form a section within the Community Affairs Department. (Although constituted over sixty years ago, the CTU was virtually moribund by 1974.) Seven new full-time officials were appointed in 1975, under a new head, John Bowis, after which there followed a spirited drive for recruitment. By the beginning of 1978 there were 250 groups, varying in size from 20 to 200 members. The 1977 annual conference was attended by over 1,200 delegates.

The CTU has been most successful in appealing to white collar workers, and is strongest in unions such as the NUT, the Civil and Public Services Association and ASTMS. Penetration of ASTMS is most striking. Many Tories (including half the Central Office staff) now belong to the union's various branches. This has worried ASTMS so much that it disbanded the Central London branch. A national Conservative trade unionists group has been formed from members of the union and a major objective is to change the basis of the union's parliamentary committee, which consists only of Labour MPs, by including some Conservative members. The CTU has also entered the fray of union elections by publicising lists of 'moderate' candidates.

Conservative encouragement of trade union membership may appear at odds with the individual self-help ideology with which the Party is identified under Margaret Thatcher's leadership. But three explanations may be offered. Firstly, much Conservative anti-unionism is aimed at the 'political' strength of the trade union movement – its apparent subversion of parliamentary power – rather than at its industrial role. Secondly, a Conservative government requires reasonable working relationships with both the trade unions and the large employers. The commitment not to legislate against the closed shop is an inducement to both these groups, and indicates the continued influence of 'collectivist' thinking in the Party.

Finally, for electoral reasons the Conservatives are compelled to seek support wherever they can. The Department of Community Affairs was set up after the election defeats in 1974 from fear that the Party was losing touch with several important sections of the electorate. Heath's confrontation with the miners in 1974, which was thought to have alienated many putative Conservative trade unionists, gave added urgency to the need to re-establish organisational links with the trade union movement. White collar groups of workers are expanding in size, are becoming more unionised and are likely to be more receptive to Conservative appeals than manual trade unionists. The electoral importance of this stratum, despite the contempt levelled at the 'new middle class' by some Conservatives, is likely to make them an important target group for the Conservative Party in the foreseeable future.

The Middle Class Association and the National Association for Freedom
The National Association for Freedom and the Middle Class Association, which became the Voice of the Independent Centre and merged with NAFF, have been little more than Conservative ginger groups seeking to push the Party towards a more individualistic and anti-union position. The substantial personal contacts between the organisations and the Party are indicated by the presence of prominent Conservatives in both the MCA and NAFF. Yet their influence on Conservative policy has proved minimal, and they are disliked by Conservatives associated with the Party's 'collectivist' wing.

The Middle Class Association was formed in 1974 by John Gorst, Conservative MP for Hendon, as much in reaction to Heath's corporatism as to an incoming Labour government (see Chapter 1). Its specific aims, however, were little different to the Conservative mainstream: opposing Capital Transfer Tax, seeking reduced public expenditure and demanding restrictions on trade union power. As approximately 80 per cent of its subscribers were either members, or lapsed members, of the Conservative Party, this is perhaps hardly surprising.[35]

Relations with the Party were never harmonious. The criticism by the MCA of Heath's 'lack of commitment to free enterprise' led to acid exchanges between Gorst and the 'Heath' wing of the Party. But the attitude of other Conservatives to the MCA was not particularly encouraging either. Although Gorst was actively associated with Thatcher's successful challenge for the Party leadership, her close associates were wary of a connection with the MCA. Many thought it would fragment Conservative support, was outside the political mainstream, and was unlikely to survive. Thatcher expressed the real fear that visible links with an organisation called the Middle Class Association would make it even more difficult to lose her middle class, suburbanite image.

NAFF, however, has received much more sympathy and tacit support from Conservatives both at national and local levels. Among the many points of contact, outlined in detail in Chapter 4, the most notable are perhaps Mrs Thatcher's appearance at a NAFF fund-raising dinner, Sir Keith Joseph's support for NAFF's stance at Grunwick and Robert Moss's contributions to Mrs Thatcher's speeches, notably the 'Iron Maiden' attack on Russian attitudes to detente. Although NAFF insists that it is a non-party organisation, its council contains a number of Tory MPs, one of whom, Rhodes Boyson, is one of the Party's spokesmen on education. Friendly Conservative backbenchers also raise questions in the Commons on NAFF's behalf or write for *The Free Nation*.

However, despite the rhetoric of Mrs Thatcher's speeches, NAFF's influence on Conservative policy is limited. Its attack on Prior's conciliatory overtures to the unions and his apparent acceptance of the closed shop has been criticised by many Tories. It has been condemned by one senior Tory MP, who has likened NAFF's activities to those of the National Front, as constituting 'extremist infiltration' of the Conservative Party.[36] Conservative leaders, even NAFF admirers, are also more interested in winning electoral support and securing willingness of trade unions to work with a Conservative government than in ideological purity. NAFF threatens the Party's institutional interests, and its methods are more of an irritant than the emollient which Party unity demands.

Moral/religious organisations

There are no institutional links between the Conservative Party and 'moral protest' groups such as the Festival of Light and NVALA, although many Tories are prominent in such organisations. It is difficult to refer to 'party policies' on moral matters, as all the major parties prefer to leave them to individual consciences and private members' bills. 'Moral' or 'religious' arguments arouse passions and deeply felt convictions, and this intensity is a potential source of internal divisiveness for the major parties and runs the risk of offending supporters.

Nevertheless, Conservatives display a more overt ideological sympathy with the 'moral protesters' than the other major parties. This is particularly noticeable in their shared commitment to preserving traditional family relationships. Many Tory aims, such as parental choice in education, the maintenance of law and discipline, the defence of the small family proprietor, and more selective welfare measures, are allegedly based upon the notion of the virtuous, productive family unit. Taxation policies, too, are sometimes justified in a similar fashion. Sir Geoffrey Howe complains that 'the present structure of Capital Transfer Tax makes insufficient allowance for the special importance of the family in the social structure'.[37]

Undoubtedly, the fears of the moral/religious groups at increasing permissiveness, the trivialisation of sex, and the decline of religious authority reflect traditional Tory concerns. Since the election of Mrs Thatcher to the Conservative leadership these groups, and especially Mrs Whitehouse, have received greatly improved access to Conservative leaders and a more sympathetic hearing. The Shadow Cabinet spent considerable time discussing Mrs Whitehouse's campaign against the use of children for pornographic purposes (ABUSE),[38] and the Child Pornography Bill was sponsored by the Conservative MP, Cyril Townsend. Of all the characteristics associated with Thatcher's leadership it is perhaps this concern for traditional moral virtues, which she shares with Sir Keith Joseph, that most clearly distinguishes her from recent Conservative leaders. Furthermore, a concern with the preservation and strengthening of family life provides the centre of her thinking on housing, taxation, thrift, self-help and less government. Not all Conservatives share these views. Strong commercial instincts within the Party militate against stricter controls on 'the selling of obscenity',[39] whilst there must be limits to the moral restrictions a party committed to individual choice can impose as increased state intervention in the moral sphere could be thought to sit uneasily with the advocacy of less governmental intervention in the market place. Young Conservatives have noted this contradiction and, regarding Mrs Whitehouse's campaign as a threat to individual liberty, have been criticised when suggesting that economic liberty should be matched by greater freedom from 'paternalistic' moral laws.[40]

There is no simple Conservative reaction to the 'middle class revolt'. Whilst most of the protesters are clearly Conservative and bitterly critical of any Labour Government, too much of their hostility is directed at the Conservative Party for them to receive an unequivocal Tory embrace. Their methods, too, are a source of disquiet, for the dissenters eschew quiet political lobbying for public demonstrations and meetings which offend the constitutionalist soul of the Conservative Party. The Party's institutional interests are challenged by internal Party divisiveness over the attitude to adopt towards NAFF, the threat posed by Ratepayers' candidates in local elections, and the syphoning of 'natural Tory' support to ostensibly non-Tory organisations.

However, the level of support in Tory ranks for the 'middle class revolt' must not be underestimated. Many Conservative MPs are willing to press some of the arguments in the Commons and a number are members of the 'middle class groups'. The Party's corporate interests in opposition were served by taking up the themes of discontent, which enabled it to embarrass the Government, please its activists, and reforge damaged links with disaffected supporters.

The stirring of middle class discontent also coincided with the resurgence of the Party's 'liberal' wing and Thatcher's successful challenge for the Conservative leadership. It was used to support the claim that the Conservatives had lost traditional supporters and that this had resulted in electoral defeat. Rhodes Boyson, for example, held that the consensual middle-ground politics of the 'one-nation' Conservatives associated with Heath did little to distinguish Conservatives from the Labour Party, and that this alienated the small businessman and the ratepayer. Sir Keith Joseph argued that compromises on the middle ground, which he distinguished from the common ground, will always be subject to irresistible pressure for even more government intervention in the interests of social justice. A 'ratchet effect' – a constant movement to the left – is generated, he claims, by *rapprochements* with the Party's collectivist opponents.[41]

But although the 'middle class revolt' coincided with the re-emergence of the Party's 'liberals', it was not directly responsible for it. Loss of office for the Conservatives often leads to leadership crises, Party introspection and a return to 'liberal' roots. There were signs of increased 'liberal' influence before the end of Heath's leadership, with restrictions on public spending and money supply in 1973, and divisions over incomes policy in the Shadow Cabinet following the February 1974 defeat.[42] In so far as middle class disillusionment with the Conservative Party contributed to the 1974 electoral defeats, which led to a crisis in the Conservative leadership and strengthened 'liberalism', it had an indirect influence in changing the Conservatives' ideological emphasis.

Thatcher is clearly more sympathetic than Heath to the 'middle class' cause. She is often identified with the suburban middle classes, and speaks approvingly of the 'middle class values' of thrift, independence and self-help. The Conservative leader is more sympathetic than Heath to small business organisations, NAFF, Mrs Whitehouse and the Ratepayers' associations, whilst the Party's links with white collar trade unionism have been strengthened under her direction.

Yet contrasts with Heath and previous Conservative leaders should not be overstated. Party leaders in opposition are closer to their supporters and activists than they are in government when civil servants exercise more influence. Free from the responsibilities of office, leaders are more open to the suggestions and attentions of groups sharing the Party's ideological universe. But once in power, the language of opposition often fails to be translated into positive proposals.

Conservative policy in May 1979 is remarkably free of detailed commitments. There are only vague promises of help to the small trader, whilst the commitment to abolish the rating system has run into substantial opposition within the Party, and policy on its replacement has yet to be announced. Moran points out that existing plans to cut public expenditure are 'considerably less distinctive than surface appearances might suggest' and much of the Party's attack on public spending after 1974 simply 'focused on the inadequacies of control procedures'.[43] Conservative economic policy, as outlined in *The Right Approach to the Economy*, reveals little sign of Josephite influence, retaining the option of an incomes policy and acceptance of the closed shop.

'Collectivist' sentiment still wields considerable authority in the Party, and has to be accommodated by Mrs Thatcher. Leading 'collectivists' have reacted to what they fear may be a return to the 'bolt-holes' of 'middle class politics' and there is support for Peter Walker's view that the Conservative Party is not a 'class party but a national party' based on middle of the road opinion.[44] In more specific terms Ian Gilmour, a member of Mrs Thatcher's Cabinet, has expressed the fear that a reduction in the role of government intervention in the name of individualism may lead to a diminution of the state's authority in the maintenance of order.[45]

The electoral implications of an appeal specifically oriented to the middle class are considerable. As Reginald Maudling once remarked, 'even your most ardent supporter cannot vote twice over . . . the votes that matter are the ones that are not committed'.[46] An electoral campaign as the saviour of the middle classes unnecessarily narrows the Conservative electoral appeal. Furthermore, Labour sympathy for the small businessman, taxpayer and householder allows less room on that part of the political spectrum for such a stance to be especially distinctive.

The Labour Party

Organised middle class disaffection was most vociferous in the two years following the return of a Labour Government in February 1974. Much of it was a response to Labour's policies and aimed at reversing or severely curtailing the Government's initial legislative programme. Fears covered a range of issues: new taxes, such as Capital Transfer Tax; the self-employed National Insurance levy; higher public expenditure; changes in the rate support provisions to favour urban areas; the restoration of trade union powers; and the extension of employees' rights. Budgets which were claimed to 'soak the rich', restrictions on income increases for higher earners, and large mortgage and rate increases combined in those first two years to ensure that for some the Labour Government was 'waging war on the middle class'.[47]

Although many in the Labour Government regarded the 'middle class revolt' as a form of disguised Toryism, their response to the varied demands was not entirely negative. Efforts were made to modify tax proposals and price controls in order to take account of small business interests, whilst ratepayers received record aid in 1974. The Government had little option but to make some response, for the middle class is no longer, if it ever was, a homogeneous grouping. The extension of the modern state has been accompanied by a 'new middle class' of public employees with attitudes to the role of the state, trade unionism and the Labour Party which differ from those of the traditional petit-bourgeoisie. Since the early 1960s and the days of 'the white heat of the technological revolution', the Labour Party has appealed to what it believes to be a more educated, meritocratic-minded middle class. Many Labour voters are ratepayers and were badly hit by the rates increases of 1974 and 1975.

Under Callaghan's leadership, the Labour Government became particularly receptive to the plight of the small businessman. Its major economic priorities, albeit under pressure from the International Monetary Fund, were the reduction of inflation and the expansion of the 'productive' manufacturing sector by shifting resources from public to private expenditure. This sprang not just from attempts to solve Britain's persisting economic malaise but also from the traditional Labour sympathy for the 'little man' – the small craftsmen in particular – and dislike of large private concentrations of economic power.

Ratepayers

The unprecedented ratepayers' protest of 1974 took the Government by surprise. The strength of feeling behind this 'new social phenomenon', as Crosland characterised it, brought a number of concessions. A subsidy of £150 million was given to ratepayers in the July budget together with an increase in the needs allowance used for calculating rebates. The Government had already been forced into promising an enquiry into local government finance (the *Layfield Committee*) following its defeat in the Commons on a Conservative rates motion the previous month. Following its return to office in October the largest rate support ever granted to local authorities was announced – an increase from 60·5 per cent to 66·5 per cent. This was larger than even the local authorities expected, and was accompanied by a once-for-all payment of £350 million to cover underestimates of inflation.

Yet the attitude of many in the Labour Party towards the Ratepayers' associations and the hard-pressed householder remained ambivalent. Labour's manifesto for the October election took a harsher line than either the Conservative or Liberal manifestos on help for the ratepayer. It 'appreciated the anxieties of ratepayers' but went on to argue that

> everybody has to face the fact that demands for better local services have to be paid for. And these have to be reconciled with demands for more local autonomy and less central direction. Public services have to be paid for by the public; the only argument is about how to share the costs, not how to avoid them.[48]

This reflected the suspicion with which the Labour Party continued to regard Ratepayers' associations, for traditionally such organisations have frequently acted with or on behalf of the Conservatives for local electoral purposes.

Nevertheless many in the Labour Party are concerned with the question because rates, by being a tax on property rather than income, contain a marked regressive element. Furthermore, rate demands often vary, in a seemingly arbitrary way, between different parts of the country. Accordingly, as increases spiralled, the rating system came under increasing examination. At Labour's local government conference in January 1974 and the Party conference in October 1974 this concern was reflected in the speeches of a number of delegates, who called for a more equitably based tax on income to replace the rating system. This was not taken up in the Party's submission to the *Layfield Committee* in 1975, which suggested the introduction of a broader based income tax, although it wished to retain the essentials of the existing arrangements. The Labour evidence also followed the Conservative proposal to transfer the cost of teachers' salaries to the central Exchequer.

The Government recognised that the Ratepayers' revolt of 1974–5 was not simply an anti-socialist movement. Some local Ratepayers' associations were hostile to all the major parties and others contained many Labour sympathisers in their ranks. Council tenants have a rates element in their housing charges, now notified by many authorities in rent books, and a number of these joined local Ratepayers' associations. In a few areas, though it was perhaps for electoral reasons rather than a reflection of their social base, protests even took place through 'Rent and Ratepayers' groups.

In addition to the genuine grievances and resentment that lay behind the 'ratepayers' revolt', two other factors explain the relative generosity of the Labour Government's response. Firstly, until October 1974, it was a minority government faced with an early election. It could not afford to ignore the substantial section of public opinion angered by rate rises. Secondly, the Conservatives produced proposals for helping the house-owner, including the plan to abolish the rating system, which shook the Government. Crosland denounced this and promised not to compete. But if it could not compete, the Government could not ignore the Ratepayers in an election year, and Labour's measures in July and October aiding the ratepayer and householder reflected this.

Perhaps as important as the rate-relief measures in dampening the 'revolt' was Labour's counter-inflation measures, especially the restrictions on public expenditure. Cash limits on local authority spending after 1975 brought down rate rises in line with lower rates of inflation. The Government's general economic policies also helped to take the wind out of the Ratepayers' organisations, although they still retain the balance of power in some council chambers.

Small businessmen and the self-employed

The change in establishment attitudes towards the small business and self-employed sector is remarkable. All influential opinion now favours more positive encouragement of small entrepreneurial activity as a way of reducing unemployment, revitalising the inner cities and aiding innovation. The change in Labour thinking is most marked, for the Party is normally identified as being hostile to the generally Tory-inclined small businessman. But the important appointment of Harold Lever with special responsibility for small firms, tax concessions, promises to alleviate the administrative burden, general praise for the efforts of the small sector and the inquiry by the Wilson Committee into Financial Institutions, which is particularly concerned with the problems faced by small and medium-sized firms in raising capital, mark the more favourable attitude of the Callaghan-led Labour Government.

This compares with the relatively scant sympathy for the economic travails of the small business sector in the first two years of the Labour administration. Early budgets contained no special relief for small businessmen, and aid to ratepayers was confined to the domestic ratepayer. The first budget which afforded specific tax concessions to the small trader, in April 1975, balanced the scales by introducing greater powers for VAT inspectors to seize business records.

This comparative disregard for small businesses in part reflected the belief that much small business and self-employed agitation was 'politically inspired' against Labour's taxation and employment protection policies. There was a genuine belief, reiterated by Shirley Williams in the passage of price control legislation, that the Labour Government should take account of the less vociferous 'consumer' interest. Nor was it felt that the smaller sector were suffering any more than other sections of society. Gregor McKenzie, Parliamentary Under-Secretary of State with special responsibility for small firms, suggested that 'the people to help small businesses are big businesses, who should pay up promptly, and the suppliers, who should stop squeezing them, and the people to see that this is done is the CBI'.[49]

Not that everyone in the Labour Party felt this way. In December 1974 a surprisingly large number of Labour peers helped to defeat the Government in the Lords over the Class 4 National Insurance levy on the self-employed. Lord George-Brown and Lord Houghton both described the proposal as 'an injustice'. Nor were all small businesses' interests ignored in the passage of legislation. The 1974 Prices Bill, after representations from the Retail Consortium, contained substantial concessions to small retailers on the plan to cut gross profit ceilings by 10 per cent. Retailers with a turnover of less than £25,000 were finally exempted from the provisions. The Government also beat a definite retreat on the more controversial features of the proposed Capital Transfer Tax. Although Mr Joel Barnett, Chief Secretary to the Treasury, argued that it was a mistake to imagine that all small businesses are good, a clutch of important concessions for small businesses were announced.

None the less, the Labour Party remained generally suspicious of the anti-union mentality of small employers, the poor working conditions of their employees, their scope for tax avoidance, and their Conservatism. The stridency of the new self-employed and small organisations in the early years of the Labour Government and the championing of the small business cause by the Conservatives added to this distrust.

Yet by the middle of 1976 the mood in the Government was much more sympathetic to small business grievances, and a number of measures were taken to help small firms. For example, the 1976 Finance Act provided Capital Transfer Tax and Corporation Tax relief at the lower levels. But it was not until the following year that the Government's quickening interest in the small entrepreneur was demonstrated by 'direct' action. The 1977 Finance Act further raised the ceiling for the reduced rate of Corporation Tax and increased the VAT threshold from £5,000 to £7,500. A Small Firms Employment Subsidy was introduced in July to encourage manufacturing firms in Special Development Areas employing fewer than fifty people to take on more staff.

In September 1977, Harold Lever and Bob Cryer were asked by the Prime Minister to make a special study of small firms. The October budget contained the first fruits of Lever's involvement: the general level at which Capital Transfer Tax became payable was raised; the rules for trading companies were eased for smaller firms; the Small Firms Counselling Service was extended; a Market Entry Guarantee scheme to encourage firms to develop a new export market was announced; the interest rates charged by COSIRA (Council for Small Industries in Rural Areas) were reduced; and the Small Firms Employment Subsidy was extended. The 1978 Budget continued the concessions aimed at helping small enterprises, notably by raising the VAT threshold. From April 1978, the self-employed benefited from the reduction in their Class 4 National Insurance contributions, from 8 per cent to 5 per cent, although employer and employee rates have risen.

It is likely, for a number of reasons, that Labour will continue to favour small businesses and the self-employed. Firstly, it is easy to exaggerate the extent of the change in the Party. A Labour Government, after all, set up the *Bolton Committee on Small Firms* in 1969, and its legislation in 1974 and 1975 included some concessions to small business interests. Traditional ideological antipathy to the small trader in the Labour movement is also over-emphasised. There is an important guild socialist tradition which idealises the self-employed small craftsman and favours self-governing small cooperatives. The Party's left wing contains many (especially those hostile to the Common Market) who are virulently opposed to larger concentrations of economic power. In June 1974, for example, Tony Benn publicly declared himself to be a 'firm believer in small and medium sized companies and I intend to make sure that industrial policies do more to help small businessmen'.[50]

Secondly, there is increasing recognition that an expanding small business sector may be the most realistic hope for quickly and noticeably reducing persisting unemployment. Restrictions on public sector employment and the shedding of labour by larger, capital-intensive firms seeking increased productivity rule out efficient labour expansion in these sectors. This argument is particularly attractive to trade unionists.

Thirdly, the Labour Government became convinced that the decay of many inner-city areas could only be alleviated by boosting small entrepreneurial activity to strengthen their social, economic and rateable bases.

Fourthly, the growth and persistence of small business feeling in new organisations such as ASP, UIC, AIB, and NFSE, but also in well-established bodies such as the CBI and the National Chamber of Commerce and Trade, has produced a source of pressure that is not easy to ignore. These groups convinced ministers that the small business sector experiences special economic distress and suffers more from Government restrictions than smaller enterprises in other industrial societies. Harold Lever operated without his own department and took considerable representation from the small business interest groups. They were particularly influential in securing Capital Transfer

Tax relief in the October 1977 budget. Finally, the Liberals also influenced Government attitudes to the small sector, especially on the need for tax concessions. However, the effect of the Lib-Lab pact on the Government's economic measures for small enterprises must not be exaggerated. Liberals were knocking on an open door with their proposals for encouraging the small entrepreneur, and reinforced rather than fundamentally altered the direction of Government thinking.

None the less, attitudes within the Labour Party to the small employer remained tinged with suspicion. Although recognising the electoral force provided by 7 million employees in the small sector, there was an unwillingness by Labour ministers and backbenchers to meet one of the central demands of the small business organisations – exemption from the provisions of the Employment Protection Act. Trade unionists are particularly unwilling to create 'two classes' of employee by allowing small firms to escape the 'social responsibilities' imposed by recent Labour legislation. Furthermore, efforts to gain union recognition in smaller enterprises could lead to more 'Grunwicks' and increase Labour suspicions of small employers. The Labour Party's traditional commitment to preserving and extending workers' rights could place limits on the amount of help a future Labour government could extend to small enterprises.

White collar trade unionism

The relationship between the Labour Party and white collar trade unionism is much more problematic than the historically close friendship between the Party and manual unions. A number of white collar unions are not affiliated to the Labour Party, which is rare for manual unions, whilst others have a substantial portion of their membership contracting out of the political levy which is paid into Party funds. White collar employees may be expected to display more 'natural Conservatism' than their manual colleagues, and the recent recruitment drive by the Conservative Trade Unionists (CTU) into ASTMS illustrates the desire by the Tories to extend their influence.

Furthermore, Labour's relationship with 'middle class' unionism has been tarnished by Government policy. Middle managers have suffered from flat-rate increases in incomes policy whilst public sector unions have found it difficult to avoid tight income restrictions when their employer – the Government – is determined to set an example to other employers in keeping to its wages guidelines. Union fears in the public sector were also aroused by the Government's 'industrial strategy' which aimed at expanding the manufacturing base and pruning public expenditure.

However, the Labour Party has recognised the need to afford representation to the increasing number of white collar unions and May points to the importance of the Liaison Committee as an important instrument in this respect.[51] Some white collar unions are also beginning to sponsor their own MPs as a way of increasing links with the Parliamentary Party. As the proportion of manual to non-manual workers in the trade union movement decreases, and as the CTU continues its renaissance, it seems likely that Labour will seek to forge stronger institutional contacts with white collar unions.

The Labour Party's reaction to both the freedom groups and the moral/religious associations need not detain us. Organisations such as NAFF and the MCA are viewed simply as Conservative pressure groups and therefore the Party is hostile to them. Attitudes to the moral/religious 'backlash' are more complex, but in general there appear to be few individual links between the Party and these groups.

It is easy to exaggerate party divisions on moral issues. Moves in the Commons to tighten the law on child pornography found all-party support in February 1978. On the abortion question many Labour members, especially Catholics, are as implacable in their opposition as the most die-hard Tory. Labour MPs are exposed through their postbags and 'surgeries' to wide constituency pressures. Electoral considerations, the sense of a swing against the so-called permissiveness of a decade ago, ensure that Conservatives are joined in their concern about moral and family life by substantial parts of the Labour Party.

In general the Party has proved most receptive to that part of the 'middle class revolt' with identifiable grievances, especially the ratepayers' and small business associations. This reflects both the intensity of feeling and real hardship of these groups, and the recognition that not all are 'anti-Labour' fronts. The ratepayers may have lost much of the force of their grievances as inflation and public expenditure have been reduced, but small businessmen and the self-employed are likely to continue to receive positive encouragement and aid under future Labour administrations as the decline of traditional industries, particularly in Scottish and Welsh Labour strongholds, continues.

The Liberal Party

One probable indicator of middle class discontent in the mid-1970s was the upsurge in the Liberal vote from approximately 2 million in the 1970 general election to almost 6 million in February 1974.[52] This continued a familiar story. In recent years Liberals have won mass support by soaking up popular disenchantment, especially with the Conservative Party. Conversion to their policies does not provide the explanation, but simply their 'otherness' from the Conservatives. This essentially negative appeal probably explains why such support is short-lived.

Parts of the disaffected middle class find the Liberals a particularly congenial retreat because they have traditionally defended the little man, squeezed between big business and powerful trade unions. Leading Liberals such as Jo Grimond and John Pardoe constantly reiterate the anti-bureaucratic themes popular with small businessmen. Yet the transitory nature of Liberal electoral support presents problems for the Liberal leadership. Since 1974 it has engaged in vigorous, albeit unsuccessful, competition with the other major parties to retain its 1974 support. Small businessmen and the self-employed have been especially courted and Liberals claim to have influenced Government concessions to the small sector. Similarly, Liberal reaction to the 'middle class revolt' has mainly concerned ratepayers and the self-employed, and it is proposed to concentrate only on these two aspects in detail.

Ratepayers

The Liberals were the only major party to advance specific proposals for reforming the rating system before the Ratepayers' storm broke in March/ April 1974. The February election manifesto argued that rates should be levied on the value of the site only, and not the house itself, as this penalised those who improved their property. It also urged that alternative sources of revenue, such as local income tax or a sales tax, should be open to local authorities, thus shifting some of the rates burden from the householder.

Ratepayers' protests reinforced the belief that the rating system was in need of reform. At the Liberal Assembly in September 1974 the Liberal leader, Jeremy Thorpe, maintained that 'the whole rating system needed radical overhaul', echoing the dissatisfaction shown by many speakers at the unfair burden of rate impositions. The Liberal manifesto of the October general election, competing with the Conservative proposal to abolish the rating system as a whole, went further than the February manifesto. Like the Conservatives, they proposed to transfer teachers' salaries to the central Exchequer, and introduced a variety of new mortgage proposals which included an index-linked mortgage plan with provision for initial low-interest payments; a low-start mortgage, to help those on low incomes; and an equity mortgage, which involved interest-free grants.

Although contacts and electoral alliances existed between the Liberals and Ratepayers' associations at local level, there were few signs of special links at national level. There was undoubted sympathy for ratepayers suffering the consequences of the massive bureaucracies created by local government re-organisation. But the Ratepayers' associations were regarded by Liberal parliamentarians as fragmented and confused, and with a tendency to exaggerate their claims. It was also increasingly difficult to outflank the Conservatives, who had moved quickly to demonstrate their support for the ratepayer. Liberal support for the small businessman has been more durable.

Small business and the self-employed

The Liberals responded enthusiastically to the self-employed and small business associations, and relations with the NFSE were particularly friendly from the start. Liberal leaders were less circumspect than Conservatives in welcoming the NFSE's aims, and the Party unambiguously sought 'the abolition of the additional eight per cent Social Security contributions imposed on the self-employed'.[53] The NFSE has held well-attended meetings at Liberal assemblies and has many Liberals among its members, including Geraint Howells, the parliamentary spokesman on small businesses.

Small business claims are generally pressed by the Liberals' Parliamentary Advisory Committee on Small Businesses formed in 1976. Its publication, *The Unfeathered Bed*, calls for tax concessions, improved credit facilities, a simplified system of form filling and legal aid and advice for the small sector.[54] More distinctively than the Conservative proposals, these demands are couched in strongly anti-bureaucratic language, and the self-employed are favourably contrasted with 'the upper echelons of the bureaucrats and public employees who are the new rich of Britain'.[55] John Pardoe has pointed to a companionship in smallness between Liberals and the small entrepreneur. Pledging his Party's full support for the NFSE in September 1975, he claimed that 'the threat from the insidious philosophy of bigness comes equally from Mr Benn and his philosophy of nationalisation and from the financiers of the City'.[56]

Not all Liberals are happy with their Party's attitudes towards the self-employed. Some younger members fear that the Party may become 'pink Tory' and others have become exasperated with the internal wranglings of the small business groups, especially the NFSE, and their lack of collective force. *The Unfeathered Bed* hints at these frustrations by urging 'the small firms sector to have one clear voice to speak for it. There should be one main channel through which its views can be expressed.'[57]

Unfortunately for the Liberals, the all-party consensus on helping the small business sector has muffled any claim for special Liberal concern with the small trader, though the Lib-Lab pact did enable the Party to translate its concern into positive action for the small sector by influencing the Government's concessions on Capital Transfer Tax in October 1977, and in helping to bring about the appointment of Harold Lever to head the Government's small business policy. The collaboration with the Labour Party may well, however, have cost them support from the predominantly anti-socialist petit-bourgeoisie.

Conclusions

The Conservative Party was the most receptive of the three parties to the idea of a 'middle class revolt'. But there was more than traditional class sympathy for the middle class behind this, for middle class support for the Conservative Party in recent years has declined more quickly than support from other social groups. Between the 1970 and February 1974 elections the Conservatives suffered a decline of 16·1 per cent amongst middle class (AB) voters, compared to declines of 8·2 per cent, 8·6 per cent and 11·2 per cent from the C1, C2 and DE categories.[58] In consequence many in the Party argued that the traditional Conservative voter had been ignored for too long, and their opinions appeared to be confirmed when the general election losses were followed by the growth of organisations representing the disaffected middle class. Although the Party in opposition developed policies that aimed to appeal to these groups, the various 'middle class' associations were not received by all Conservatives with total enthusiasm. Their methods in particular were often regarded as divisive, ineffective and veering towards the illegal.

The Liberals were less concerned than the Conservatives with the decline of traditional middle class morality or the growth of white collar unionism, but have supported the NFSE and the small business sector with fewer reservations than the other two parties. Their influence on the Labour Government is difficult to guage, though there is no doubt that the Government proved remarkably sympathetic to specific 'middle class grievances', especially those of the small entrepreneur and the ratepayer.

The influence of the middle class protesters on party policies generally is difficult to estimate, for such policies are formulated within a welter of influences. Would the Conservative Party have championed the cause of the ratepayer and small businessman in 1974 without the Ratepayers' or small business associations jogging its arm, but simply as a consequence of electoral defeat? In the same way it is difficult to calculate how much effect the 'revolt' had on overall public policy formation. At the very least it created a climate of 'establishment' opinion which is much more favourably disposed to its aims. There is in the late 1970s a general fashion for 'smallness', a reluctance by policy-makers to create larger structures in the name of efficiency and rational-isation. Company mergers are regarded now with a leery eye by government and the organisational top-heaviness that accompanied the reorganisations of local government and the National Health Service ensures that 'bigness' is no longer beautiful. There is a general reaction, too, against the liberal sixties, in favour of traditional middle class virtues.

In conclusion, all the major parties responded to the intensity of feeling that characterised many middle class activists in the 1970s. Most space has been devoted here to the Conservative Party. Their reaction to the 'middle class revolt' was the most important and the most interesting. The middle class provide the bulk of Conservative supporters and 'middle class' virtues are very often Conservative virtues. Indeed many have considered the 'revolt' to be a Tory revolt, aimed at a Labour government and its trade union allies. Yet this is too simple. Middle class anger can be at its most venomous when directed at the Party that should be its firmest political supporter. Conservative links with the various 'middle class' groups remain stronger than those between the groups and the other parties. But mutual suspicion exists. Will the Tories forget their friends now power has been regained? Conversely, are the 'middle class' dissi-dents so contemptuous of proper procedure and the requirements of social order that they might divide the Party or pose a threat to political stability?

Thus the Conservative response has been fuller and more ambivalent than those of the other parties. They share an ideological sympathy with the 'middle class revolt' which, although matched to some extent by the Liberals, finds little echo in the Labour Party. Labour's response is simpler and more openly instrumental. 'Here are groups that have votes; what can we do to cater for them?' But the Conservatives and the 'middle class' protesters demand more of each other, and this raises expectations and therefore tensions not found in the other parties.

NOTES

1 See Peter Jenkins, *Guardian*, 19 April 1974.
2 Ibid.
3 See, for example, Harris, N., *Competition and the Corporate Society*, Methuen, 1972.
4 Moran, M., *The Price for Conservatism: The Conservative Party and the Economy Since 1974*, paper presented at the British Politics Group of the Political Studies Association, January 1978, p. 3. Moran refers specifically to Gamble, A., *The Conservative Nation*, Routledge, 1974; and Gamble, A., and Walton, P., *Capitalism in Crisis*, Macmillan, 1976, pp. 194–7. A Conservative reference to the belief that government and the big groups are collectivist in this way is J. Bruce-Gardyne's *Myths and Magic in Economic Management*, Centre for Policy Studies, 1976.
5 See, for example, Stewart, M., *The Jekyll and Hyde Years: Politics and Economic Policy Since 1964*, Dent, 1977, p. 217.
6 See Sir Keith Joseph, *Stranded on the Middle Ground*, Centre for Policy Studies 1976; and Rhodes Boyson, 'The Fallacy of the Middle Ground', *The Daily Telegraph*, 9 July 1975, p. 16.
7 For statements of their respective positions at this time, see articles by Sir Keith Joseph and Margaret Thatcher on 'My Kind of Tory Party' in *The Daily Telegraph*, 28 January 1975, and 30 January 1975.
8 *The Times*, 9 May 1974, p. 10.
9 Ibid, 14 June 1974, p. 2.
10 Ibid, 12 August 1974, p. 1.
11 Conservative Election Manifesto, October 1974.
12 Butler, D., and Kavanagh, D., *The British General Election of October 1974*, Macmillan, 1975, p. 64.
13 *The Times*, 29 August 1974.
14 Ibid.
15 See, for example, Sam Brittan's criticisms in *The Times*, 31 August 1974, p. 13.
16 Freeman, R., *The Rates Riddle*, Bow Group Publication, 1978.
17 Such as Horace Cutler, Conservative leader on the GLC. See *The Times*, 23 April 1974, p. 3.
18 See King, R., and Nugent, N., 'Ratepayers' Associations in Newcastle and Wakefield', in Garrard, J., *et al.* (eds), *The Middle Class in Politics*, Teakfield, 1978; and Grant, W., *Independent Local Politics in England and Wales*, Saxon House, 1977, pp. 98–100.
19 Grant, op. cit., p. 100.
20 *Guardian*, 3 June 1977, p. 16.
21 *The Times*, 9 October 1975, p. 6.
22 Bechhofer, F., *et al.*, 'The Petits Bourgeois in the Class Structure: the Case of the Small Shopkeepers', in Parkin, F. (ed.), *The Social Analysis of Class Structure*, Tavistock, London, 1974, p. 123.
23 'Small firms', *Report of the Committee of Inquiry on Small Firms*, Cmnd 4811, HMSO, 1971, p. 71.
24 For accounts of Liberal support in the 1974 general elections see Alt, J., *et al.*, 'Angels in Plastic: The Liberal Surge in 1974', *Political Studies*, XXV, 3, pp. 343–68; and Limieux, P., 'Political Issues and Liberal Support in the February 1974 British General Election', *Political Studies*, same issue.
25 *The Times*, 1 April 1974, p. 10.
26 Ibid, 11 September 1974, pp. 4–5.
27 Ibid, 25 November 1974, p. 3.
28 Ibid, 25 October 1975, p. 10.
29 *Small Business, Big Future*, Conservative Central Office, 1977.
30 *The Right Approach to the Economy*, Conservative Central Office, London, 1977.
31 *Small Business, Big Future*, op. cit., p. 7.

32 Criticism voiced at the Small Business Bureau's annual conference, Caxton Hall, March 1978.
33 See *Guardian*, 31 October 1977. The Association of Independent Businesses was especially incensed and also complained of a similar practice by British Petroleum.
34 Criticism voiced at the Small Business Bureau's annual conference, Caxton Hall, March 1978.
35 Much of this information is based on an interview with Mr Gorst, March 1978.
36 W. van Straubenzee, quoted in the *Guardian*, 27 May 1978.
37 *The Times*, 15 November 1975.
38 See reports in *The Sunday Times*, 23 October 1977, and *The Times*, 15 November 1977.
39 See *Guardian*, 12 October 1977, for such criticisms voiced at a 'fringe' meeting at the Conservative Party Conference addressed by Mrs Whitehouse.
40 See the article by Ronald Butt on the Federation of Conservative Students, *The Times*, 5 May 1977, p. 18.
41 Sir Keith Joseph, *Stranded on the Middle Ground*, op. cit.
42 Moran, op. cit., p. 27.
43 Ibid, p. 28.
44 See Walker's speech at Droitwich in 1974, reported in *The Times*, 4 November.
45 *The Times*, 7 October 1975.
46 Ibid, 31 January 1978.
47 Sir Keith Joseph, op. cit.
48 Labour Party Manifesto, October 1974.
49 *The Times*, 12 November 1974.
50 Ibid, 15 June 1974.
51 See Chapter 5.
52 Butler and Kavanagh, op. cit.
53 See the Liberal document on small businesses, *The Unfeathered Bed*, Liberal Publications, 1975, p. 7.
54 Ibid, p. 7.
55 Ibid, p. 3.
56 *The Times*, 22 September 1975.
57 Ibid, p. 4.
58 Wilson, M., and Phillips, K., 'The Conservative Party: from Macmillan to Thatcher', in Nugent, N., and King, R., *The British Right*, Saxon House, 1977, p. 31. Their figures are based on Nuffield General Election Studies.

Roger King and Neill Nugent

8.   Conclusions

If the phrase 'the middle class revolt' is useful it is because it points to the increased willingness of certain sections of an undeniably fragmented class to organise in the 1970s so as to protect their interests. Some of the more obvious examples have been examined in the preceding chapters. We have witnessed the surge of ratepayer and small business associations, successive attempts by a range of organisations to stem the alleged tide of permissiveness and secularisation, the creation of NAFF with a view to establishing a popular base for the defence of British 'freedoms', and the continuing embrace of collectivism in the form of increased trade unionism amongst non-manual workers.

This greater activism has been accompanied by an increased propensity to engage in more demonstrative, combative and direct forms of political action than is characteristic of most orthodox pressure group activity. The vociferousness and aggression of the ratepayer and self-employed campaigns during 1974–6 are the clearest examples of this. The militant pronouncements of their spokesmen, which are all the more remarkable when compared with the relative timidity of their predecessors, sprang from deep grassroots anger and strong feelings of injustice. In the early stages many of their proposals and actions bordered on the illegal and even when the peak of their 'revolt' passed they continued to show a general contempt for the institutionalised political processes of bargaining and compromise.

Most of the other organisations examined in the preceding chapters have also displayed a predilection for boisterous and occasionally belligerent political action. NAFF, for example, has been much more populist than most of its forerunners; the NFOL has displayed a taste for mass rallies and demonstrations; whilst middle class unions, as the impact of high levels of inflation, increased taxation and restrictive pay policies have accelerated employees' grievances, have become increasingly willing to use forms of 'direct action' which in the past have been more associated with traditional manual unionism.

The case 'for' a middle class revolt is thus based primarily on the increased activism and militancy of certain sections of the middle class. It is further bolstered by the increased willingness of virtually all the organisations discussed in this book to move outside the normal channels of party politics. Their 'non-party' stance may legitimately be regarded with suspicion, but it is not entirely spurious. Certainly there are closer links between the ratepayers, small businessmen, NAFF and NVALA on the one hand and the Conservative Party on the other than there are with either the Labour or Liberal parties. Nevertheless, disillusionment with the Conservatives' past performance in government has led to a general scepticism and suspicion as to their future intentions.

But though a case can be made for there having been a 'middle class revolt' in Britain in the 1970s it must be seen as having been of a very limited nature. Doubt was cast in Chapter 1 on the very concept of a *generalised* 'middle class revolt' since this implies a collective class identity that simply does not exist. Class boundaries cannot be precisely drawn and any attempt to pinpoint the middle class – or any class, for that matter – must be somewhat arbitrary. This is highlighted by the way in which some interests and beliefs cut across conventional class boundaries. To take one of our examples, the puritan backlash is not the prerogative of one section of society. It runs from people such as Mrs Whitehouse and the 'blue rinse', middle class suburbanites she is generally portrayed as representing, to working class Baptists, Jehovah's Witnesses and West Indian Pentecostals.

But even if it is supposed, despite the problems of identification, that the middle class 'exists', internal divisions make it difficult to talk of there being a 'class identity', or 'class consciousness'. The middle class is simply too diffuse to act as a class even though it is the smaller of the two broad classes and even though it votes more solidly for one party than does the larger working class. The support for the organisations examined in the preceding chapters may be drawn primarily from sections of society usually thought of as being middle class, but conflicting interests have precluded the foundations of common action. In terms of their aims and roles *general* divisions exist over and above the obvious *specific* differences of interest. For example, in ideological terms, NAFF and ASP propound what they call a 'radical libertarian' philosophy and see a major part of their function as being to move the whole political spectrum to the right. The NFSE and the unions, however, do not subscribe to the libertarian doctrine of non-governmental interventionism. Their role is much more instrumental in that they are primarily concerned, like many other conventional pressure groups, simply to advance the immediate social and economic interests of their members. This is not seen to require the advocacy of a global ideological view, and, far from demanding a general withdrawal of the State, its positive intervention is frequently sought. Much of the assistance it can provide is warmly welcomed.

Thus neither the middle classes as a whole, nor our particular activists, display a unity of purpose warranting the description 'middle class revolt' *per se*. There are too many strands being pulled in too many directions, and in any event those pulling the strands are frequently not as numerous or representative as they may appear to be. Close inspection reveals that overtly impressive levels of support sometimes cover minimal levels of activity. Indeed, geographical and organisational isolation often results in local branches and groups of apparently vigorous national bodies being dependent for their survival on a few key individuals.

Our organisations are further distinguished by the circumstances in which they arose, which, in turn, are linked to their likely futures. The 'revolt' of the ratepayers and self-employed was a reaction to specific measures and events: the sharp increase in rate demands in 1974 and 1975 and the introduction of the special Class 4 National Insurance contribution in the same period. As the

Government and the Conservative and Liberal parties took evasive action – by adopting the measures outlined in Chapter 7 – then so did much of the steam go out of their protests. For, as we have shown in Chapter 2, rating in itself, although controversial, is less resented than is often believed and is not, of its own accord, capable of sustaining vigorous political activity. The Ratepayers' electoral successes of 1974–6 thus increasingly appear as years of respite in the long-term 'nationalisation' of local party politics. Similarly, support for ASP and NASE has declined since 1976, whilst efforts by the NFSE to increase its membership have been unsuccessful. The Class 4 contribution still rankles, but perhaps less so since its level was reduced from 8 per cent to 5 per cent in 1978 by the Labour Government. There are, of course, long-term trends that will continue to sustain small business anxieties, notably the extension of state activity in the social and economic fields, the concentration of resources into larger units, and the presence of a powerful trade union movement. On the whole, however, it seems likely, with the climate in all the major parties being much more sympathetic to the small business case than it was prior to 1974, that lobbying will increasingly take a more quiescent 'insider' approach.

Middle class unionism, by contrast, is of a more durable quality. As Chapter 5 has shown, an element of protest and dissatisfaction has also fuelled the growth of non-manual unionism. Nevertheless, the increase in influence and density dates from the mid-1960s and can be related to longer term developments such as the increase in large, bureaucratically structured working environments and increasing governmental support of unionism. There is clearly a much greater solidity and permanence about middle class unionism than is the case with any of our other movements.

At the same time the 'moral/religious' militants are also symptomatic of long-term changes, though in their case these are cultural rather than economic. They are not simply a reaction to the 'permissiveness' of the late 1960s and early 1970s but are, more generally, a response to the decline in 'the Protestant ethic'. Furthermore, it seems likely that as long as figures for divorce, delinquency, violent crime etc. continue to rise, then so will such organisations maintain, and perhaps even increase, their support.

NAFF's future is more difficult to gauge, for though it too is a response to long-term changes in British society, in particular post-1945 collectivism, the experience of its most obvious forerunner, Edward Martell's Freedom Group, suggests that it may have difficulty in retaining popular and financial support over a period of years. Moreover, as Chapter 4 makes clear, its fortunes are probably much more attuned to the vagaries of election results and party politics than is the case with the unions or the morality groups. At the least, however, it may be said that its future is probably not so dim as that of the national Ratepayers' organisations, if only because it differs from them in having been organised from the centre to the periphery, with its leaders seeking to tap the mass sympathy they believe to be available for their cause. A strong, centralised organisational nub, supported by a steady income – such as NAFF enjoys but NARAG does not – provides some basis of security, even though local branch activity may atrophy.

Closely linked to the differing backgrounds and natures of the organisations is an important distinction between the commitments of the activists themselves. Many, particularly those who were drawn into the ratepayer and self-employed movements at the height of the 'revolt', had not previously directly participated in political activity. They displayed the three major features commonly associated with what Dowse and Hughes have called 'sporadic interventionists'. Firstly, their eruption into the political arena was brief and they attracted little support outside their own particular point of attention. Secondly, they lacked previous political experience. Thirdly, they possessed an initial naivety about their political efficacy which, when not realised, resulted in cynicism and withdrawal. The odds are stacked against 'sporadic interventionists' from the start as they are usually in the position of having to respond to policies from well-established organisations or even publicly announced governmental/local authority decisions. The resources required to sustain long campaigns accelerate disillusionment. Hardly surprisingly, they frequently come to recognise that the redress of perceived grievances depends more on creating a lot of noise and propaganda than on reasoned argument with politicians.[1]

But not all ratepayer or self-employed activists are 'sporadic interventionists'. Many supporters have adjusted to falling membership by coming to resemble in their methods the pre-1974 'respectability seeking' groups of whom they were previously scornful. In so doing they have perhaps further contributed to their associations' decline. Be that as it may, there is no doubt that many, who felt uncomfortable in their erstwhile role of rebel, feel more at ease in calmer surroundings. So, many have established close links with politicians and officials, have exhibited a desire to be taken as serious-minded representatives of community or occupational interests, and have generally pulled back from the flamboyancy that marked the search for publicity during 1974–6. Such a metamorphosis does, of course, take time. It can also be a source of great friction. The cross-pressures of 'insider-outsider' considerations have, for example, provided a persisting source of turbulence within the NFSE.

Partly as a result of the loss of popular steam in 1976, many of the ratepayer and small business organisations have broadened their range of interests. Most of the 'new' 1974 Ratepayers' groups have increasingly lobbied on a variety of community matters and have established a more general concern with the rating system than simply the size of the annual rate demand. Similarly small business and self-employed organisations have campaigned on many matters other than the Class 4 contribution – the alleged handicaps of the Employment Protection Act and the 714 builders' certificate being the most obvious examples. Small business pressure group activity is increasingly 'orthodox', particularly as the CBI Small Firms Division and the National Chamber of Trade enter the fray, and as the more radical groups – ASP and NASE – lose ground.

Beyond the ratepayers and the self-employed it is even more evident that many of our activists are not 'sporadic interventionists'. That is most clearly so with the middle class unions, but it is also apparent with many of the political sophisticates in NAFF and the morality groups. They often have long-standing goals, reflected in well-articulated programmes and considerable political experience, which suggests that if NAFF, for example, were to fail, similar bodies would attract many of its activists. Indeed, many joined NAFF itself because of the decline of the Monday Club. NAFF, like the NVALA and increasingly the NFSE, is also becoming increasingly structured and this too distinguishes it from groups of the pure 'interventionist' variety. This process does not, of course, protect NAFF from the dilemma, which is not confined to middle class groups, that associations which do acquire the organisational strength to become effective spokesmen for their cause may risk forfeiting vigorous grassroots participation.

It is thus apparent that though the middle class organisations examined in this book share a number of common features it is unlikely that coordinated effort, even if it were to exclude the middle class unions – in many ways the 'odd men out' – will ever be forthcoming. NAFF's attempts to assume ideological and organisational leadership have not been successful and the prospect of a 'third force' to match the CBI and TUC is remote. There is an essential fragmentariness about middle class protest which results in an issue which may be of burning interest to one section being, at best, of marginal importance to another.

Small business and self-employed organisations appeal to individuals in their occupational roles and come into conflict with other middle class groups, notably white collar trade unionists, over issues such as the Employment Protection Act and levels of public expenditure. Ratepayers' associations and 'moral' groups, on the other hand, appeal to individuals in a different role – as householders or moral beings. In so doing they have the potential to overcome the occupational diversity that characterises the middle class. But they often find themselves confronting educated, publicly employed sections of their class. At the same time a group such as the NVALA is frequently at odds with the commercial interests of entrepreneurs. NAFF and the other 'freedom groups' are primarily attractive to Conservative sympathisers and, as such, are regarded as political opponents by middle class supporters of other parties. They are even seen by some Conservatives as being divisive.

Ratepayers, small business, 'moral' and 'freedom' groups will remain a feature of British political life for the foreseeable future, whilst non-manual unionism will, doubtless, continue to expand. Yet, unless the special features of the mid-1970s reappear, most of the organisations are likely to eschew aggressive publicity-seeking in favour of 'insider' politics, concentrating on a broad set of issues with, in some cases, reduced support.

Of course, much depends on the actions of future governments. We have noted at various points in the book how in the 1970s the actions and fortunes of some of our organisations have been affected by the increasing responsiveness of both Government and Opposition to many of their demands. Most retain at least a residual sympathy for Mrs Thatcher's brand of Toryism, but scepticism is not far beneath the surface. If the Conservative Government elected in May 1979 pursues policies that do not match the rhetoric of opposition, there could be a further period of disenchantment with Conservatism and a possible boost to 'non-political' middle class organisations outside the Tory Party.

It is even possible that the other parties may benefit, for there is by no means total antipathy to either Labour or the Liberals. Rather do many of the groups with which we have been concerned reflect the emerging instrumentality of electoral behaviour, the idea of choosing between parties as opposed to unswerving loyalty to one. The decline in uncritical political allegiances, coupled with the 'non-party' assertiveness of many middle class dissidents, suggests that the major parties will have to continue to work hard if they are to convince putative supporters of their efficiency and competence.

NOTE

1 Dowse, R. E., and Hughes, J. A., 'Sporadic Interventionists', *Political Studies*, Vol. 25, No. 1 (March 1977), pp. 84–92.

Bibliography

This bibliography makes no attempt to be exhaustive. It lists only what the respective authors consider to be the most useful material in the various areas. Where it has seemed useful, a distinction has been made between primary and secondary sources.

CHAPTER 1 – The middle class in revolt?

Bechhofer, F., and Elliott, B., 'The Voice of Small Business and the Politics of Survival', *Sociological Review*, Vol. 26 (February 1978).

Bechhofer, F., *et al.*, 'Structure, Consciousness and Action: A Sociological Profile of the British Middle Class', *British Journal of Sociology*, Vol. 29, No. 4 (December 1978).

Bell, D., *The Cultural Contradictions of Capitalism*, Heinemann, 1975.

Butler, D., and Stokes, D., *Political Change in Britain*, Macmillan, 1974.

Carroll, J., *Puritan, Paranoid, Remissive,* Heinemann, 1977.

Crouch, C. (ed.), *British Political Sociology Yearbook*, Vol. 3: *Participation in Politics*, Croom Helm, 1977.

Galbraith, J., *The New Industrial State*, Penguin, 1969.

Gallie, D., *In Search of the New Working Class*, Cambridge University Press, 1978.

Gamble, A., *The Conservative Nation*, Routledge, 1974.

Garrard, J., *et al.* (eds), *The Middle Class in Politics*, Saxon House, 1978.

Goldthorpe, J., *et al.*, *The Affluent Worker*, 3 vols, Cambridge University Press, 1969, 1970, 1971.

Goldthorpe, J. H., and Bevan, P., 'The study of social stratification in Great Britain; 1946–1976', *Social Science Information*, Vol. 16, 1977.

Habermas, J., *Legitimation Crisis*, Heinemann, 1976.

Harris, N., *Competition and the Corporate Society*, Methuen, 1972.

Hutber, P., *The Decline and Fall of the Middle Class: and how it can fight back*, Penguin, 1977.

Lewis, R., and Maude, A., *The English Middle Classes*, Phoenix House, 1949.

McKenzie, R., and Silver, A., *Angels in Marble*, Heinemann, 1968.

Mills, C. W., *The Power Elite*, Oxford University Press, 1965.

Parkin, F., *Middle Class Radicalism*, Manchester University Press, 1968.

Parkin, F. (ed.), *The Social Analysis of Class Structure*, Tavistock, 1974.

Poulantzas, N., *Classes in Contemporary Capitalism*, New Left Books, 1975.

Roberts, K., *et al.*, *The Fragmentary Class Structure*, Heinemann, 1977.

Webb, D., 'Research Note: Some Reservations on the Use of Self-Rated Class', *Sociological Review*, Vol. 21, No. 2 (1973).

Westergaard, J., and Resler, H., *Class in a Capitalist Society*, Penguin, 1976.

CHAPTER 2 – The Ratepayers

Dowse, R. E., and Hughes, J. A., 'Sporadic Interventionists', *Political Studies*, Vol. 25, No. 1 (March 1977).

Grant, W., '"Local" Parties in British Local Politics: A Framework for Empirical Analysis', *Political Studies*, Vol. XIX, No. 2 (1971).

Grant, W., 'Non-Partisanship in British Local Politics', *Policy and Politics*, Vol. 1, No. 3 (March 1973).

Grant, W., *Independent Local Politics in England and Wales*, Saxon House, 1977.

Gyford, J., *Local Politics in Britain*, Croom Helm, 1976.

King, R., and Nugent, N., 'Ratepayers Associations in Newcastle and Wakefield', in Garrard, J., *et al.* (eds), *The Middle Class in Politics*, Saxon House, 1978.

Newton, K., *Second City Politics: Democratic Processes and Decision Making in Birmingham*, Oxford University Press, 1976.

Report of the Committee of Inquiry on Local Government Finance (Layfield Committee), Cmnd 6463, HMSO, 1976. Evidence submitted by National Association of Ratepayers' Action Groups and by National Union of Ratepayers' Associations.

Royal Commission on Local Government in England (Redcliffe-Maud Report): Written Evidence of Private Citizens, Amenity, Ratepayers' and Residents Organisations and Other Witnesses, HMSO, 1969.

Sharpe, J., *Voting in Cities*, Macmillan, 1967.

Stanyer, J., *Understanding Local Government*, Fontana, 1976.

Steed, M., 'Ratepayers' Associations and Local Politics', Parts 1 and 2, *Insight*, June and July 1965.

Weightman, G., 'The Politics of Rates', *New Society*, 1 January 1976.

CHAPTER 3 – The self-employed and the small independent entrepreneur

Primary

Annual Report of the National Chamber of Trade, 1974–8.

Counterattack (newspaper of the Association of Self-Employed People).

Department of Employment Gazette, Vol. 134, No. 12 (December 1976).

First Voice (newspaper of the National Federation of the Self-Employed).

Report of the Committee of Inquiry into Industrial and Commercial Representation (Devlin Report), The Association of British Chambers of Commerce/The Confederation of British Industry, November 1972.

Report of the Committee of Inquiry on Small Firms (Bolton Report), HMSO, Cmnd 4811, 1971.

Report of the National Federation of the Self-Employed, First National Delegates Conference, 1977.

Secondary

Bechhofer, F., and Elliott, B., 'Associating for Freedom: Bourgeois Social Movements and British Politics', paper given to the International Political Science Association Round Table on Pluralism, Paris, 1978.

Bechhofer, F., and Elliott, B., 'The Voice of Small Business and the Politics of Survival', *Sociological Review*, Vol. 26 (February 1978).

Bechhofer, F., *et al.*, 'The Petits Bourgeois in the Class Structure: The Case of the Small Shopkeepers', in Parkin, F. (ed.), *The Social Analysis of Class Structure*, Tavistock, 1974.

Black, S., 'The Rise of Small Businesses', *Spectator*, 29 April 1978.

Britain's Small Firms, CBI, 1970.

Enterprise Into the Eighties, CBI, 1977.

Hamilton, R. T., 'Government Decisions and Small Firms', unpublished manuscript of the London Business School, 1975.

McCarthy, M. A., 'Organising the Independent Centre', *Political Quarterly*, Vol. 49, No. 3 (July 1978).

CHAPTER 4 – The National Association for Freedom

Primary
The British Gazette (journal of the Self-Help Organisation since 1976).
The Free Nation (newspaper of the National Association for Freedom).
Freedom First (journal of the Society for Individual Freedom).
Majority (irregularly produced newspaper of Self-Help prior to Ross McWhirter's murder).
Moss, R., *The Collapse of Democracy*, Sphere Books, 1977.
Watkins, K. W., *In Defence of Freedom*, Casswell, 1978.
In addition to the above there are innumerable leaflets, pamphlets and booklets published by the various organisations.

Secondary
Davis, G., 'Inside Self-Help', *Isis*, 7 October 1977.
Davis, G., 'Behind the Scenes', *New Statesman*, 16 December 1977.
Dunn, P., 'NAFF in Thurberland', *New Statesman*, 15 July 1977.
Labour Party Research Department, Information Paper No. 9: *National Association for Freedom*.
Mount, F., 'Freedom and the "Free Nation"', *Spectator*, 19 February 1977.
Nugent, N., 'The Freedom Groups', *New Society*, 2 September 1976.
Rogaly, J., *Grunwick*, Penguin Books, 1977.
Thayer, G., *The British Political Fringe*, Anthony Blond, 1965.
Ward, G., *Fort Grunwick*, Maurice Temple Smith, 1977.
Watt, D., 'Mr. Martell and the Tories', *Spectator*, 26 June 1964.

CHAPTER 5 – Middle class unionism

Primary
First Annual Report of the Certification Officer 1976, HMSO, 1977.
Annual Report of the Certification Officer 1977, HMSO, 1978.
Economic Policy and Collective Bargaining – Report of a Special TUC, March 1973, TUC, 1973.
The Industrial Relations Bill – Report of the Special Trades Union Congress, TUC, 1971.
Reports of the Annual Trades Union Congress, TUC, 1965–77.

Secondary
Bain, G. S., *The Growth of White Collar Unionism*, Clarendon Press, 1970.
Bain, G. S., *et al.*, *Social Stratification and Trade Unionism*, Heinemann, 1973.
Bocock, J., 'The Politics of White Collar Unionisation', *Political Quarterly*, Vol. 44, No. 3 (July/September 1973).
Coates, R. D., *Teachers' Unions and Interest Group Politics*, Cambridge University Press, 1972.
Dickens, L., 'UKAPE: A Study of a Professional Union', *Industrial Relations Journal*, Vol. 3, No. 3 (Autumn 1972).
Goldthorpe, J. H., and Llewellyn, C., 'Class Mobility in Modern Britain: Three Theses Examined', *Sociology*, Vol. 11, No. 2 (May 1977).
Lockwood, D., *The Blackcoated Worker*, Allen & Unwin, 1958.
Lumley, R., *White Collar Unionism in Britain*, Methuen, 1973.
Moran, M., *The Politics of Industrial Relations*, Macmillan, 1977.
Price, R., and Bain, G. S., 'Union Growth Revisited: 1948–1974 in Perspective', *British Journal of Industrial Relations*, Vol. 14, No. 3 (November 1976).
Roberts, B. C., *et al.*, *Reluctant Militants*, Heinemann, 1972.
Roberts, K., *et al.*, *The Fragmentary Class Structure*, Heinemann, 1977.
Taylor, R., *The Fifth Estate*, Routledge, 1978.
Thakur, M., and Naylor, M., *White Collar Unions*, Institute of Personnel Management, 1976.

CHAPTER 6 – Religion, morality and the middle class

Bell, D., *The Cultural Contradictions of Capitalism*, Heinemann, 1976.
Belson, W., *Television, Violence and the Adolescent Boy*, Saxon House, 1978.
Berger, P., and Kellner, H., 'Marriage and the Social Construction of Reality', in Open University reader *School and Society*, Routledge, 1971.
Brothers, J., *Religious Institutions*, Longmans, 1971.
Capon, J., . . . *And There Was Light*, Butterworth, 1972.
Caulfield, M., *Mary Whitehouse*, Mowbrays, 1975.
Cohen, A., 'The Elasticity of Evil: Changes in the Social Definition of Deviance', in Hammersley, A., and Woods, P. (eds), *The Process of Schooling*, Routledge, 1976.
Gusfield, J., *Symbolic Crusade and Status Politics: The American Temperance Movement*, University of Illinois Press, 1976.
Halsey, A. H., Reith Lecture No. 5, *Listener*, 9 February 1978.
Harris, C. C., 'Family and Societal Form', in Scase, R. S. (ed.), *Industrial Society: Class Cleavage and Control*, Allen & Unwin, 1977.
Longley, C., 'Casting Some Much Needed Light on the Festival of the Same Name', *The Times*, 9 July 1973.
Milson, F., *Youth in a Changing Society*, Routledge, 1972.
Morrison, D., and Tracey, M., *Opposition to the Age: A Study of NVALA*, report to the SSRC, 1978.
Munyham, G., and Pearson, G. (eds), *Working Class Youth Cultures*, Routledge, 1976.
Musgrave, F., *Margins of the Mind*, Tavistock, 1977.
Norman, E., 'Church and State: Establishment versus Radicals', *Spectator*, 12 December 1970.
Pym, B., *Pressure Groups and the Permissive Society*, David & Charles, 1974.
Raynor, J., *The Middle Class*, Longmans, 1969.
Robertson, R., *The Sociological Interpretation of Religion*, Blackwell, 1970.
Rock, P., *Deviant Behaviour*, Hutchinson, 1973.
Seagrave, J. R., 'A Model of Organised Group Behaviour for the Church in British Politics', *Parliamentary Affairs*, Vol. 27 (Autumn 1974).
Shorter, E., *The Making of the Modern Family*, Fontana, 1977.
Taylor, L., 'The Significance and Interpretation of Replies to Motivational Questions: The Case of Sex Offenders', in Wiles, P. (ed.), *The Sociology of Crime and Delinquency in Britain*, Vol. II, Martin Robertson, 1976.
Thomas, W. I., *Social Behaviour and Personality* (ed. Volkhart, E. H.), Social Science Research, 1951.
Tudor, A., *Image and Influence*, St Martin's Press, 1975.
Wallis, R., 'Dilemma of a Moral Crusade', *New Society*, 13 July 1972.
Wallis, R., 'Moral Indignation and the Media – An Analysis of NVALA', *Sociology*, Vol. 10 (1976).
Wallis, R., 'A Critique of the Theory of Moral Crusades as Status Defence', *Scottish Journal of Sociology*, Vol. 1, Part 2 (1977).
Weber, M., *The Protestant Ethic and the Spirit of Capitalism*, Allen & Unwin, 1930.
Whitehouse, M., *Who Does She Think She Is?*, New English Library, 1970.
Whitehouse, M., *Whatever Happened to Sex?*, Wayland Publishers Ltd, 1977.
Willmott, P., and Young, M., *The Symmetrical Family*, Penguin, 1975.

CHAPTER 7 – The middle class revolt and the established parties

Primary
Bruce-Gardyne, J., *Myths and Magic in Economic Management*, Centre for Policy Studies, 1976.
Freeman, R., *The Rates Riddle*, Bow Group Publications, 1978.
Joseph, K., *Stranded on the Middle Ground*, Centre for Policy Studies, 1976.

Report of the Committee of Inquiry on Small Firms (Bolton Report), Cmnd 4811, HMSO, 1971.
The Right Approach to the Economy, Conservative Central Office, 1977.
Small Business, Big Future, Conservative Central Office, 1977.
The Unfeathered Bed, Liberal Publications, 1975.

Secondary
Alt, J., *et al.*, 'Angels in Plastic: The Liberal Surge in 1974', *Political Studies*, Vol. 25, No. 3 (1977).
Butler, D., and Kavanagh, D., *The British General Election of October 1974*, Macmillan, 1975.
Gamble, A., *The Conservative Nation*, Routledge, 1974.
Gamble, A., and Walton, P., *Capitalism in Crisis*, Macmillan, 1976.
Grant, W., *Independent Local Politics in England and Wales*, Saxon House, 1977.
Harris, N., *Competition and the Corporate State*, Methuen, 1977.
Limieux, P., 'Political Issues and Liberal Support in the February 1974 British General Election', *Political Studies*, Vol. 25, No. 3 (1977).
Nugent, N., and King, R., *The British Right*, Saxon House, 1977.
Stewart, M., *The Jekyll and Hyde Years; Politics and Economic Policy Since 1964*, Dent, 1977.

List of Abbreviations

ABUSE	Action to Ban the Sexual Exploitation of Children
ABCC	Association of British Chambers of Commerce
ACAS	Advisory, Conciliation and Arbitration Service
ACTT	Association of Cinematograph, Television and Allied Technicians
AIB/SBA	Association of Independent Businesses/Small Businesses Association
AIMS	Aims for Freedom and Enterprise
APEX	Association of Professional, Executive, Clerical and Computer Staff
APST	Association of Professional Scientists and Technologists
ASDAG	All Sunderland District Action Group
ASEE	Association of Supervisory and Executive Engineers
ASP	Association of Self-Employed People
ASTAG	All South Tyneside Action Group
ASTMS	Association of Scientific, Technical and Managerial Staffs
AUEW	Amalgamated Union of Engineering Workers
BFLA	Bristol Family Life Association
BIM	British Institute of Management
BMA	British Medical Association
BUI	British United Industrialists
CA	Civil Assistance
CBI	Confederation of British Industry
CIR	Commission on Industrial Relations
COFACE	Committee of Family Organisations in the Community of Europe
CONRAG	Consortium of Newcastle Rates Action Groups
COPPSO	Conference of Professional and Public Service Organisations
CORA	Consortium of Ratepayers' Associations
COSIRA	Council for Small Industries in Rural Areas
CPSA	Civil and Public Services Association
CSA	Community Standards Association
CTU	Conservative Trade Unionists
EMA	Engineers and Managers Association
GMWU	General and Municipal Workers Union
IEA	Institute of Economic Affairs
IPCS	Institute of Professional Civil Servants
IRSF	Inland Revenue Staff Federation
MCA	Middle Class Association
MPSL	Managerial and Professional Staffs Liaison Group
NABM	National Association of British Manufacturers
NAFF	National Association for Freedom (now The Freedom Association)
NALGO	National and Local Government Officers' Association
NARAG	National Association of Ratepayers' Action Groups
NAS	National Association of Schoolmasters
NASE	National Association of the Self-Employed
NATFHE	National Association of Teachers in Further and Higher Education

NATKO	National Trade and Kindred Organisations Committee for National Insurance
NCCL	National Council for Civil Liberties
NCT	National Chamber of Trade
NEC	National Executive Committee of the Labour Party
NFOL	National Festival of Light
NFSE	National Federation of the Self-Employed
NTRAG	North Tyneside Rates Action Group
NUBE	National Union of Bank Employees
NUPE	National Union of Public Employees
NURA	National Union of Ratepayers' Associations
NUT	National Union of Teachers
NVALA	National Viewers and Listeners Association
OCU	Order of Christian Unity
PAL	Paedophile Action Liberation
PLP	Parliamentary Labour Party
RS	Responsible Society
SBB	Small Business Bureau
SIF	Society for Individual Freedom
SRHA	Sunderland Ratepayers and Homebuyers Association
SSRC	Social Science Research Council
TASS	Technical, Administrative and Supervisory Section of the AUEW
TAWRAG	Tyne and Wear Rates Action Groups
TUC	Trades Union Congress
UIC	Union of Independent Companies
UKAPE	United Kingdom Association of Professional Engineers
UPW	Union of Post Office Workers
VAT	Value Added Tax

Index